T0305068

Religion and Consumer Behaviour in
Developing Nations

Religion and Consumer Behaviour in Developing Nations

Edited by

Ayantunji Gbadamosi

Senior Lecturer, Royal Docks School of Business and Law, University of East London, UK

Ayodele Christopher Oniku

Senior Lecturer, Department of Business Administration, University of Lagos, Nigeria

Cheltenham, UK • Northampton, MA, USA

Published by
Edward Elgar Publishing Limited
The Lypiatts
15 Lansdown Road
Cheltenham
Glos GL50 2JA
UK

Edward Elgar Publishing, Inc.
William Pratt House
9 Dewey Court
Northampton
Massachusetts 01060
USA

A catalogue record for this book
is available from the British Library

Library of Congress Control Number: 2020950288

This book is available electronically in the **Elgar**online
Business subject collection
http://dx.doi.org/10.4337/9781839101038

ISBN 978 1 83910 102 1 (cased)
ISBN 978 1 83910 103 8 (eBook)

Printed and bound by CPI Group (UK) Ltd, Croydon, CR0 4YY

Contents

Figures

Tables

Contributors

Rula M. Al-Abdulrazak is a branding and global marketing specialist with diverse experience in the oil industry, business consultancy, and higher education. She spent over a decade working with Royal Dutch Shell and the European Commission before joining academia at Royal Holloway, University of London, and the University of East London, UK as Senior Lecturer. At Royal Holloway, Rula completed an MBA in international management and marketing and a PhD in marketing ('The Branded Nation: A Comparative Review with Reference to Syria and the United Arab Emirates'), in addition to a postgraduate degree in teaching and learning. She is currently studying positive psychology and coaching. Al-Abdulrazak researches branding, nation and place marketing, cultural branding, and cross-cultural marketing. She is interested in digital marketing and the impact of digitalisation on growth and well-being. Her studies include an examination of cultural diplomacy and art with reference to the United Arab Emirates, the Arab Spring and nation image, nation-brand state and public diplomacy, brand and social trust, and religiosity and branding. Rula is an editor and conference organiser and champions business collaborations and professional training, while also chairing research ethics.

David J. Bamber is Director of PhD Studies at Bolton Business School, University of Bolton, UK. He has worked as a research fellow in organisational learning at the University of Salford, senior lecturer in international marketing, Liverpool Hope University, and is external examiner in international marketing and business at several other UK universities. He is a foundation member of the Chartered College of Teaching and has been track Co-Chair for Organisational Studies with the British Academy of Management for 15 years and has presented academic papers at 40 international peer-reviewed conferences. He is a reviewer for the *International Journal of Contemporary Hospitality Management*.

Mohamed Djemilou is a PhD candidate and researcher at the School of Business and Finance, University of the Western Cape, South Africa. His research areas include consumer behaviour, marketing management, halal research, entrepreneurship, and international trade. He has authored, published, and reviewed several articles and research papers for journals and conferences in the above-mentioned areas.

Gift Donga completed his PhD in the Department of Business Management at the University of Venda, South Africa. His thesis focused on the area of consumer behaviour, specialising in the adoption of mobile commerce among young consumers. His research interests are in the areas of e-commerce, technology, green marketing, and culture.

Kathy-Ann Fletcher is Lecturer in Marketing at Abertay University, UK. Her teaching focuses on areas such as digital marketing and customer relationship management. She conducted research on the development of consumer identity with social media brand communities in support of a PhD in business. Her research interests include consumer behaviour, sustainable consumption, digital media, and brand relationships.

Chahid Fourali has a background in marketing, psychology, and education and has published extensively in all three areas. He led the consultation with the UK government to set up the Marketing and Sales Standards Setting Body, which he then led for eight years, as well as the development of three sets of world-class national occupational standards (in marketing, sales, and social marketing) that were supported by many internationally recognised marketing/business gurus. These standards are now the basis for all nationally recognised qualifications in the UK in the three professional areas. Fourali leads the Business Management and Marketing course at the London Metropolitan Business School, UK and his experience has covered being an examiner and subject expert for several institutions including Cambridge University and the University of Hertfordshire, UK and the Universities of Gdansk and WSEIZ, Poland. Fourali is lead editor of *The Palgrave Encyclopaedia of Social Marketing*, the first international encyclopaedia of social marketing. He has published over 60 articles, chapters, and books. He has achieved fellowship or professional membership status from several international organisations including the Royal Society of Arts, Chartered Institute of Marketing, Higher Education Academy, and the British Association for Behavioural and Cognitive Psychotherapies.

Ayantunji Gbadamosi lectures at Royal Docks School of Business and Law, University of East London, UK. He once served as Research Coordinator and Chair of the Research and Knowledge Exchange Committee in the school. He received his PhD from the University of Salford, UK and has taught marketing courses at various institutions including the University of Lagos (Nigeria), University of Salford (UK), Manchester Metropolitan University (UK), Liverpool Hope University (UK), and various professional bodies.

'Tunji Gbadamosi has written over 100 publications – journal articles, chapters in edited books, edited books, monograph, conference papers, and case studies. He has previously authored or edited eight books including *Contemporary Issues in Marketing* (2019), *Young Consumer Behaviour* (2018), *The Handbook of Research on Consumerism and Buying Behaviour in Developing Nations* (2016), *Principles of Marketing: A Value-Based Approach* (2013), and *Entrepreneurship Marketing: Principles and Practice of SME Marketing*, 2nd edition (2020). Gbadamosi is an editorial board member of several journals. He has supervised several students including 12 PhD students to successful completion and served as an examiner for 28 doctorate degree examinations. He is the current Programme Chair of the Academy of African Business Development. His research interests lie in consumer behaviour, small to medium enterprise marketing, marketing to children, and marketing communications. His paper won the Emerald Best Paper Award at the International Academy of African Business Development Conference, 2014. He is a Fellow of some prestigious professional bodies, namely Higher Education Academy (FHEA), Chartered Institute of Marketing (FCIM), and Chartered Management Institute (FCMI). He is listed in Who is Who in the World.

Nashaat H. Hussein is Assistant Professor of Sociology in Alsun and Mass Communication Department of Misr International University in Cairo. He has published extensively in *Cairo Papers in Social Sciences*, *Journal of the History of Childhood and Youth*, and *International Journal of Sociology and Social Policy*. He is the author of 'The Social Stigma of Divorce' in *The Cultural Sociology of Divorce: An Encyclopedia* (2013), 'Sport and Schools' in *The Sociology of Education: An A–Z Guide* (2013), and *Contemporary Issues in Marketing* (2019).

Ayodele Christopher Oniku is Senior Lecturer in the Department of Business Administration at the University of Lagos, Nigeria. He gained his PhD from the Royal Docks School of Business and Law, University of East London, UK. Ayo Oniku is a seasoned lecturer with experience that cuts across both the industry and academia and equally between African and European markets. He has contributed to many reputable academic journals, edited books, and international conferences on marketing and other business-related issues. Oniku is a seasoned consultant and trainer in marketing fields and other business-related areas and is presently Senior Consultant/Partner with Ayo Oniku Consulting and Ayo Oniku & Associates.

Roshan Panditharathna is Lecturer of Business at OLC (Europe), UK. He completed his PhD in marketing and innovation from the University of Bolton. His main research interests are marketing, entrepreneurship, and innovation. He gained his BSc degree in ecobusiness management from the Sabaragamuwa University of Sri Lanka. He is also an expert in qualitative (case study and grounded theory) and quantitative (partial least squares structural equation modelling) methods in marketing research.

Kareem Sani obtained a BSc in marketing from the University of Uyo, Nigeria and an MSc in international marketing management from the University of East London. His experience spans over a decade in the banking industry before joining academia. Sani focuses on consumer behaviour, relationship marketing, and service marketing. He is currently a doctoral researcher and a part-time lecturer in marketing at the University of East London.

Richard Shambare is Associate Professor in Entrepreneurship and Marketing at the School of Business and Finance at the University of the Western Cape, South Africa. He teaches various entrepreneurship and management subjects in both the undergraduate and postgraduate programmes and also supervises master and PhD students. His research interests are in the broad area of the entrepreneurship–marketing interface. Of note, Shambare takes a keen interest in research that looks at how entrepreneurs seek to promote their businesses through marketing (i.e., small to medium enterprise marketing philosophies, small business marketing approaches, and the ubiquitous adoption of technologies by entrepreneurs). He has published in peer-reviewed journals, books, and book chapters as well as presenting his research at numerous international conferences.

Preface

Religion is notably pervasive in its impacts in people's lives and relevant to virtually every aspect of human endeavour including consumption. The dynamics of its role in consumption is markedly interesting in that there are different religious faiths and in most cases with different tenets that guide believers' actions. Religious affiliations in the form of communities of consumers are prescriptive to a great extent. Accordingly, more often than not, members' decisions around consumption activities of goods and services are closely linked to the notion of trust and commitment in their religious relationships. So, it is not surprising that the tenets that bind members of specific religious faith together are spread across different contexts. This explains why religion is described as some form of cultural globalisation. The choices of specific products, brands, labelling, and packaging, how these market products and services are priced, the mode of distribution, and how their value is communicated to the target audience are becoming increasingly moderated by religious values. While the literature is awash with publications on religion and its link to consumption, surprisingly, not so much has been written around this phenomenon and its links to consumption, specifically in developing nations' context, which leaves us with many unanswered questions.

Meanwhile, the fundamental discourse of developing nations often revolves around the fact that they are nations with lower economic development compared with developed nations. However, increasing evidence continues to emphasise that consumption issues in developing nations cannot be discounted. This contention is underpinned by the increasing activities of several multinationals in these nations which suggests that these contexts could not be considered inconsequential in the global marketing system. Simply put, the landscape of consumer behaviour is changing rapidly, and there is a compelling need not only to keep up with this pace but also to make a meticulous link between this, religion, and religiosity towards extending the current understanding around this research theme. Accordingly, there are gaps in the extant literature on the dynamics of consumption patterns vis-à-vis religion in relation to developing nations. Hence, this edited book which combines eclectic perspectives on the topic is being introduced to address these gaps.

SCOPE OF THE BOOK

Essentially, this book, *Religion and Consumer Behaviour in Developing Nations*, focuses on exploring consumer behaviour in relation to religion and religiosity in developing nations. The chapters address different aspects of consumption activities in relation to religion at the individual level such as motivation and involvement, perception, learning, attitude, the self, and personality. Similarly, chapters on consumer behaviour in social settings contextualised to developing nations ranging from culture, sub-culture, income and social class, family, to reference groups will be incorporated into the book. It also explores the discourse around branding, ethics, and digital marketing in relation to consumption and developing nations as the contextual platform. Hence, contributions on these will be critically and robustly featured in the book. In this book, the discourse around religion is reasonably broad as examples, illustrations, and postulations are teased out from various religious practices including Christianity, Islam, Jehovah's witnesses, Hinduism, Buddhism, Judaism, Sikhism, Atheism, and African Traditional Religion, among others, as relevant to consumption and specific topics. Meanwhile, developing nations, as will be covered in this book, are those that are considered to have lower economic development compared with developed nations. This includes sub-Saharan African countries, China, India, Mexico, and several others that fit the criteria.

TARGET AUDIENCE

This comprehensive publication is intended as a compendium of research materials that will constitute an essential reference source, building on the extant literature in the field of marketing and consumer behaviour. Essentially, the primary target markets of the book are postgraduate students, researchers, managers, and policy makers for insight into consumption practices within a religious context and the relevance of these to business and societal developments.

The secondary target market of the book consists of students studying marketing at the undergraduate level that will need to deepen their knowledge on how religion impacts consumer behaviour in developing nations. By and large, it is hoped that this text will illuminate the field and serve as a key source of research material for these target markets.

OBJECTIVES OF THE BOOK

This book seeks to achieve these broad objectives:

1. Enable readers to develop a coherent understanding of basic underpinnings of religion and consumer behaviour as they relate to individual and group-oriented consumption decisions.
2. Provide readers with insight into how the interlinkage of religion and consumer behaviour concepts may be amenable to developing nations' contemporary real-life situations.

In more specific terms, the text aims to:

1. Highlight the individual aspects of consumers from perception to motivation, personality, learning, the self, and attitude in relation to religion.
2. Discuss consumers' religiosity and consumption in the context of cultural and social settings to cover social class, culture, sub-culture, values, and how these factors interrelate to influence family and societal consumption issues.
3. Examine consumer decision-making processes through the use of relevant models and family consumption dynamics in relation to religion and religiosity in developing nations.
4. Discuss the ethical issues in consumption vis-à-vis religion in developing nations.
5. Explore the place of religion in brand, branding, and brand culture in relation to consumer behaviour in developing nations.
6. Examine the nexus of religion and digital marketing in relation to consumption activities in the context of developing nations.
7. Provide enriched details that will be of good value to all the stakeholders including marketers, consumers, academics, and others.

Dr Ayantunji Gbadamosi
University of East London, UK

Dr Ayodele Oniku
University of Lagos, Nigeria

Acknowledgements

As the editors of *Religion and Consumer Behaviour in Developing Nations*, we have received great support from many people in diverse ways. Most notably the contributions and enthusiasm of our colleagues, the chapter contributors, are invaluable. They are inspiring and committed scholars to work with. Likewise, we would like to appreciate the team at Edward Elgar, especially Ellen Pearce, Catherine Cumming and Beatrice McCartney, who supported the project from proposal to the final stage: their effort and time make this book a reality. Moreover, we acknowledge our students who are always keen to discuss marketing issues with us and thereby ensure teaching the subject remains interesting and gratifying. To others whom we have not explicitly mentioned, we think of you and thank you also. By and large, it is notable that the inspiration and empowerment for this book come from God for which we are eternally grateful.

Dr Ayantunji Gbadamosi
University of East London, UK

Dr Ayodele Oniku
University of Lagos, Nigeria

1. A critical overview of religion, culture and consumption in developing nations

Ayantunji Gbadamosi

INTRODUCTION

Religion is an enigma. It is interestingly complex in that it has a global relevance in various ways. It is closely interlocked with many other phenomena such as politics, ethics, culture, and consumption. Relating it to consumption specifically opens up a number of spectacular avenues for discussion. In the marketing parlance, consumption is presumably related to every individual and consumer segment in one form or another. It applies to old as well as the young, rich and the poor, various educational categories, all geographical locations, and in various seasons, to mention but a few cases. For instance, while the Covid-19 pandemic may have changed consumption patterns of many households as a specific phase of humanity, it does not in any way remove the discourse outright.

Meanwhile, in a somewhat related way, the discourse of religion is wide-ranging. Those who are not affiliated to any religion have reasons for their stance and their religiosity as well as reasons for such a disposition to make the explication of religion to consumption very intriguing. The interrelated nature of both religion and consumption indicates a varying dynamic of consumer behaviour in different contexts. Hence, it is judicious to show interest in developing countries as a context rather than having a broad and overly generalised focus on the subject. Such undue generalisation will constrain the extent of meticulosity that could be applied to studying the nitty-gritty of such an important phenomenon. Meanwhile, nations are categorised on the basis of their economic conditions. Broadly speaking, countries are categorised as developed economies, developing countries, and economies in transition (UN, 2013). Statistically, one of the commonly used indicators of the economic position of nations is gross national income (GNI). Hence, for the year 2020, the low-income economies are noted as those countries with a GNI per capita of no more than $1,025 in 2018, while those with a GNI that ranges between $1,026 and $3,995 are categorised as falling into the lower middle-income category, and those regarded as upper middle-income economies are characterised by a GNI of between $3,996 and $12,375 (World Bank, 2020). Accordingly, and as stated in the same source, those with more than $12,375 GNI are known as high-income economies (World Bank, 2020). In addition to the statistical calculation, another useful indicator of developing countries which will give us a more qualitative understanding of the context and serve the operational definition of the term is to define such countries as those with a GNI lower than those of developed countries. Besides, some of the common characteristics of developing economies have been shown as low per capita income, overpopulation, high unemployment rate, high level of illiteracy, low level of technological development, and people tend to be caste-minded and religious (Knowledge Team, 2017). Hence, cases and illustrations will be drawn from this context to discuss the interactions of religion and consumer behaviour. This chapter, which sets the pace for others in this book, covers a number of key issues including emerging issues in contemporary consumer behaviour, the consumer decision-making process, main influences on consumer behaviour, and a critical overview of culture and religion. Other issues addressed in the chapter are religion and consumption in developing nations as well as the dynamics of this consumption pattern in the twenty-first-century developing nations.

CONTEMPORARY CONSUMER BEHAVIOUR AND THE EMERGING ISSUES: A CRITICAL OVERVIEW

Consumer behaviour has been considered an interesting phenomenon from different perspectives. Whether we consider it from the perspective of the consumers whose behaviour is the focus in the discourse or from the viewpoint of business organisations that use the knowledge for decision making, it remains a fascinating issue. In summing up, Asem (2018) describes it as involving identification, consumption, and the removal of products and services as well as the processes that give rise to these actions and those following them. This perspective is elaborate and aligns very well with several other contributions on this subject such as those offered by Hoyer et al. (2018), Babin and Harris (2018), Solomon (2018), and Schiffman and Wisenblit (2019). Hence, it could be a good platform upon which the discussion in this segment and the chapter could be based. Consumer behaviour as a phenomenon is even more interesting when considering the discourse in relation to the contemporary consumer who is awash with choices and strategies for fulfilling her needs. This is the point made by Singhal (2018), who indicates that the consumer of today is confronted with the dilemma of gauging the balance between the risks and benefits of innovation. As indicated in the literature, we experience innovation every day. The food we eat and the mode of serving it, the fashion items we use for different occasions, the automobile we use in various ways, and services of various professionals are some of the areas in which we can see pointers of the innovative developments in society in recent times. Similarly, our experiences in the gig economy have taken the contemporary consumption story to a whole new level far above the traditional terrain. We react to these innovations differently in that some are enthusiastic about the new technological breakthrough while others are not (Singhal, 2018). For instance, one category of consumer will not only be willing to pay a premium to acquire a new invention but will also willingly stay in the queue to be among the first set of consumers that will get the product on the same day it is launched. Conversely, another group could show no interest at all in new market offerings as they are considered to be risky in various ways (economically, socially, physically, or in other ways) due to their newness. It is therefore not surprising that having a good knowledge of consumer behaviour is sine qua non to successful business practice in the contemporary competitive marketing environment (Shaw et al., 2017).

The interest in consumer behaviour is not only applicable to the process associated with the acquisition and consumption of goods and services but also in the disposition of products. So, issues around recycling and reusage are becoming more and more relevant to the discourse of consumerism. Ting et al.'s (2019) study on the disposition of smartphones in an emerging economy provides some insight into this interesting area. The study focuses on students in a developing country and finds that product attachment and compatibility are key influencing factors in such decisions. Specifically, they noted that students are strongly connected to their smartphone until the point when it breaks or loses compatibility. They indicate that the decision to dispose of the smartphones is not linked to the price paid for it or the brand of the phones. This study which revolves around Malaysia as a developing country challenges the conventional understanding that places undue emphasis on prices and brands as core factors in consumption dynamics. It underscores the increasing relevance of not only studying consumer behaviour in a contemporary context but also in different research contexts such as developing nations, and exploring relevant influencing factors that underpin the decisions such as the key role of religion.

Consumer Decision-Making Process: Emerging Issues

Exploring consumer behaviour as a process beginning with need recognition all the way to post purchase evaluation has been a popular discussion in marketing literature. Although the detailed discussion of this in relation to religion in developing countries is presented in Chapter 4, this segment simply teases out the emerging issues in the subject towards presenting a robust foundation for the phenomenon addressed in this book.

Something so fundamental about consumer behaviour is the need which also by implication indicates that the stage of need recognition is essential. This is the stage where the gap between the current state and the desired state of the consumer becomes highlighted. Our needs in life are diverse and vary in many ramifications. The need for the basic essentials of life like food and water is considered crucial. There is also the need for products that bring us close to others, usually discussed as social needs. There are a good number of studies around consumers' needs such as Maslow (1943), Adams (1963), McClelland (1978); these are some of the studies that emphasise the diversity of our needs as discussed in different contexts. For example, it could be argued that consumers in different cultural contexts could exhibit different types of needs. The specific factors that differentiate developing countries from developed ones could also be reasons to account for differences in their needs. Hence, consumers' needs in developing countries such as Malaysia, Nigeria, Ghana, Mexico, and the Philippines could be dissimilar to those in developed countries like the United States, United Kingdom, Canada, and France. Some of these needs are linked to taboos, ceremonies, and sacrifices as emphasised by Rihtaršič and Rihtaršič (2017) in their paper on the model of consumer behaviour with a focus on feminine hygiene.

In a bid to satisfy the identified needs, consumers explore various sources of information that could give them details around products and services market offerings that could be used to solve the identified problems. These sources could be commercial or non-commercial. More often than not, marketers provide information about products and services to make favourable mention of their offerings. Hence, such details around product suitability and functionality are embedded in marketing communication messages in the form of advertising, sales promotion, publicity and public relations, personal selling, and direct marketing. Also, the increasing use of digital technology has widened the sources of commercial messages for consumers. The internet usage in the world has seen a significant increase in recent times as the figure is given as 4.65 as at May 31, 2020 (Internet World Stats, 2020). As shown in this source, this represents a 59.6 per cent penetration rate for the entire population. This could help in a number of ways to provide some crucial details that could help consumers concerning the likelihood of usefulness of products or services to consumers. Nonetheless, given that there is a limit to the usefulness of the information obtained by consumers from these sources, they often find non-commercial sources of information handy. These include sources such as family, friends, co-workers, government agencies, and non-governmental organisations. Given the typical close ties within the family systems in most of the developing countries, this is an interesting explanation that will be vital to decisions within these societal systems. In Hofstede's national cultural typology, the notion of collectivism fits this scenario. An example of this is the notion of *Umbutu* which was explained as indicating that it is society that emphasises the existence of an individual. As explained in Kruger et al. (2009: 161), it is an African term which means 'my humanity is bound to your humanity', meaning 'one'. This plays a key role in how people share information on purchases and consumption activities. Since these sources do not have commercial motives, they tend to have more credibility than commercial sources.

At the stage of evaluation of alternatives, consumers screen the options available in relation to the applicable criteria. A good number of criteria could be used, depending on the nature of the products. For example, fuel efficiency, price, and comfort could be used for the selection of cars, while location, price, and closeness to amenities could be the criteria for the selection of houses. Apart from the nature of the product, the context where decisions are being made such as developed nations versus developing nations could influence or distinguish the criteria that consumers use to evaluate the appropriateness of the products or services to be selected. Religion and culture that constitute the key elements of this book could also be the key criteria. For instance, more often than not, what to eat and what to wear are influenced by religious values. Religion is increasingly becoming a defining factor in people's choices of goods and services in recent times. Further details about this are discussed later in the chapter.

The stage of decision making is fundamental to this process as it is the stage where the actual selection of the market offering which emanates from the evaluation stage takes place. The dynamics of the consumption system indicating how decisions about consumptions are made tend to be different from one society to another. For example, the question of who makes the decisions could be society-related and this also changes with time. We can draw illustration on this from the notion of family-buying roles which addresses how family members interact to play the roles of initiator, influencer, gatekeeper, decider, and user of the products or services involved. The extant literature (Munroe and Munroe, 1972; Harvey et al., 2000) indicates that decision-making roles in most developing countries are played by spouses, unlike in other contexts where children's decision-making power is stronger. Interestingly, some studies have cautioned on this postulation indicating that children could also make decisions in some circumstances. A good example here is the study of Gbadamosi (2012) who argues that children in Nigeria, especially in cosmopolitan cities, are sometimes given free will to choose when the products involved are routinely consumed items such as snacks. Similarly, the notion of e-shopping also creates a twist to the issues of purchase decisions. There are indications that e-shoppers and traditional shoppers could be similar or dissimilar in how they approach their purchase decisions (Dennis et al., 2009). This understanding is needed for effective discussion of contemporary marketing and societal dynamics.

At the stage of post-purchase evaluation, consumers compare their experience after the use of the products with the expectations they had before buying the products. This could lead to satisfaction and dissatisfaction. The outcome of this also determines whether a repeat purchase will take place or not. Also, repeat purchase is most likely to result in loyalty to the brand or the organisation. Many factors could be useful to trigger loyalty among consumers. Fundamentally, the market offerings should satisfy the needs but one of the challenges for businesses today is that more firms are also looking into satisfying customers. Hence, additional benefits such as warranties and excellent customer service would be needed to keep customers 'locked' into a firm's transaction system. Shaw et al.'s (2017) study into Czech consumer behaviour and warranty claims found that young consumers have a positive tendency for warranty claims. Interestingly, they show more satisfaction with warranty procedure. Apart from this study which relates to specific consumer segments, providing some degree of assurance over purchases made could be significantly beneficial for both parties in a transaction. In the same vein, just as consumers use religion at the stage of evaluation to screen which item to buy and which to avoid, they also tend to use religious belief as a guide to know whether a particular market offering has provided the needed value in specific transactions. As an example, the promise of a food vendor that the items offered for sale are compliant with halal standards of practice will be expected to hold true. To discover that this was actually not the case after consumption will be greatly disappointing to such consumers and will understandably result in dissatisfaction and in some cases negative word of mouth.

Consumer Behaviour: What Are the Main Influences?

Fundamentally, a number of factors influence consumer behaviour. Broadly speaking, we can categorise them as psychological and sociological factors. The former consists of factors such as attitudes, perceptions, self, personality and self-concept, and learning. The impact of these factors could be interactive in terms of how individuals, whether based in developing nations or developed countries, make their day-to-day consumption decisions. On the other hand, the sociological factors relate to how consumers' decisions are underpinned by other people in one form or another. These are mainly reference groups, culture, social class, and family. Meanwhile, another classification which features prominently in this chapter is the categorisation into personal factors, social-cultural factors, and marketing stimuli (see Figure 1.1).

Egan and Taylor (2010), in their study on shoplifting, unethical behaviour, and personality, found that all dimensions of consumers' personality are

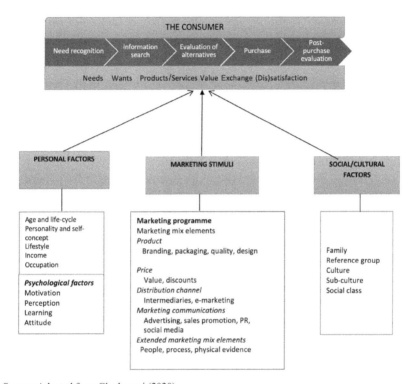

Source: Adapted from Gbadamosi (2020).

Figure 1.1   Major influences on consumer decisions

related to shoplifting and the consumer ethical belief scale. Another interesting finding in the literature is in the area of ethical consumerism, organic products, and sustainability. A study found that young students in Brno are willing to pay a premium for the freshness and better taste of organic products as well as the associated quality and are positively inclined to information relating to the moral and health issues associated with this purchase type (Švecová and Odehnalová, 2019). This is interesting to note, especially when compared to the commonly reported findings around ethical consumerism which tends to suggest somewhat different behaviour patterns from young consumers. On the issue of sustainability, it is reported that the motivation of consumers to embrace sustainable consumption such as switching to green electricity and limiting the use of private cars by switching to public transportation is rather limited. According to Hartmann et al. (2018), this involves costs to individuals and does not provide notable short- or medium-term personal benefits. Hence, in their study of the role of psychological empowerment in climate-protective behaviour, Hartmann et al. (2018) suggest that the behaviour of an individual in favour of the environment could be kindled by psychological empowerment which could be emphasised in various marketing messages designed to reach these consumers. So far, irrespective of the classification used, the notion of culture and religion remains core to the deeper part of the consumption system. Hence, these are now discussed in detail in the next section.

CULTURE AND RELIGION: A GENERAL OVERVIEW

As established earlier, consumption behaviour is influenced by a myriad of factors which can also be categorised in a number of ways. Meanwhile, one of the defining influences on consumption is culture. We will examine some of the interesting definitions of culture before going further into how the phenomenon is linked to religion as this intersection constitutes the focal part of this book. Culture is seen as a source of learning the symbolic system represented in the arts, aesthetics, drama, music, ritual, dance, and cosmetics by members of a society (Mansori et al., 2015). Another interesting definition of this phenomenon is the one proposed by Solomon (2020), it is seen as the personality of a particular society. Since personality is unique to an individual and specifies his or her personal being, it is understandable why this author applies this phenomenon at a wider or cultural context to indicate the specificity of that system. Meanwhile, far earlier than this, culture has been explained as the distinctive attitudes which distinguish a group of people from another (Temin, 1997). Hence, in a study on an analysis of how culture and religion affect perceived corruption in a global context, Mensah (2014) argues that viewing culture in this sense indicates that it is expressed through a variety of issues such as institutions, language, history, and religion, and both culture and religion contribute independently to the level of perceived corruption at the global level (Mensah, 2014). From the foregoing, we can infer that defining culture could be done in a number of ways. For example, we can have a definition of how it relates to an individual and how it underpins the dynamics of groups of people. This is linked to the claim that culture could be seen as the social and cognitive processes relating to individuals that underline several settings that individuals encounter in their endeavours (Abu-Nimer, 2001). A good number of scholarship effort corroborates this core role of culture in consumer behaviour. Examples include Mooij (2003), Arnould and Thompson (2005),

Mokhlis (2006), Alam et al. (2011), Nayeem (2012), Polese and Seliverstova (2020), and Chatterjee and Mandal (2020).

Meanwhile, as can be inferred from these key highlights, there is a considerable link between religion and people's culture. So, by and large, narratives are closely related to us as people in terms of who we are, where we come from, and give cohesion to our shared beliefs of common origin identity and how this is transmitted among members (Andrews et al., 2015). This implies that narration is linked to our religions and cultures. For example, Jamal and Sharifuddin (2015) note the nature of Muslim communities to be collectivist which makes it more amenable to word-of-mouth and in-group recommendations for choices of products and services in the marketplace. Gbadamosi (2019a) notes a similar point for Christianity in his study which revolves around Pentecostalism, women entrepreneurship, and Black African consumerism in the United Kingdom. A similar pattern was noted in an earlier study (Gbadamosi, 2015). In these cases, adherents engage in solidarity with respect to consumption, business patronage, and recommendation in the form of word-of-mouth communication. This suggests that the link between religion and culture is beyond superficial.

Interestingly, with a critical review of the activities of religious faiths such as Sikhism, Islam, Hinduism, and Buddhism, it has also been pointed out that religion could be key to peace making (Cox et al., 1994; Abu-Nimer, 2001). This is closely related to the claim by Abu-Nimer (2001) that effective interfaith interactions could emphasise a number of things including ensuring that the facilitation team has the knowledge of different groups and exploring what makes each of the religions unique. For example, it has been noted that Islamic adherents are idealists who were brought up to follow a Malay philosophy that emphasises being cautious in decision making, which ensures that their actions result in fewer mistakes (Cornwell et al., 2005). Moreover, the effectiveness in interfaith dialogue would stress that scripture and sacred texts enrich this dialogue and that rituals and symbols could be useful to enhance this interaction. Also, in such interfaith dialogue, spirituality is quite significant to changing the attitudes of participants.

The study of Jamal and Sharifuddin (2015) presents a useful addition to the discourse of religion and culture in relation to food consumption. Drawing from the extant literature (Ahmed, 2008) they note that, since Islam indicates some food types to be unlawful (haram), while others are lawful (halal), businesses owned by Muslims as well as some mainstream retailers offer packaged halal food in areas with a considerable number of Muslims in the British marketing environment. This corroborates the observation noted by Winter (2006) that just as we cannot have a society without a culture, no culture exists without some form of religion. In his study that revolves around religion, culture, and the human rights of women, the issue of the Islamic headscarf, known as the *hijab*, is highlighted. Controversies surrounding this dressing mode have been documented in several places. The core arguments around these religious issues resonate with the global citizenship phenomenon which is a sense of belonging to a wider community and common humanity that embodies political, cultural, and social interconnectedness and interdependence among the local, national, and global systems (Haynes, 2019). By and large, the interplay of religion and culture comes to the fore more often than not in various societies. Meanwhile, from the perspective of Mokhlis (2009), religion and consumer behaviour are closely interlocked to the extent that it is impossible to see the influence of other factors on consumption choices.

When considering how religion impacts consumption in developing countries, it is relevant to discuss the notions of in-groups and out-groups. A seminal study on this is the work of Tajfel. With reference to Sherif (1966), it is argued in this publication that whenever members of certain groups interact with other groups, it results in in-group behaviour (Tajfel, 1982a: 2). So, members of a particular group are identified to be among the 'in-group' and people outside this are known as 'out-group'. Hence, people of a specific religious group, say Christianity, would see fellow adherents as in-group members while people outside of this religion are the 'out-group'. As indicated by Tajfel (1982a), three components of group identification can be highlighted as cognitive, evaluative, and emotional investment. According to him, the cognitive aspect revolves around members' sense of awareness of their group, whereas the evaluative element indicates that the awareness is linked to some connotations and the third emphasises the members' emotional investment in both the awareness and evaluations. This knowledge is linked to the Social Identity Theory in that social identity explains that part of an individual's self-concept which emanates from their knowledge of being members of a social group(s) (Tajfel, 1982b: 2). In the context of this book and the notion of Social Identity Theory, apart from the consumer's religiosity, the relevance of social norms associated with the religion would influence his or her choices of products and services. This explains why Shavitt et al. (2006) claim that conformity in the choice of market offerings may be unique to vertical collectivism, which emphasises deference to authority figures and the wishes of the in-group.

From a broad perspective, using medicine or healthcare consumption as the contextual platform, Hordern (2016) indicates that it is important to consider religion, belief, and culture as potential sources of personal strength and moral purpose in the healthcare system. This system encapsulates the welfare of patients vis-à-vis their experience of ill health, sufferings, healing, and dying as well as the welfare of clinicians. Hordern (2016) suggests further that it is important to consider the associated sensitivities as there could be conflict between the clinical judgement, religion, belief, and culture of an individual. As argued in this publication, it is possible for the belief of an individual to not be totally in alignment with his or her religion and cultural normative teachings. Hence, the dynamics should be managed without making any assumptions. This brings in the notion of religiosity. Religiosity is defined as the degree to which an individual adheres to the values, beliefs, and practices of his or her religion and uses them in daily living (Worthington et al., 2003; Jamal and Sharifuddin, 2015). This is not a radical departure from the definition of Patel (2012) which sees it as the degree to which someone is attached to a specific religious group. From the perspective of McDaniel and Burnett (1990), as cited by Mansori et al. (2015), while religious affiliation is about adhering to a particular religious group, religiosity is about the psychological and behavioural phenomenon that indicates an individual's degree of commitment and belief in specific religious values and ideals. In his study on the relevance and measurement of religiosity in consumer behaviour research, Mokhlis' (2009) findings show that religiosity has an influence on consumer behaviour in relation to factors such as price, quality, and impulse buying. Similarly, a more recent study conducted by Nasse et al. (2019) indicates a probable link between consumer behaviour and consumers' religiosity. This is an interesting finding which relates to Burkina Faso, a developing country. According to this group of authors, religion plays an important role in consumption in this country.

On the question of moral guidance and principles as embedded in religion, culture, and politics, Yagboyaju examines corruption within some of the key religious faiths in the Nigerian context. He traces corrupt practices to the disobedience of Adam and Eve who ate the forbidden fruit in the Garden of Eden as indicated in Genesis 3:5–24. Nonetheless, it is noteworthy that the Holy Bible underscores penitence and retribution for immoral and corrupt practices (Yagboyaju, 2017). He positions this discourse within the lens of the Pentecostal movement in Nigeria, in which churches speak to the material and spiritual needs of the people with a promise of life-changing breakthroughs and miracles. This tends to foster multi-religious competition in relation to those who believe this and fuels the insatiable appetite for primitive accumulation and is closely linked to the acts of those benefiting from the corrupt system.

The African Traditional Religion is characterised by multiple practices, doctrines, and experiences. In this discourse, there is a distinction between the High God, who is the supreme being that is the creator of all things and the source of all power, and the other small gods. These are commonly held beliefs in most African countries, including Nigeria and Ghana. In this context, most of the small gods are associated with nature such as rivers, rocks, iron, lagoons, and mountains. Drawing from the extant literature such as Egberongbe (1988: 69–87) and Aiyede et al. (2011: 228–9), these religious practices have elaborate moral systems and discipline for most of the society. One example cited by Egberongbe (1988) is that of Ifa, a type of god in Yoruba, notably in the south

west of Nigeria, which stipulates 'dos' and 'don'ts' for followers such as promoting honesty, hard work, and detesting dictatorial actions over others. For
Islamic religion, Yagboyaju (2017) indicates that the faith is expected to per-
meate every facet of the life of adherents, and he emphasises that it is a culture
that connotes a way of worship, an approach to running a business, an economic system, an approach to business management, and many other aspects
of life. Hence, it hardly omits any part of human existence. In fact, the close
relationship between culture, religion, and corruptions which could encourage
the abuse of power by public officials is part of the reason why Yagboyaju
(2017) advocates a separation of politics and religion. Logically, this explains
why its impact on consumption is notably significant and enduring.

RELIGION IN DEVELOPING NATIONS: PERSPECTIVE
ON CONSUMPTION

It could be argued that religion is a pervasive phenomenon with wide implications on our day-to-day decision making linking issues such as values, beliefs,
ethics, and consumption as shown in Figure 1.2. Its impact is worldwide which
explains why it has a wide scope. Based on an eclectic review of literature
including materials from the BBC, *Encyclopaedia Britannica*, and the specific
websites of each of the religions, Table 1.1 shows some useful details about
some common religions of the world.

   While so many issues remain unclear about each of the religious groups, it
is clear that there are some differences in how each influences its adherents.
However, it is important to state that despite the variation in people's specific
values and beliefs concerning various religious faiths, the behavioural patterns of the followers and the correlation between religiosity and values are
considerably consistent across monothetic religions (Mansori et al., 2015). It
is indicated that religious rituals, characterised by sacredness, constitute an
important factor influencing an individual and groups (Suhrke, 1971). The
complexity on this becomes more pronounced when considered in relation to
the contextual factors around consumer behaviour. For example, it is believed
that certain factors differentiate developing nations from developed countries.
The sub-Saharan African region, which constitutes an example of developing
nations, is characterised by stability challenges such as poverty, lack of democracy, and ineffective institutions (Pokimica et al., 2012). These tend to reflect
in the consumption of this consumer group to a great extent.

   In view of this claim, there are some specific studies that have been conducted in relation to developing nations on their consumption dynamics. The
study of Amine et al. (2012), which revolves around consumers' opposition
motives to the modern retailing format in Tunisia, found that when compared
to developed nations, consumers in this context are prone to avoid and defect

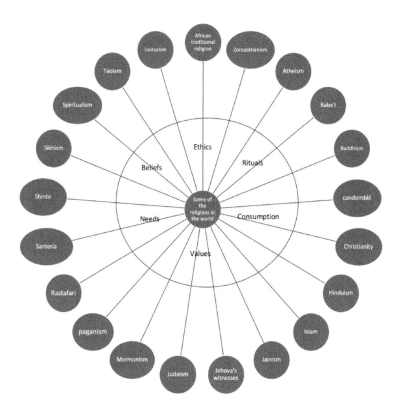

Figure 1.2   The nexus of religion and consumption: selected examples in perspective

from mass retailing. These authors indicate that this is linked to culture, education, and religion. With reference to a body of literature (Sow, 2005; Dumbili, 2013; Porter 2013), Nasse et al. (2019), whose study revolves around Burkina Faso, indicate that industrial drinks such as Coca-Cola or Fanta could be used for medical functions, food functions, and religious functions which explains their use in various events such as wedding ceremonies, funeral rites, religious rituals, and many others. Thus, consumption and religion are markedly linked as shown in this context.

Table 1.1   Religions and their dynamics

Religion	Basic description	Further comments
African Traditional Religion	Can be traced back to prehistoric times. It is characterised by a reliance on oral stories which have been passed down from generations about gods, superhuman entities, and ancestors.	Followers acknowledge the existence of the Supreme God who created everything and other small gods. Although they do not have any major doctrinal teachings, their beliefs revolve around issues like the existence of deities, divination, and ancestor veneration.
Atheism	Those following this religious stance are known as Atheists, and hold that God or gods are man-made ideas.	Adherents have no relationship with God or any other gods.
Baha'i	Founded in the nineteenth century by Bahá'u'lláh.	Emphasises that human kind be united spiritually.
Buddhism	A way of living based on the teachings of the founder, Siddhartha Gautama.	Uses an understanding of cause and effect through the use of practical approaches like meditation for gaining insight towards achieving enlightenment. It focuses on shaping future through thought, actions, and words.
Candomblé	Its root could be traced back to the slave trade and it originated in Brazil.	This is a combination of elements of Catholicism and some aspects of Indigenous African religion and focuses on the belief of a supreme creator as well as several minor deities. It holds that everyone has their deity that serves to protect them and guide their destiny.
Christianity	The world's biggest faith, with a focus on the teachings of Jesus Christ.	As indicated on the Christianity.org website, Christianity should not be equated with going to church but is about having a relationship with God. It revolves around acknowledging the fact that Jesus died for the sins of the world. Hence, the religion is known as 'Good News' in that trusting in Jesus Christ makes it possible for anyone to have a relationship with God.
Hinduism	A collection of faiths entrenched in the religious ideas of India.	Hinduism revolves around a belief in reincarnation. It emphasises following righteousness through spiritual practices, called yogas, and prayers which are also known as *bhakti*.

Religion	Basic description	Further comments
Islam	Revealed in its final form by the Prophet Muhammad, in the seventh century CE.	The followers of Islam are called Muslims and believe in only one God, translated as *Allah* in Arabic. They believe that God sent many prophets to provide direction on how to live and the final Prophet was Muhammad. They believe that there are five pillars of Islam, namely, declaration of faith that there is no other God apart from God and Mohammed is his messenger (Shahadah), praying five times daily, fasting, giving to charity, and pilgrimage to Mecca.
Jainism	An early philosophy and moral teaching that developed in the seventh–fifth century BCE in India.	The name was formed from the word '*jina*' which refers to 'victor' or 'liberator' in the spiritual context. It focuses on achieving liberation and bliss through living a life of renunciation and harmlessness.
Jehovah'sWitnesses	A Christian-oriented evangelistic religious movement that originated around the nineteenth century in the United States.	The followers of this religion hold many of the beliefs consistent with the traditional Christian perspective but also believe in some that are unique to the religious group. They believe that Jehovah (God) is the most high and the Holy Spirit is the active force of God in this world, while Jesus Christ is the agent of God who reconciles sinful humans to God. They also believe that those who accept Jehovah will be rewarded with membership of the millennial kingdom, while those who do not acknowledge him will not go to hell but become totally exterminated.
Judaism	Judaism originated in the Middle East over 3,500 years ago and is about the covenant relationship of the Jewish people with God.	It revolves around the belief that there is only one God who appointed Jews to be his chosen people to set the example of ethical behaviour and holiness to the world. Their religious document is called the Torah and religious leaders are addressed as Rabbi.

Religion	Basic description	Further comments
Mormonism	Founded by Joseph Smith in 1830 CE in the United States. It is known as the Church of Jesus Christ of Latter-Day Saints.	The followers of this religion are known as Mormons and they believe that they are Christians but with some differences to mainstream Christianity. They do not acknowledge the notion of trinity but hold the view that the Father, Son, and Holy Ghost are three distinct gods. They believe in an afterlife and that individuals can become gods. The Mormons use 'Temple garment', an underwear with special religious significance often used by adult members for hallowed promises to God.
Paganism	A topical religious movement with a philosophical perspective on reverence for nature.	The focus of Pagans revolves around the natural world and they worship many deities. Most of them are eco-friendly thereby keenly interested in minimising damage to the natural environment. Some simply define Paganism as having no specific religion.
Rastafari	Originated in the 1930s and has its roots in Jamaica.	It combines mysticism, Protestant Christianity, and a pan-African political consciousness. Members, are called Rastas and most of them believe that Haile Selassie I, who was crowned the King of Ethiopia in 1930, is God who came to redeem all Black people. Part of their religious rituals are prayer sessions and all-night drumming ceremonies.
Santeria	Afro-Caribbean syncretic religion that originated from Cuba.	It is not fixed on a set of beliefs but revolves around a blend of several faiths and cultures. It displays a combination of Catholicism, West African Yoruba spirituality, and Caribbean tradition.
Shinto	Japanese traditional worldview and ritual with no specific founder.	Adherents are not expected to follow it as the only religion. It focuses on the belief that there are no absolutes as the action taken by people, whether good or bad, is accessed in relation to the context in which they take place.

Religion	Basic description	Further comments
Sikhism	Founded in the fifteenth century CE in India by Guru Nanak.	Adherents believe that there is only one God and equality among humans. They are focused on avoiding materialism, anger, covetousness and greed, lust, and pride, but embrace working, praying, and giving.
Spiritualism	Originated in the United States in the mid-nineteenth century and Spiritualists hold that it is possible to communicate with the dead.	It holds that people survive the deaths of their bodies and move into a spirit world. Adherents believe that those who have died and are in the spirit world have an interest in the lives of those that are alive.
Taoism	Developed from several religious and philosophical customs in early China.	Taoism, which is also known as Daoism, has its philosophical root in nature worship as well as the divination of Chinese ancestors. It holds that it is imperative for man to put his will to be in harmony with nature.
Unitarianism	A liberal religious movement with its origin in the United States.	Even though it has its origin from Jewish and Christian practices, it is open-minded to accommodate insights from other beliefs and is grounded in rational enquiry as opposed to external authority. It revolves around inclusivity and is open to all races, ages, sexual orientations, and religions.
Zoroastrianism	Founded by the Iranian Prophet Zoroaster.	Adherents believe in the supremacy of God, called Ahura Mazda, and are traditionally keen about protecting the natural environment as they believe that all creations should be loved and respected.

Sources: Adapted from BBC (2002, 2009, 2020a, 2020b), Christianity (n.d.), Diamond Day Buddhism (2020), Duchesne-Guillemin (2020), Encyclopaedia.com (2020), Godbey (n.d.), History (2018), McAlister (2020), Melton (n.d.a, n.d.b), MysticalBee (n.d.), Pagan Federation International (n.d.), Shah et al. (nd), SikhNet (n.d.), Unitarians (n.d.), Wigington (2019).

RELIGION AND CONSUMER BEHAVIOUR IN THE TWENTY-FIRST-CENTURY DEVELOPING NATIONS

Religion plays a key role in how consumers make sense of their purpose in life and responsibilities to themselves, others, and God but the narrative around religion is still considered controversial to an extent (Johnson, 2000; Mansori et al., 2015). It is important for marketers to be sensitive to their values, otherwise actions taken could be deemed offensive and result in a negative impression of the organisation and its brands. As an example, it has been noted that religion has significant implications among Africans with traditional religious beliefs playing a potent role in their pattern of day-to-day living and social interactions with various groups (Opoku, 1978; Addai et al., 2013). Its influence permeates virtually every aspect of life such as travelling, farming, eating, and drinking (Addai et al., 2013). The link between religion, trust and relationship marketing has also been established (Al-Abdulrazak and Gbadamosi, 2017). Overall, it is argued that religious affiliation constitutes a key determinant of people's interpersonal trust (Addai et al., 2013). The study of Cornwell et al. (2005), which revolves around cross-cultural study of the role of religion in consumers' ethical position, emphasises the significance of trust. They show that when business organisations participate to foster social integration which also engenders relationship and trust among consumers, these consumers will also exhibit loyalty to those businesses.

Meanwhile, these differences in how religion influences consumption generally emphasise the divide between developing and developed nations which seems to have been disrupted in some way by globalisation in which consumers are becoming increasingly exposed to the cultural values and mores of others through civilisation, immigration, and technological breakthroughs. Sheth (2006) indicates that the globalisation experienced in the twenty-first century is at variance from its first-wave counterpart in the 1800s. In the article 'Clash of Cultures or Fusion of Cultures?', Sheth (2006) argues that contemporary globalisation features a lack of economic growth of affluent countries that are predominantly aging which prompts their economic integration with emerging economies that are notably young. In this contention, it is argued that emerging economies, especially China and India, will rival the developed economies. He cites examples of evidence of such developments as major Western awards won by Indian writers and artists. Consequently, it was projected that this will result in a fusion of cultures rather than a clash of cultures. While this publication is now over a decade old, the current state of affairs in the world economy corroborates this projection. For example, Amine et al. (2012) note that the main actors in modern retailing are now making incursions into emerging nations as these countries offer decent growth prospects and returns on investment which could be attributed to a number of developments such as improvements in gross development product and an increasing middle class. The same argument is made by Rihtaršič and Rihtaršič (2017) who claim that the globalisation, continuous migration of people, and access to information make the boundary between rural and urban populations rather blurred.

The link between religion, religiosity, and consumer behaviour in developing countries remains of keen interest. In a study on religiosity and consumer behaviour, with a specific focus on Muslims in Burkina Faso, Nasse et al. (2019) raise a crucial question on why Muslims, who are expected to be less tolerant of the consumption of alcoholic drinks, are rather beginning to consume them. They conclude that the notion of religiosity should be taken into consideration by marketers of non-alcoholic drinks in the country.

CONCLUSION

Consumption activities constitute a key role in defining human systems. Irrespective of categories of life that we belong to, we consume various products and services to 'keep going'. Essentially, this is linked to the fact that these market offerings are designed by various organisations to satisfy needs of different categories. These could be described in a number of ways such as basic, sophisticated, social, personal, cultural, esteem-related, religion-related, and many others. Meanwhile, apart from the fact that consumers' needs are numerous, these needs vary in relation to time and several other contexts such as developed and developing countries. Hence, the nature of products and services consumed several decades ago would most likely be different from what is needed now. Hence, having an understanding of the contemporary consumer behaviour is a worthy endeavour. As there are changes in the nature of the market offerings so will such changes be evident in the process associated with buying them. Fundamentally, extant literature has established that consumption follows a decision-making process which consists of need recognition, search for information, evaluation of alternatives, purchase, and post-purchase evaluation. While the fundamental scholarship efforts establishing this contention date back several decades, there are emerging issues in the dynamics of how consumers move through them. From a very broad perspective, consumers' choices of products and services are influenced by a number of factors that could be categorised as personal, social-cultural, and marketing stimuli. These factors are interrelated in how they influence consumption. Nonetheless, the prominent examples of changes to the consumer decision-making process are the relevance of digital technologies and prominence of religion. Consumers' need for products associated with religions is diverse and continues to grow in line with the multiple religious groups all over the world. Similarly, while searching for information that could help the choice and evaluation of the available options, the role of religion is crucial especially for those with a high level of religiosity. Similarly, the specific choice to buy and the perception of how the object fits personal use are increasingly being tuned by religion. At the stage of post-purchase evaluation when consumers review the decisions to gauge whether the identified needs have been met or not, the relevance of religion in that process could be very significant.

While culture depicts the way and pattern of life of members of a particular society, its close link to religion could be pivotal in the explication of consumption decisions. The link emphasises the logic behind the study of consumption issues and processes in developing nations. The contemporary developing nations exhibit some similarities in consumption patterns that mirror those noted for developed nations (Gbadamosi, 2019b). Nonetheless, there are still some useful interesting differences. Arguments in either direction constitute part of the discourse that make the study of consumption intriguing. Adding the twist of religion to this enriches the excitement associated with the subject vis-à-vis the context of developing nations. It has been established that consumers in developing nations tend to be more religious when compared to those in developed societies. Meanwhile, consumers' attachment to their religious beliefs culminates in the trust they have for specific products and brands that ultimately reflects in preferences for such market offerings. Hence, by implication, both local and international marketers have great opportunities in the developing nations as communities with great and diverse needs. As different factors influence consumption, exploring the dynamics of religious beliefs in the strategic planning for businesses could yield handsome returns on investment.

REFERENCES

Abu-Nimer, M. (2001). Conflict resolution, culture, and religion: Toward a training model of interreligious peacebuilding. *Journal of Peace Research*, 38(6), 685–704.

Adams, J. S. (1963). Toward an understanding of inequity. *Journal of Abnormal and Social Psychology*, 67, 422–36.

Addai, I., Opoku-Agyeman, C., & Ghartey, H. T. (2013). An exploratory study of religion and trust in Ghana. *Social Indicators Research*, 110(3), 993–1012.

Ahmed, A. (2008). Marketing of halal meat in the United Kingdom: Supermarkets versus local shops. *British Food Journal*, 110, 655–70.

Aiyede, E. R., Simbine, A. T., Fagge, M. A., & Olaniyi, R. (2011). Religion, ethics and attitudes toward corruption in Nigeria. *Research for Development*, 25(1–2), 205–37.

Al-Abdulrazak, R., & Gbadamosi, A. (2017). Trust, religiosity, and relationship marketing: A conceptual overview of consumer brand loyalty. *Society and Business Review*, 12(3). DOI: 10.1108/SBR-03-2017-0014.

Alam, S. S., Mohd, R., & Hisham, B. (2011). Is religiosity an important determinant on Muslim consumer behaviour in Malaysia? *Journal of Islamic Marketing*, 2(1), 83–96.

Amine, A., & Hendaoui Ben Tanfous, F. (2012). Exploring consumers' opposition motives to the modern retailing format in the Tunisian market. *International Journal of Retail and Distribution Management*, 40(7), 510–27.

Andrews, M., Kinnvall, C., & Monroe, K. (2015). Narratives of (in)security: Nationhood, culture, religion, and gender: Introduction to the special issue. *Political Psychology*, 36(2), 141–9.

Arnould, E. J., & Thompson, C. J. (2005). Consumer culture theory (CCT): Twenty years of research. *Journal of Consumer Research*, 31(4), 868–82.

Asem, N. R. (2018). Consumer behaviour approach under the aspect of concept evolution. *Business and Administration*, 366(1), 51–66.

Babin, B. J., & Harris, E. J. (2018). *CB*. Boston, MA: Cengage Learning.

BBC (2002). Pagan beliefs. www.bbc.co.uk/religion/religions/paganism/beliefs/beliefs .shtml (accessed 17 May 2020).

BBC (2009). God, Zoroaster and immortals. www.bbc.co.uk/religion/religions/ zoroastrian/beliefs/god.shtml (accessed 15 May 2020).

BBC (2020a). Ethics in Shinto. www.bbc.co.uk/religion/religions/shinto/shintoethics/ ethics.shtml (accessed 16 May 2020).

BBC (2020b). Islam. www.bbc.co.uk/religion/religions/islam/ataglance/glance.shtml (accessed 15 May 2020).

Chatterjee, S., & Mandal, P. (2020). Traveler preferences from online reviews: Role of travel goals, class and culture. *Tourism Management*, 80, 104–8.

Christianity (n.d.). The basics of Christianity. https://christianity.org.uk/the-basics (accessed 28 April 2020).

Cornwell, B., Chi Cui, C., Mitchell, V., Schlegelmilch, B., Dzulkiflee, A., & Chan, J. (2005). A cross-cultural study of the role of religion in consumers' ethical positions. *International Marketing Review*, 22(5), 531–46.

Cox, H., Sharma, A., Abe, M., Sachedina A. L., Oberoi, H., & Idel, M. (1994). World religions and conflict resolution, in D. Johnston & C. Sampson (eds), *Religion: The Missing Dimension of Statecraft*. Oxford: Oxford University Press, pp. 266–84.

Dennis, C., Merrilees, B., Jayawardhena, C., & Tiu Wright, L. (2009). E-consumer behaviour. *European Journal of Marketing*, 43(9/10), 1121–39.

Diamond Day Buddhism (2020). What is Buddhism? www.diamondway-buddhism .org/buddhism/ (accessed 8 April 2020).

Duchesne-Guillemin, J. (2020). Zoroastrianism: Religion. 17 July. www.britannica .com/topic/Zoroastrianism (accessed 30 July 2020).

Dumbili, E. (2013). Changing patterns of alcohol consumption in Nigeria: An exploration of responsible factors and consequences. *Journal of the BSA MedSoc Group*, 7(1), 20–33.

Egan, V., & Taylor, D. (2010). Shoplifting, unethical consumer behaviour, and personality. *Personality and Individual Differences*, 48(8), 878–83.

Egberongbe, W. (1988). Ifa, the arrow: Pointer to nation – Building, in C. S. Momoh, C. O. Onikpe, & V. ChukwuDozie (eds), *Nigerian Studies in Religion and Tolerance*, Lagos: Centre for African and Black Arts Civilization.

Encyclopaedia.com (2020). African traditional religions. *Wordmark Encyclopaedia of Religious Practices*, 18 June. www.encyclopedia.com/religion/encyclopedias -almanacs-transcripts-and-maps/african-traditional-religions (accessed 8 July 2020).

Gbadamosi, A. (2012). Exploring children, family, and consumption behaviour: Empirical evidence from Nigeria. *Thunderbird International Business Review*, 54(4), 591–605.

Gbadamosi, A. (2015). Exploring the growing link of ethnic entrepreneurship, markets, and Pentecostalism in London (UK): An empirical study. *Society and Business Review*, 10(2), 150–69.

Gbadamosi, A. (2019a). Postmodernism, ethnicity, and celebrity culture in women's symbolic consumption. *International Journal of Market Research*. DOI: 10.1177/1470785319868363.

Gbadamosi, A. (2019b). Women entrepreneurship, religiosity, and value-co-creation with ethnic consumers: Revisiting the paradox. *Journal of Strategic Marketing*, 27(4), 303–16.

Gbadamosi, A. (2020). Buyer behaviour in the 21st century: Implications for SME marketing, in S. Nwankwo & A. Gbadamosi (eds), *Entrepreneurship Marketing: Principles and Practice of SME Marketing*, 2nd ed., Abingdon: Routledge, pp. 72–96.

Godbey, J. C (n.d.). Unitarianism and universalism. *Encyclopaedia Britannica*. www .britannica.com/topic/Unitarianism (accessed 17 May 2020).

Hartmann, P., Apaolaza, V., & D'Souza, C. (2018). The role of psychological empowerment in climate-protective consumer behaviour: An extension of the value-belief-norm framework. *European Journal of Marketing*, 52(1/2), 392–417.

Harvey, J., Carter, S., & Mudimu, G. (2000). A comparison of work values and motives among Zimbabwean and British managers. *Personnel Review*, 29(6), 723–42.

Haynes, J. (2019). Religion, education and security: The United Nations Alliance of Civilisations and Global Citizenship. *Religions*, 10(1), 51.

History (2018). Mormons. 21 August. www.history.com/topics/religion/mormons (accessed 30 June 2020).

Hordern, J. (2016). Religion and culture. *Medicine*, 44(10), 589–92.

Hoyer, W. D., MacInnis, D. J., & Pieters, R. (2018). *Consumer Behaviour*, 7th ed. Boston, MA: Cengage Learning.

Internet World Stats (2020). Usage and population statistics. www.internetworldstats .com/stats.htm (accessed 8 July 2020).

Jamal, A., & Sharifuddin, J. (2015). Perceived value and perceived usefulness of halal labelling: The role of religion and culture. *Journal of Business Research*, 68(5), 933–41.

Johnson, E. L. (2000). Describing the self within redemptive history. *Journal of Psychology and Christianity*, 19(1), 5–24.

Knowledge Team (2017). What are the characteristics of developing countries. *Knowledgiate*. www.knowledgiate.com/characteristics-of-developing-countries/ (accessed 8 July 2020).

Kruger, D. P., Gandy, S. K., Bechard, A., Brown, R., & Williams, D. (2009). Writing a successful Fulbright group projects abroad grant: Voices from a journey to South Africa. *Journal of Geography*, 108(4–5), 155–62.

Mansori, S., Sambasivan, M., & Md-Sidin, S. (2015). Acceptance of novel products: The role of religiosity, ethnicity and values. *Marketing Intelligence and Planning*, 33(1), 39–66.

Maslow, A. H. (1943). A theory of human motivation. *Psychological Review*, 50, 370–96.

McAlister, E. A. (2020). Rastafari: Political and religious movement. *Encyclopaedia Britannica*, 23 July. www.britannica.com/topic/Rastafari (accessed 30 July 2020).

McClelland, D. C. (1978). Managing motivation to expand human freedom. *American Psychologist*, 33(3), 201.

McDaniel, S. W. & Burnett, J. J. (1990). Consumer religiosity and retail store evaluative criteria. *Journal of the Academy of Marketing Science*, 18(2), 101–12.

Melton, J. G. (n.d.a). Jehovah's Witness. *Encyclopaedia Britannica*. www.britannica .com/topic/Jehovahs-Witnesses (accessed 28 April 2020).

Melton, J. G. (n.d.b). Spiritualism: Religion. *Encyclopaedia Britannica*. www .britannica.com/topic/spiritualism-religion (accessed 17 May 2020).

Mensah, Y. M. (2014). An analysis of the effect of culture and religion on perceived corruption in a global context. *Journal of Business Ethics*, 121(2), 255–82.

Mokhlis, S. (2006). The effect of religiosity on shopping orientation: An exploratory study in Malaysia. *Journal of American Academy of Business*, 9(1), 64–74.

Mokhlis, S. (2009). Relevancy and measurement of religiosity in consumer behavior research. *International Business Research*, 2(3), 75–84.

Mooij, M. D. (2003). Convergence and divergence in consumer behaviour: Implications for global advertising. *International Journal of Advertising*, 22(2), 183–202.

Munroe, R. L., & Munroe, R. H. (1972). Obedience among children in an East African society. *Journal of Cross-Cultural Psychology*, 3(4), 395–9.

MysticalBee (n.d.). 10 beliefs of Taoism religion. https://mysticalbee.com/beliefs-of -taoism-religion/ (accessed 15 May 2020).

Nasse, T. B., Ouédraogo, A., & Sall, F. D. (2019). Religiosity and consumer behavior in developing countries: An exploratory study on Muslims in the context of Burkina Faso. *African Journal of Business Management*, 13(4), 116–27.

Nayeem, T. (2012). Cultural influences on consumer behaviour. *International Journal of Business and Management*, 7(21), 79–91.

Opoku, K. A. (1978). West African traditional religion. Accra: FEP International Private.

Pagan Federation International (n.d.). What is Paganism. Paganism Federation International. www.paganfederation.org/what-is-paganism/ (accessed 30 June 2020).

Patel, M. (2012). Influence of religion on shopping behaviour of consumers: An exploratory study. *Abhinav National Monthly Refereed Journal of Research in Commerce and Management*, 1(5), 68–78.

Pokimica, J., Addai, I., & Takyi, B. K. (2012). Religion and subjective well-being in Ghana. *Social Indicators Research*, 106(1), 61–79.

Polese, A., & Seliverstova, O. (2020). Luxury consumption as identity markers in Tallinn: A study of Russian and Estonian everyday identity construction through consumer citizenship. *Journal of Consumer Culture*, 20(2), 194–215.

Porter, C. A. (2013). The religion of consumption and Christian neighbor love. Doctoral dissertation, Loyola University, Chicago.

Rihtaršič, T., & Rihtaršič, M. (2017). Model of consumer behaviour: Feminine hygiene. *Economics*, 5(1), 125–36.

Schiffman, L. G., & Wisenblit, J. (2019), *Consumer Behaviour*, 12th ed. Harlow: Pearson Education.

Shah, U. P., Strohl, G. R., & Dundas, P. (n.d.). Jainism. *Encyclopaedia Britannica*. www.britannica.com/topic/Jainism/Festivals (accessed 9 July 2020).

Shavitt, S., Lalwani, A. K., Zhang, J., & Torelli, C. J. (2006). The horizontal/vertical distinction in cross-cultural consumer research. *Journal of Counseling Psychology*, 16, 325–56.

Shaw, S., Chovancová, M., & Bejtkovský, J. (2017). Consumer behaviour and warranty claim: A study on Czech consumers. *Economics and Sociology*, 10(3), 90–101.

Sherif, M. (1966). *Common Predicament: Social Psychology of Intergroup Conflict and Cooperation*. Boston, MA: Houghton Mifflin.

Sheth, J. N. (2006). Clash of cultures or fusion of cultures? Implications for international business. *Journal of International Management*, 12(2), 218–21.

SikhNet (n.d.). Who are Sikhs? What is Sikhism? www.sikhnet.com/pages/who-are -sikhs-what-is-sikhism (accessed 16 May 2020).

Singhal, N. (2018). A study of consumer behaviour towards genetically modified foods and the moderating effects of health consciousness. *Vision*, 22(3), 306–15.

Solomon, M. R. (2018). *Consumer Behaviour: Buying, Having, and Being*, 12th ed. Harlow: Pearson Education.

Solomon, M. R. (2020). *Consumer Behaviour: Buying, Having, and Being*, 13th ed. Harlow: Person Education.

Sow, D. M. (2005). *Alimentation et boisson au Burkina Faso: au-delà de la survie*. Geneva: International Labour Organization.

Suhrke, A. (1971). Political rituals in developing nations: The case of the Philippines. *Journal of Southeast Asian Studies*, 2(2), 126–41.

Švecová, J., & Odehnalová, P. (2019). The determinants of consumer behaviour of students from Brno when purchasing organic food. *Review of Economic Perspectives*, 19(1), 49–64.

Tajfel, H. (1982a). Social psychology of intergroup relations. *Annual Review of Psychology*, 33, 1–39.

Tajfel, H. (ed.) (1982b). *Social Identity and Intergroup Relations*. Cambridge: Cambridge University Press.

Temin, P. (1997). Is it kosher to talk about culture? *Journal of Economic History*, 57(2), 267–87.

Ting, H., Thaichon, P., Chuah, F., & Tan, S. R. (2019). Consumer behaviour and disposition decisions: The why and how of smartphone disposition. *Journal of Retailing and Consumer Services*, 51, 212–20.

UN (2013). World economic situation and prospects 2014: Global economic outlook, December, www.un.org/en/development/desa/publications/wesp2014-firstchapter.html (accessed 8 July 2020).

Unitarians (n.d.). Unitarianism explained. www.unitarian.org.uk/pages/unitarianism-explained (accessed 17 May 2020).

Wigington, P. (2019). What is Santeria? www.learnreligions.com/about-santeria traditions-2562543, 13 February (accessed 3 May 2020).

Winter, B. (2006). Religion, culture and women's human rights: Some general political and theoretical considerations. *Women's Studies International Forum*, 29(4), 381–93.

World Bank (2020). World Bank Country and Lending Group. https://datahelpdesk.worldbank.org/knowledgebase/articles/906519 (accessed 12 May 2020).

Worthington, E. L., Wade, N. G., Hight, T. L., Ripley, J. S., McCullough, M. E., Berry, J. W. et al. (2003). The religious commitment inventory – 10: Development, refinement and validation of a brief scale for research and counselling. *Journal of Counselling Psychology*, 50, 84–96.

Yagboyaju, D. A. (2017). Religion, culture and political corruption in Nigeria. *Africa's Public Service Delivery and Performance Review*, 5(1), 1–10.

2. Religion and psychological influences on consumer behaviour: Perspectives on developing nations

Nashaat H. Hussein

INTRODUCTION

There is no doubt that religion plays a significant role in people's consumer behaviour. In addition to the psychological effect of religion on individuals, it either legitimizes or disdains the use or consumption of certain items on the basis of belonging to a specific community of believers. In her article written in 2001 titled "Coffee and Coffee Merchants in Cairo: 1580–1630," Nelly Hanna drives the attention to the fact that the introduction of coffee to Egypt during the late sixteenth and early seventeenth centuries was not at all appreciated by the Islamic religious community at that time. Both public and private consumption patterns were adversely affected. The religious community insisted that coffee consumption was a form of deviation from the mainstream orientation of Islam, and considered, from their perspective, that coffee consumption strongly resembled the use of alcohol (which is restricted in Islam) since it negatively affects the human brain. Hanna stated that "controversies arose between the al-Azhar scholars, many of whom were not sympathetic to Sufi practices (of consuming coffee collectively to keep Sufis awake during Sufi rituals) and quick to criticize coffee which they considered intoxicating" (Hanna, 2001: 94).

Obviously, any identified threat to religion becomes a critical factor which influences the adoption and public (or even private) consumption of new products; and consequently, individual motivations and attitudes would be adversely affected. In societies where religion is a dominant component of culture, newly introduced products may experience scrutiny if their introduction beholds any religiously questionable attributes that may be perceived as potential risks to the religious order. Religious men often take positions for or against the introduction of new products to their religious communities by referring them to religious norms and values; despite the fact that the power of those religious trends may decline if the new products grow in popularity over time or become accepted by other members of the ruling classes, which is exactly what happened to coffee in Egypt. Nelly Hanna referred to the ultimate positive shift of religious orientation towards coffee by saying that "the power of coffee merchants resulted in the flourishing of coffee trade in Egypt" (Hanna, 2001: 96).

The above socio-cultural and religious factors are essential for understanding the economic and consumer behavior of a particular religious community to the use and consumption of certain items, since they directly relate to and influence the psychology of the individuals. Religion influences a variety of consumer behaviors, such as information seeking and product innovativeness (Hirschman, 1990). Understanding the impact of religion on consumer behavior is vital because consumers communicate their religious identities to others and express the strength of their beliefs through their consumption choices. In *The Varieties of Religious Experience*, William James (1902) suggested that studying religious experience offers the potential for breakthroughs in understanding fundamental human psychology. If we investigate consumer behavior, we can easily realize that "the internal influences that have effect on consumer behaviour consist of an individual's perception, learning, memory, motives, personality, emotions and attitudes" (Hawkins and Mothersbaugh, 2010: 274–5). All of these mental processes are highly affected by the socialization process as well as the socio-cultural and religious contexts that make them possible, especially in the developing countries. Human perception, for example, plays a decisive role in the processing of information and consumer decision making since it initiates consumer exposure and attention to marketing stimuli and ends with interpretation and behavior. The stimulus that does enter the conscience is not processed objectively in most cases and is interpreted differently from person to person and influenced by unique biases, needs and experiences (Solomon et al., 2006). When predetermined by factors that influence the formation of the conscience, consumer orientation is more likely to be affected. In communities where religion becomes a major part of culture, and therefore the conscience, the psychology of the individual becomes predisposed, whether positively or negatively, towards the consumption and use of certain items.

Marketers always face a challenge when they market to a country with various religious groups. Religious consumers are more likely to be offended when faced with controversial products than less religious ones (De Run et al., 2010). Belligerent responses may occur if faced with certain products that contradict with their value systems and religions. Therefore, perceptions of brands and products often influence consumer consumption patterns (Fam et al., 2004). Muslims, for example, are completely forbidden from eating pork or any of its derivatives, while conservative members of the Catholic Church deem contraceptive products totally unacceptable (Ruiz, 2004). Being religious is usually based on adherence to a certain worldview and on the way a person is committed to religious teachings and beliefs (Essoo and Dibb, 2004).

This chapter aims to elucidate the relationship between religion, worldview and consumer behavior. It also highlights the link between the psychology of the individual and consumer behavior. Then, there will be a discussion concerning consumer behavior in developing nations, followed by concluding remarks.

RELIGION, WORLDVIEW AND CONSUMPTION

Although some of the issues discussed here are addressed in Chapter 3, given the significant link between religion, worldview, consumption and psychological influences on consumer behavior, this discussion is present to lay the foundation for the discourse on psychological influences on consumer behaviour. "Religion" and "worldview" are two terms that are used interchangeably. The term "worldview" is the English translation of the German term *Weltanschauung*, which can be defined as "a term for an intellectual conception of the universe from the perspective of a human knower" (Naugle, 2002: 59). Accordingly, every religion can be called a worldview, or at least plays a major role in formulating the worldview of its adherents. But, not all worldviews are religious. For instance, the main world religions like Christianity, Islam, Buddhism, and Hinduism can be treated as worldviews from the point of view of their adherents, whereas "Humanism" is not a religion, it is a worldview (Vroom, 2006). The distinction is found in the fact that religions are mainly based on the existence of spirituality and transcendence, while this is not a necessary characteristic of a worldview.

Although the term "worldview" can be defined in various ways, Artur Nilsson defines it as "those mental states that, in comparison with those of other individuals, make the individual intelligible and predictable as a rational system, to other rational agents" (Nilsson, 2013: 70). Worldviews, therefore, determine not only the conceptual basis of a person's internal mental framework of consciousness and cognitive learning about reality and life meaning, but also human thoughts and behavior. They regulate the way a society operates, or has to operate, especially in societies where religion is a dominant component of culture and everyday life. The effect of a worldview can be recognized in various aspects of life like ethics, philosophies, beliefs, economics, and so on. Daniel Hausman (2012), in his book titled *The Philosophy of Economics: An Anthology*, argues that the worldview is responsible for organizing relationships among people, such as education, political and economic orientations, production and distribution of the goods and services they need, and people's consumer lifestyles (Hausman, 2012). Moreover, it provides answers to existential questions about the world through which people interpret their reality and make meanings of their lives. By providing answers to many of life's intrinsic questions, a worldview affects many psychological processes including contingencies, expectations, goals, motivations and emotions (Silberman, 2005). Additionally, it provides more general but similarly beneficial feelings of certainty and control about day-to-day experiences (McGregor et al., 2010). Thus, the worldview serves many important cognitive and psychological functions.

Many scholars have attempted to investigate the relationship between religion, worldviews and economics. Max Weber (1864–1920) in his book *The Protestant Ethic and the Spirit of Capitalism* (1904–5), along with other early papers on Confucianism, Hinduism and Buddhism, explained the way Western civilization developed, compared to Eastern ones. He emphasizes the idea that the religious ethic of the Calvinist Protestantism strongly affected the emergence and development of capitalism in Western countries, especially in Northern Europe, and concluded that the religious ethic of Protestantism paved the way for understanding the "spirit" of capitalism. Therefore, religion has helped to shape a distinct worldview that affected the adoption of a specific economic orientation called capitalism (Weber, 1930). When examining the economic orientations, worldviews and consumer behaviors in developing countries, religion can be perceived as a dominant constituent since "the resilience of religion in developing countries is now plain to see. In Africa, religion shows no sign of disappearing or diminishing in public importance, as development theorists have generally supposed" (Ter Haar and Ellis, 2006: 351). It sets the boundaries for any process of economic development, as long as those development processes do not contradict with religious alignments.

Although religion has a significant influence in many people's lives since it affects human behavior in terms of thoughts, values, moral standards and attitudes, and religiosity affects consumer decision making, ethical beliefs and judgments, the study of the link between religion and consumption is still a sensitive issue. Sensitivity of religion and problems related to the theoretical conceptualization and measurement of religious faith, religiosity as it relates to consumer behavior has been under-researched (Swimberghe et al., 2011). There is still a need to develop a more robust theoretical understanding of how individual religiosity impacts consumer behavior (Vitell, 2009). On the other hand, the worldviews of people in one culture or society cannot be treated as a homogenous whole. There is a difference between organized and personal worldviews. Sven Hartman (1986) argues that an organized worldview can be considered as a view on life that has developed over time as a more or less coherent and established system with certain sources, traditions, values, rituals, or ideals, while a personal worldview refers to someone's personal views on life and humanity, which does not necessarily have to be based on religiosity (Hartman, 1986). One can denote that although people may belong to a certain religion that has its coherent organized worldview, they may also develop their personal worldviews which may contradict or coincide with the overall organized worldview of religion. The existence of both organized and personal worldviews can help explain the dichotomy in social, economic and cultural orientations among members of one nation or even members of one religion since people do not follow a precise predetermined orientation of live events similarly. However, in both cases, people cannot surpass the trajectories stipulated by religion.

Worldviews usually develop through the socialization process. They pass from one generation to another and help formulate certain ways of thinking and behaving including those related to consumer behavior (Kwan et al., 2015). Society shapes the beliefs, values and norms that largely define tastes and preferences. People absorb, almost unconsciously, the worldview that defines their relationship to themselves, to others, to organizations, to society, to nature and to the universe (Kotler and Keller, 2006). A survey of followers of Islam, Christianity and Hinduism in Mauritius Islands was carried out by Essoo and Dibb (2004) to evaluate shopping behavior based on consumer religion. Survey results revealed that religion has a major effect on shopping behavior, with highly religious consumers across religions showing a greater sense of discipline in their shopping habits. They came to the conclusion that religious affiliation should be included in future cross-cultural research and that there is considerable potential for extending research into the influence of religious affiliation on consumer behavior.

The general theory of marketing ethics (Vitell and Hunt, 1990) tackles the notion in which consumers confront issues perceived to have ethical implications (Vitell, 2009). The theory argues that individuals perceive alternatives and evaluate those alternatives based on their personal characteristics, cultural environment, professional environment, industrial environment and organizational environment (Vitell and Hunt, 1990). An individual forms ethical judgments based on the evaluation of the alternatives and consequences, which results in attitudes and behaviors. The theory stresses that ethical judgments are not the same as intentions because intentions are finalized after making ethical judgments. The theory denotes that religion is represented in the theory under the cultural environment and personal characteristics. According to Scott Vitell (2009), the theory proposes several situations where religiosity may affect ethical decision making. The first determines whether or not there is an ethical issue which needs to be resolved. The second determines whether or not there is an impact on a person's moral philosophy or norms. The third determines a person's ethical judgments regarding a particular situation and various courses of action. The fourth determines a person's intention in a particular situation involving moral choices. The fifth occasion determines the actual behavior in particular situations (Vitell, 2009).

Identification of the effect of religion and religiosity on consumer behavior is vital to marketers who work in multi-religious countries. Accordingly, understanding the similarities and differences of consumer behavior across different religious groups is necessary. In order for marketers to develop effective marketing strategies in those cultures, an inclusive understanding of consumer behavior of different religious groups, religious devotion or religiosity, and its effect on consumer behavior, influence the individual in his/her buying habits. It is widely acknowledged that the knowledge problem consumers of a particular religion may encounter can be dealt with through religious consumption norms, since each religion provides a distinctive blueprint of consumption norms for its followers. Idiosyncratic styles and varieties in food, clothing, religious symbols, and ornamentation that mark religious festivities are all set by religions. People use those blueprints of consumption norms to express and stress their commitment to religions. These blueprints need to be internalized in people's minds in order to become effective. This is where the role of socialization and norms begin to emphasize and provide limitations and social sanctions if violated.

The worldviews of consumers precede any model marketers can depict and abstractly represent to optimally make use of such information in meeting ever changing needs and wants (McFarlane, 2013). Therefore, without an understanding of the various consumer worldviews and social class differences in society, the impact and influence of advertising and promotional activities would decline. Demands, psychological preferences and consumption patterns are shaped by those worldviews and other significant socio-cultural values and backgrounds, in addition to other factors like income variations. Major social class differences in society seem to be explained or even justified on the basis of people's worldviews. Social distinctions are complex across societies and the factors that go into categorizing social classes also vary across cultures and society and can range from very simple, to very complex and overlapping social, economic and political issues (Solomon, 2004). The social structure of the society and class-based characteristics seem to reflect different values, interests and behaviors (Norcia and Rissotto, 2013; Manning and Reece, 2004), which will automatically have a direct impact on the way consumption is defined and practiced. Psychological influences on consumer behavior usually coincide with those worldviews, and accordingly, psychological factors cannot be studied in isolation from the worldviews of the people that shape them and make them meaningful.

All religions have their explanations for poverty and social inequality (Beyers, 2014). Religions also provide remedies for poverty and legitimize resistance (De Jong, 2009). Economists, sociologists, political scientists and researchers attempt to describe and analyze information about poor and rich people, investigating the religious dimensions of poverty and wealth. There is a consensus that "what religious people say and do is important to them because their beliefs about rich people and poor people are essential to their identity – the core of their religious message disappears without their tradition of preaching and caring for rich and poor" (Kollar and Shafi, 2016: xxviii). Among Muslims, for example, "Islamic teachings assert that it is not scarcity, but misuse of existing wealth and material possessions which leads to poverty and inequality. Solutions require re-distribution of wealth from the rich to the poor and not accumulation of more wealth" (Zaman, 2018: 87). One main solution in Islam to face income disparity is *zakat* (alms), in which the rich are obliged to share a certain amount of their wealth with the poor, especially during the holy month of Ramadan.

Understanding the effect of religion on economic lives is essential to deeply understand the role religion plays in formulating people's worldviews (Montoro-Pons and Cuadrado-García, 2018). As with the case of Buddhism and Christian monks and nuns, intense commitment to religion is character-ized by minimal consumption patterns and norms. The application of those consumption norms refers to the existence of formal and informal rules that limit the spectrum of choices available for self-expression of intense religious adherents. Formal and informal rules also provide a model for others to follow. Those consumption norms facilitate conveying messages and replace exten-sive reasoning since less effort is required to communicate and to generate meanings that stimulate desired reactions. Consumption norms thus assist us to cope with uncertainty by reducing the scope of our problems of choice. They simplify the required knowledge. No individual has to start from scratch or place unreasonable demands on his or her cognitive powers. Individuals who have only limited knowledge of the religious identities and commitments of others can nevertheless relate to each other through intersubjectively shared categories of communication provided by consumption norms (Coşgel and Minkler, 2004).

In sum, research that focuses on the relationship between religiosity and consumer behavior and decision-making processes endorses the idea that religion is essential to consumer perception, attitude and behavioral processes. Research also confirms that utilizing religious commitment or religious affili-ation to measure religiosity gives a comprehensive description of the relation-ship between religiosity and consumer behavior. It is vital to examine a wider effect of religiosity constructs on consumers' perceived risk as an important aspect of consumer behavior (Delener, 1990). It is therefore argued that a need exists to empirically improve the understanding of the relationship between religiosity and different dimensions of consumer risk perception.

PSYCHOLOGICAL INFLUENCES ON CONSUMER BEHAVIOR

Consumer behavior can be regarded as "the study of the processes involved when individuals or groups select, purchase, use or dispose of products, services, ideas or experiences to satisfy needs and desires" (Solomon et al., 2006: 6). It can also be defined as "the behavior that consumers display in searching for, purchasing, using, evaluating, and disposing of products and services that they expect will satisfy their needs" (Schiffman and Kanuk, 2007: 3). Consumers can take many profiles, ranging from a young child who wants to have a piece of candy to an adult who decides to buy a new house. Consumed items can be anything ranging from food items to ideas and different forms of services. Needs and desires to be satisfied range from hunger and thirst to love, status or even spiritual fulfillment (Solomon et al., 2006).

Generally, consumer behavior is a holistic term that covers every aspect of human lives since it is based on human consumption of goods and services. It includes different factors as it focuses on the whole consumption process, including issues that affect the consumer before, after and during buying a single item. And as long as a discussion of a person's usage of goods and services is required, there is a need to investigate the psychological aspects or factors that either motivate or discourage a person to use or not to use certain items. Psychologists interested in consumption deal with the way individuals or groups are involved with consumer activities and the effect consumption has on human personality. It is hard to understand consumer psychology without having an understanding of the way individuals process information and make decisions.

The internal influences that have a direct impact on consumer behavior consist of "an individual's perception, learning, memory, motives, personality, emotions and attitudes" (Hawkins and Mothersbaugh, 2010: 274–5). Perception is responsible for the processing of new information and consumer decision making, since it initiates with consumer exposure and attention to marketing stimuli and ends with an attitude to buy or not to use certain items, which formulate the psychological process of perception. Although the meaning of a stimulus can be interpreted differently from person to person and is influenced by unique biases, needs and experiences (Solomon et al., 2010), the stimulus that enters the conscience may not be processed objectively. Processing information is a process whereby stimuli are perceived, transformed into meaningful information and then stored. It normally starts with exposure which is when a stimulus leads to a response of sensory receptors, particularly sight, smell, hearing, touch and taste (Solomon et al., 2010). Exposure to a certain stimulus is also determined by experience. Previous experiences of an individual affect perception and what the consumer chooses to process (Solomon et al., 2010). This explains the reason why consumers become highly selective in what they buy when they enter a store. Consumers process a stimulus that has relevance to their personal requirements. However, different cultures show different buying habits. Many studies have found that culture affects marketing and consumer buying behavior (Wursten and Fadrhonc, 2012; Durmaz et al., 2011). Culture, along with its various constituents such as values, religion, norms and sanctions, helps shape and direct consumer behavior into more culturally acceptable channels.

Since personality traits, motives and emotions influence consumer behavior and buying habits, and because the three processes seem to be affected by culture and religion, then, there is a direct link between religion and personality, motives and emotions. People's perceptions, motivations and emotions usually get affected by culture, and if religion is a dominant part of culture, people's perceptions, motivations and feelings toward or against certain items or services would be curtailed by the way religion perceives those items or services. In Islam, for example, using alcoholic beverages or using alcohol in food is forbidden. Once alcohol is used for cooking or is incorporated into making any type of food, a Muslim is not supposed to approach it, even if he/she likes it. Importing chocolate, for example, might be acceptable, but not alcoholic chocolate, or chocolate with a certain percentage of alcohol. A Muslim's perception, motives or emotions would automatically turn against buying or even handling (e.g. importing) those items for fear of religious reprimand. On the other hand, if a Muslim is exposed accidently to alcoholic foods or beverages (without a person's willingness or knowledge), that person does not need to be sanctioned or purified.

Motivation is a "process that influences the direction, persistence, and vigor of goal-directed behaviour" (Passer and Smith, 2008: 364). If motives, whether intrinsically or extrinsically, match with norms and values in society, and a person feels that his/her behavior is acceptable and gratified by the society in which he/she lives, emotions will react accordingly. If the behavior contradicts with the norms and values of the mainstream culture or worldview or is being penalized or threatened, negative feelings may develop accordingly (Lazarus, 2001). A person's mental health and wellbeing is usually affected by positive affect or pleasant emotions, negative affect or unpleasant emotions, and a cognitive component of life satisfaction (Diener et al., 1999). Religion plays a main role in generating and regulating emotional experience, emphasizing positive emotional experience, which is unquestionably the role of every religion. Motivation, personality and emotion are all interrelated, and therefore difficult to detach. They are all influential factors that affect consumer decision making and buying habits. Understanding that motivation is the driving source of behavior, needs and motives that influence consumers' perception of what is relevant and can impact their feelings and emotions. Needs and motives affect a consumer's perception of what is relevant and can influence feelings and emotions.

Marcus Orji et al. stated that "an individual or a consumer is always influenced by his culture, subculture, social class, reference groups, family, personality, and his psychological factors" (Orji et al., 2017: 7). Consumers usually buy products that reflect their personality: houses, cars, jewelry, etc. These products reflect and are influenced by a person's gender, age, culture, social class (based on the social structure he/she belongs to), family, friends, etc. Personality can be defined as "an individual's characteristic patterns of thought, emotion and behaviour, together with the psychological mechanisms – hidden or not – behind those patterns" (Funder, 2007: 5). The personality factors that affect consumer buying behavior are social character, compliance, aggressiveness, ethnocentrism and dogmatism (Orji et al., 2017). These factors have an impact on the way consumers perceive, learn, feel and develop an attitude to buy or use a certain item. For example, Bob Altemeyer (2002) asserts that dogmatism refers to relatively unchangeable, unjustified certainty. Therefore, consumers who have a low level of dogmatism are likely to be more open to marketing communication than those who have a high level of dogmatism who may not appreciate new foreign goods.

Marketers usually target certain personality traits to be able to sell their commodities, and to gain popularity among potential consumers. Accordingly, the advertisements they make need to target those, for example, who believe in "being different" or "unique," those who prefer to have "adventure" or a "sense of oneness," etc. Therefore, understanding personality traits can help predict potential buying and the behavior of consumers. Different personality traits can provide a clear guidance of the characteristics consumers have that define their behavior.

Pre-dispositional attributes of the trait theory can be of great help to marketers. Many psychologists emphasize that "more prototypic for a trait are constructs such as neuroticism (temperamental), intelligence (cognitive), or the achievement motive (motivational) that comprise many characteristic behaviours in many situations and that are stable over many years for most adults" (Corr and Matthews, 2009: 44). Raymond Cattell's (1996) early pioneering work to develop a lexicon for personality traits called the Five Factor Model of personality structure, which develop in humans through early childhood learning, includes (traits) labeled as neuroticism, extraversion, openness, agreeableness and conscientiousness. These five factors (called the Big Five) were generated from various factor analytic studies of self-reports, peer reports and questionnaire personality-related data. A trait can be defined as "a distinguishable way in which an individual can be differentiated from another" (Engel et al., 1995: 201). Marketers find traits such as risk taking and self-consciousness useful when planning strategies. Three assumptions describe the trait theory. First, all consumers have traits that are different from others which allow marketers to segment consumer markets. Second, these traits are stable throughout an individual's lifetime. Finally, traits can be gathered from the measurement of behavioral signs. Although the Big Five model can be criticized on the basis that two individuals from one classified category (such as openness) may exhibit different characteristics and behave differently, the theory still gains popularity among marketers. Religions and culture-specific values are more likely to create what can be termed as "core personalities" to illuminate and clarify the required personality traits of their adherents, which may not coincide with the theory of the Big Five.

Emotions can be defined as "processes of causally linked mental (appraisal, action tendency, subjective experience) and behavioral (physiological reactions, facial and vocal expression) elements" (Reisenzein, 2007: 426). Accordingly, they are closely related to motivation and personality. Once consumer needs and desires are not satisfied, negative emotions usually develop causing frustration, anger and aggression. The opposite is true. Once needs and desires are satisfied, feelings of happiness and satisfaction will arise. Unless a person has a justification for not being able to satisfy his/her needs and desires (which can be provided through religion and religious orientation), a person may experience a low self-esteem due to the fact that his or her ability does not support attaining his or her needs. Islam, for example, has an explanation for divergent social stratifications, poverty and wealth, and reasons for the creation of non-homogenous social structures. Such an explanation provides a consolation against a lack of ability, and would directly influence the emotions of Islamic adherents. This does not mean that Islam is based on conformity to the status quo. On the contrary, it provides outlets for an individual to change his or her economic status through work and faith.

Generally, emotions play a major role in consumer arousal. Consumers are more likely to look for products that bring beneficial emotional arousal (Ruth, 2001), which can be found in music, videos, new cars, etc. Advertising campaigns of many brands target the emotional arousal of consumers. Emotional arousal can be triggered by various means, including targeting the senses of consumers. Odors, for example, can stir the emotions. They can affect and regain memories or deal with stressful events. Association with other experiences can affect our responses to odors (Rimkute et al., 2016). The same thing applies to vision, hearing, touch and taste. Sound and music are important to marketers, who tend to link certain types of items they advertise with particular types of music to arouse the emotions of consumers.

Attitudes, on the other hand, are determined by previous experiences, personality, motivations and emotions. They can be defined as "a favorable or unfavorable evaluative reaction toward something or someone (often rooted in one's beliefs, and exhibited in one's feelings and intended behaviour)" (Eagly and Chaiken, 2005: 745). An attitude is "lasting because it tends to endure over time. It is general because it applies to more than a momentary event" (Solomon et al., 2006: 138). Consumers develop attitudes towards certain products based on positive experiences with those products, which are more likely to remain unchanged for a certain amount of time until customers are exposed to new products that can alter their persistent or long-lasting attitudes. In order to market a product, marketers need to comprehend that "in decision-making situations, people form attitudes towards objects other than the product itself that can influence their ultimate selections" (Solomon et al., 2006: 137). People's buying habits and routine may affect their buying behavior to a large extent, not particularly the type of products themselves. Also, attitudes towards consumption are usually linked to self-identities, regardless of a person's religious orientation, especially if a person feels that his or her self-identity is at risk. When a person feels that his or her self-identity is threatened, he or she is more likely to try to regain self-worth by a variety of means, including "compensatory consumption" (Rucker and Galinsky, 2013). This is when attitudes towards consumption become intensified to reimburse self-esteem.

There is no doubt that a religion and its associated worldview have a direct impact on the attitudes of its adherents, whether Christianity, Islam, Buddhism, Hinduism, etc. Fam and his colleagues stated that "religion defines the ideals for life, which in turn are reflected in the values and attitudes of societies and individuals. Such values and attitudes shape the behaviour and practices of institutions and members of culture" (Fam et al., 2004: 538). Therefore, religion is responsible for attitude formation, including people's consumer behavior. Attitudes cannot be examined in isolation from the social context where the individual lives. His or her main attitudes need to match with those of the dominant mainstream culture, especially in the developing world where the family or tribe represents a major determinant in attitude formation and preferences. Attitudes towards consumption, on the other hand, are largely based on affiliations and recognition of society; otherwise he or she will be treated negatively by the people around him or her for misbehavior and sometimes for violation of religious rules. In the Arab World, for example, even when a person is wealthy, he or she cannot reveal that in public for fear of disapproval from the community in which he or she lives. If the three-component attitude model is to be applied as a guideline for understanding the components of attitudes, one can understand that the model suggests three elements (or components) of attitudes: affect, behavior and cognition (Rosenberg at al., 1960). Affect refers to the individual's feelings, behavior refers to the individual's intentions to do something guided by an attitude and cognitive means the beliefs an individual has about a certain object or a particular type of service.

CONSUMER BEHAVIOR IN DEVELOPING COUNTRIES

If the term "developing countries" is compared to terms like "developed countries," "industrialized countries" and so on, a "developing country" is defined in the *Cambridge English Dictionary* as "a country with little industrial and economic activity and where people generally have low incomes." Regardless of the problems associated with that definition, research suggests that people in developing countries have become increasingly interested in the consumption of foreign goods (Batra et al., 2000). This raises questions over the behavior of consumers in the developing world and the way ethnocentrism affects their consumer orientation, and how they overestimate foreign products over nationally produced ones. Previous research conducted in several developing countries reveals that there is a common belief among consumers that foreign manufactured products are superior to those made by local producers (Wu et al., 2010). This widely shared attitude among consumers of developing countries goes back to concurrent dominant conceptions of colonialism when consumers endorsed the inferiority of their domestic products compared to foreign ones based on their economic variations and exploitation of their economies. In sociology, ethnocentrism is a social construct that describes the tendency of people to reject others who are not culturally similar to them and at the same time to favor those who are more like themselves. This can be explained in light of the conception that social comparison and acquiring and maintaining social status and self-esteem are found in all societies, including countries of the developing world. High self-esteem is acquired by showing off and buying foreign goods. Such concern with status display is even more important in developing countries, where interpersonal relationships are of prime importance (Ger et al., 1993: 105). Rajeev Batra and his colleagues (2000), for example, clarify that "consumers in developing countries often seek to emulate the apparently glamorous Western consumption practices and lifestyles and purchase the brands they are exposed to through movies and TV channels, Western tourists, their own workers gone overseas, and their own travel abroad" (Batra et al., 2000: 85).

Changes associated with the perception of consumption have altered dramatically in developing countries, whereas consumption has started to play a distinctive role. There is no doubt that the development of market economy, globalization, technological innovations and the rising living standards of certain social strata in developing countries have created a kind of consumer culture in which people strive to best meet their needs (Michałowska and Danielak, 2015). Those factors have resulted in major shifts from collectivism, which is one of the characteristics of countries of the developing world, into individualism with its capitalist orientation. Individualism is more likely to create separate identities, behaviors, attitudes and distinctive preferences. At the same time, the Internet and globalization have affected people in developing countries, increased their exposure to brands and online shopping potentials and at the same time modified their consumer behaviors. These indicators led Martinez-Ruiz and Moser (2019) to claim that understanding the psychology behind online consumer behavior is a key to competing in today's markets which are characterized by ever increasing competition and globalization. They stressed that "in an online context, consumer responses are no longer dependent on the physical environment while at the same time entirely new factors come into play such as the device through which consumers interact, and the way products and services are sold and presented online which often differs significantly from traditional offline marketing strategies" (Martinez-Ruiz and Moser, 2019: 1). Online consumer behavior necessitates re-evaluation of various other disciplines, such as psychological approaches and concepts. Therefore, "in the age of globalization, the main problem seems to be the diversity of consumer behavior determinants, which are subject to nationality, cultural and religious affinity" (Makarewicz, 2013: 106).

Recognizing that religion plays a main role in this emerging economic mosaic of importation of foreign products in the developing world, and that religiosity still applies a similar role even when it gets to imports of online goods from foreign countries, the role of religion and worldview cannot be overlooked. In terms of the relationship between religiosity and buying behavior in the developing countries, studies of purchase decision (Ilyas et al., 2011) and taboo advertisement came to the conclusion that religiosity has a positive effect in marketing areas. In a study carried out by Nasse et al. titled "Religiosity and Consumer Behavior in Developing Countries: An Exploratory Study on Muslims in the Context of Burkina Faso," the authors came to the conclusion that "There is an emergency for the authorities to set up some mechanisms to tackle the counterfeit industrial drinks on the market and to help protect the environment from the excessive pollution by drinks packaging for a sustainable development" (Nasse et al., 2019: 126). The authors highlight the importance of culture in management and marketing products such as "halal" (permitted in Islam) products. Although religion plays a decisive role in Burkina Faso, the authors claim that a number of people with little religious faith contribute to increasing the consumption of industrial alcoholic drinks, which will adversely affect the consumption of industrial non-alcoholic ones.

Understanding the role of religion as one of the key elements of culture, especially in the developing world (Sood and Nasu, 1995), and the way religion has an influence upon marketing decisions and consumer behavior (Maheswaran and Shavitt, 2000), the perception may be that religious rulings and religious norms affect only purchasing decisions and choices which are related to products considered prohibited for religious reasons. For example,

Hinduism prohibits the consumption of beef products, while in Islam, religious values and norms prohibit gambling. However, the influence of religion on marketing and consumer decision making is an issue far more complex than one which is simply limited to product prohibition, or services which are contentious within individuals' or communities' religious norms (Vitell, 2009). In this sense, religion cannot be perceived as an obstructing factor in the developing world, but as a regulator between local values and consumer demands.

Personal and socio-cultural factors cannot be treated separately when discussing consumer behavior in the developing world. The individual psychological factors we discussed above seem to be universal; however, social and culture-specific reasons differ from one country or social context to another. They, including religion, affect the way consumers develop their distinctive consumer behavior. It is apparent that "religion exerts a significant influence in developing countries, whether in Catholicism in Latin America, Islam in the Middle East and Africa, Islam, Buddhism and Hinduism in Asia, or other less dominant" (Austin, 1990: 65). Alidou and Verpoorten (2019), for example, refer to the idea that several cultural factors affect the way people tend to have children in Sub-Saharan Africa, which indicates that group affiliation and socialization play a major role in the way people perceive their surrounding socio-economic and cultural contexts, including developing ideas towards consumption. It has been noted that in different parts of the developing world, respect and obedience to elders and tribal affiliation are the main factors that typify values and motives. Factors like age, gender, family, reference groups and social class all determine the range and types of consumption in the developing world. These factors, if treated separately, can affect economic and consumption orientations of individuals, who have been brought up to conform to the overall collectivist orientation of society regardless of the emerging tides of individualism.

In the Arab World, for example, male and female choices of fashion are rather limited, despite income variations and class differences, to various cultural factors that affect the way an Arab should appear to the public. Therefore, self-presentation cannot be understood in isolation from the various cultural and associated psychological factors that intervene with the way men and women should dress in society.

CONCLUSION

Religion is perceived as a powerful social force that affects people's values, habits and attitudes, which in turn affects their behaviors as consumers. It is considered as a sacred value that strongly influences a person's emotional experience, thinking, behavior and psychological well-being as a consumer (La Barbera and Gurhan, 1997). Religion consolidates values and attitudes among its adherents and socializes members into a community, while at the same time suppressing deviant behavior. Bell and Richerson explain that religion is a "powerful device by which people are absorbed into a tribe and psychically strengthened" (Bell and Richerson, 2008: 307). Religion also attempts to link social life to faith, and fosters social group unity.

Ter Haar and Ellis (2006), in their publication titled "The Role of Religion in Development: Towards a New Relationship between the European Union and Africa," argue that religion and religious activities can influence society in two ways. First, religious activities establish networks that could be of use for economic activities and could also be helpful for establishing trading relations with partners from other countries who belong to the same religious group, which can stimulate economic growth. Second, the values that are taught by the adherents or most important leaders of the religion concerned could influence actual behavior and thus the functioning of society (Ter Haar and Ellis, 2006). These factors are all based on religious commitment, in which "there are five types of religious factors, which frequently examine buying behaviour, namely religious affiliation, religious commitment, religious motivation or orientation, religious knowledge, as well as awareness of the social consequences of following a religion" (Musadik and Azmi, 2017: 139).

In order to make decisions like buying new products, consumers must engage in many psychological processes beforehand, which are based on their buying habits and worldviews such as motives, abilities and the chance to meet with, perceive and attend to the given information concerning a certain item. As consumers, they think about the given information, develop attitudes about it and shape memories. They can also be motivated or discouraged by the cultural environment and the impact of other variables like age, gender, social class, ethnicity, families and friends, which all affect consumer values and lifestyles and, in turn, influence the decisions that consumers make. In their book *Consumer Behavior*, Hoyer and MacInnis explain the psychological aspects related to buying decisions by saying that before consumers can make decisions, they must have some source of knowledge or information upon which to base their decisions. This source, known as the psychological core, "covers motivation, ability, and opportunity, exposure, attention, and perception, categorization and comprehension of information, and attitudes" (Hoyer and MacInnis, 2008: 10–11).

People's perception of consumption in the developing countries has changed dramatically. Development of the market economy, globalization, technological innovations and rising living standards have created a kind of consumer culture in which people strive to best meet their needs, despite the conventional understanding that developing nations are characterized with low development in many areas; globalization and civilization are introducing many changes into these societies (Gbadamosi, 2016). Those factors have resulted in major shifts from collectivism, which is one of the characteristics of countries of the developing world, to individualism, with its capitalist orientation. Individualism is more likely to create separate identity, behavior, attitudes and distinctive preferences. At the same time, the Internet and globalization have affected people in developing countries, increased their exposure to brands and online shopping potentials and at the same time modified their consumer behaviors. That led Martinez-Ruiz and Moser to claim that understanding the psychology behind online consumer behavior is key to competition in today's markets which are characterized by ever increasing competition and globalization. They stressed that "in an online context, consumer responses are no longer dependent on the physical environment while at the same time entirely new factors come into play such as the device through which consumers interact, and the way products and services are sold and presented online which often differs significantly from traditional offline marketing strategies" (Martinez-Ruiz and Moser, 2019: 1). Online consumer behavior necessitates a re-evaluation of various other disciplines, such as psychological approaches and concepts.

REFERENCES

Alidou, Sahawal and Verpoorten, Marijke (2019) Family size and schooling in sub-Saharan Africa: testing the quantity-quality trade-off, *Journal of Population Economics*, 32: 1353–99.

Altemeyer, Bob (2002) Dogmatic behaviour among students: testing a new measure of dogmatism, *Journal of Social Psychology*, 142(6): 713–21.

Austin, James (1990) *Managing in Developing Countries: Strategic Analysis and Operating Techniques*. New York: Free Press.

Batra, Rajeev, Ramaswamy, Venkatram, Steenkamp, Jan-Benedict and Ramachander, S. (2000) Effects of brand local and nonlocal origin on consumer attitudes in developing countries, *Journal of Consumer Psychology*, 9(2): 83–95.

Bell, Adrian and Richerson, Peter (2008) Charles J. Lumsden and Edward O. Wilson, Genes, mind, and culture: 25th anniversary edition, *Journal of Bio Economics*, 10: 307–14.

Beyers, Jaco (2014) The effect of religion on poverty, *HTS Theological Studies*, 70: 1–10.

Cattell, Raymond (1996) Personality and structured learning. *European Review of Applied Psychology*, 46: 73–5.

Corr, Philip and Matthews, Gerlad (2009) *The Cambridge Handbook of Personality Psychology*. New York: Cambridge University Press.

Coşgel, Metin and Minkler, Lanse (2004) Religious identity and consumption, *Review of Social Economy*, 62: 339–50.

De Jong, Eelke (2009) *Culture and Economics: On Values, Economics, and International Business*. London: Routledge.

De Run, Ernest, Butt, Muhammad, Fam, Kim and Jong, Hui (2010) Attitudes towards offensive advertising: Malaysian Muslims' views, *Journal of Islamic Marketing*, 1(1): 25–36.

Delener, Nejdet (1990) The effects of religious factors on perceived risk in durable goods purchase decisions, *Journal of Consumer Marketing*, 7(3): 27–38.

Diener, Ed, Suh, Eunkook, Lucas, Richard and Smith, Heidi (1999) Subjective well-being: three decades of progress. *Psychological Bulletin*, 125: 276–302.

Durmaz, Y., Celik, M. and Oruç, R. (2011) The impact of cultural factors on the consumer buying behaviors examined through an empirical study, *International Journal of Business and Social Science*, 2(5): 109–14.

Eagly, Alice and Chaiken, Shelly (2005) Attitude research in the 21st century: The current state of knowledge. In Dolores Albaraccín, Blair Johnson and Mark Zanna (Eds), *The Handbook of Attitudes* (pp. 743–67). Hillsdale, NJ: Erlbaum.

Engel, James, Blackwell, Roger and Miniard, Paul (1995) *Consumer Behavior*, 8th Edition. Forth Worth: Dryden Press.

Essoo, Nittin and Dibb, Sally (2004) Religious influences on shopping behaviour: an exploratory study, *Journal of Marketing Management*, 20(7–8): 683–712.

Fam, Kim, Waller, David and Erdogan, B. Zafer (2004) The influence of religion on attitudes towards the advertising of controversial products, *European Journal of Marketing*, 38(5/6): 537–55.

Funder, David (2007) *The Personality Puzzle*, 4th Edition. New York: W. W. Norton & Company.

Gbadamosi, Ayantunji (2016) Consumer behaviour in the developing world: a conceptual overview. In Ayantunji Gbadamosi (Ed.), *Handbook of Research on Consumerism and Buying Behaviour in Developing Nations* (pp. 1–29). Hershey, PA: IGI Global.

Ger, Gnliz, Belk, Russell and Lascu, Dana (1993) The development of consumer desire in marketing and developing economies: the cases of Romania and Turkey, *Advances in Consumer Research*, 20: 102–7.

Hanna, Nelly (2001) Coffee and coffee merchants in Cairo, 1580–1630, In Tuchscherer Michel (Ed.), *Le commerce du café avant l'ère des plantations coloniales: espaces, réseaux, sociétés (XVe–XIXe siècle)* (pp. 91–101). Cairo: IFAO.

Hartman, Sven (1986) *Children's Philosophy of Life*. Malmo: CWK Gleerup.

Hausman, Daniel (2012) *The Philosophy of Economics: An Anthology*. Cambridge: Cambridge University Press.

Hawkins, D. and Mothersbaugh, D. (2010) Consumer behaviour, *Building Marketing Strategy*, 11th Edition. New York: McGraw Hill Irwin.

Hirschman, E. (1990) Secular immortality and the American ideology of affluence, *Journal of Consumer Research*, 17(1): 31–42.

Hoyer, Wayne and MacInnis, Deborah (2008) *Consumer Behaviour*, 5th Edition. Mason, OH: Cengage Learning.

Ilyas, Saqib, Hussain, Muhammad and Usman, Muhammad (2011) An integrative framework for consumer behavior: evidence from Pakistan, *International Journal of Business and Management*, 6(4): 120–8.

James, W. (1902) *The Varieties of Religious Experience*. London: Longman.

Kollar, Nathan and Shafi, Muhammad (2016) *Poverty and Wealth in Judaism, Christianity, and Islam*. New York: Palgrave MacMillan.

Kotler, Philip and Keller, Kevin (2006) *Marketing Management*, 12th Edition. Upper Saddle River, NJ: Pearson Prentice Hall.

Kwan, Virginia, Li, Yexin and White, Andrew (2015) Culture, worldview and religion, in Sharon Ng and Angela Lee (Eds), *Handbook of Culture and Consumer Behaviour*. Oxford: Oxford University Press.

La Barbera, P. and Gurhan, Z. (1997) The role of materialism, religiosity and demographics in subjective well-being. *Psychology and Marketing*, 14(1): 71–97.

Lazarus, Richard (2001) Relational meaning and discrete emotions. In K. R. Scherer, A. Schorr and T. Johnstone (Eds), *Appraisal Processes in Emotion: Theory, Methods, Research* (pp. 37–67). New York: Oxford University Press.

Maheswaran, Durairaj and Shavitt, Sharon (2000) Issues and new directions in global consumer psychology, *Journal of Consumer Psychology*, 9(2), 59–66.

Makarewicz, Anna (2013) Consumer behaviour as a fundamental requirement for effective operations of companies, *Journal of International Studies*, 6(1): 103–9.

Manning, Gerald and Reece, Barry (2004) *Selling Today*. Upper Saddle River, NJ: Prentice Hall.

Martinez-Ruiz, Maria and Moser, Karen (2019) Studying consumer behavior in an online context: the impact of the evolution of the world wide web for new avenues in research, *Frontiers in Psychology*, 10(2731): 1–4.

McFarlane, Donovan (2013) Consumer worldviews, social class differences, and source attractiveness in promotion, advertising, and marketing, *International Journal of Marketing*, 2(6): 1–11.

McGregor, I., Nash, K. and Prentice, M. (2010) Reactive approach motivation (RAM) for religion, *Journal of Personality and Social Psychology*, 99, 148–61.

Michałowska, Mariola and Danielak, Wiesław (2015) *The Impact of Globalization on Consumer Behavior in Lubuskie*. Lublin: Wydawnictwo Naukowe Uniwersytetu Marii Curie-Sklodowskiej.

Montoro-Pons, Juan and Cuadrado-García, Manuel (2018) Religiosity and cultural consumption, *International Journal of Consumer Studies*, 42: 704–14.

Musadik, Siti and Azmi, Ilhaamie (2017) A conceptual paper: The effect of Islamic religiosity on impulse buying behaviour, *Journal of Global Business and Social Entrepreneurship*, 1(2): 137–47.

Nasse, Théophile, Ouédraogo, Alidou and Sall, Fatou (2019) Religiosity and consumer behavior in developing countries: An exploratory study on Muslims in the context of Burkina Faso, *African Journal of Business Management*, 13(4): 116–27.

Naugle, David (2002) *Worldview: The History of a Concept*. Cambridge: Eerdmans.

Nilsson, Artur (2013) *The Psychology of Worldviews: Towards a Non-Reductive Science of the Personality*. Lund: Lund University.

Norcia, M. and Rissotto, A. (2013) How religious faith affects beliefs on poverty: a study in Italy, *International Journal of Social Science and Humanity*, 3(2): 180–5.

Orji, Marcus, Sabo, Belo, Abubakar, Muktar and Usman, Abubakar (2017) Impact of personality factors on consumer buying behaviour towards textile materials in South Eastern Nigeria, *International Journal of Business and Economics Research*, 6(1): 7–18.

Passer, Michael and Smith, Ronald (2008) *Psychology: The Science of Mind and Behaviour*, 4th Edition. New York: McGraw-Hill Higher Education.

Reisenzein, Rainer (2007) What is a definition of emotion? And are emotions mental behavioral processes? *Social Science Information*, 46(3): 424–8.

Rimkute, Justina, Moraes, Caroline and Ferreira, Carlos (2016) The effect of scent on consumer behaviour, *International Journal of Consumer Studies*, 40(1): 24–34.

Rosenberg, M. J., Hovland, C. I., McGuire, W. J., Abelson, R. P. and Brehm, J. W. (1960) *Attitude Organization and Change: An Analysis of Consistency among Attitude Components*. New Haven, CT: Yale University Press.

Rucker, Derek and Galinsky, Adam (2013) Compensatory consumption, in Russell Belk and Ayalla Ruvio (Eds), *The Routledge Companion to Identity and Consumption* (pp. 207–15). New York: Routledge.

Ruiz, Carolina (2004) The church, the state and women's bodies in the context of religious fundamentalism in the Philippines, *Reproductive Health Matters*, 12(24): 96–103.

Ruth, Julie (2001) Promoting a brand's emotional benefits, *Journal of Consumer Psychology*, 11(2): 99–113.

Schiffman, Leon and Kanuk, Leslie (2007) *Consumer Behaviour*, 9th Edition. Harlow: Pearson.

Silberman, Israela (2005) Religion as a meaning system: implications for the new millennium, *Journal of Social Issues*, 61: 641–63.

Solomon, Michael (2004) *Consumer Behavior: Buying, Having, and Being*. Upper Saddle River, NJ: Pearson Education.

Solomon, Michael, Bamossy, Gary, Askegaard, Soren and Hogg, Margaret (2006) *Consumer Behaviour: A European Perspective*, 3rd Edition. Upper Saddle River, NJ: Prentice Hall.

Solomon, Michael, Bamossy, Gary, Askegaard, Soren and Hogg, Margaret (2010) *Consumer Behaviour: A European Perspective*, 4th Edition. Harlow: Pearson Education.

Sood, J. and Nasu, Y. (1995) Religiosity and nationality: an exploratory study of their effect on consumer behaviour in Japan and the United States, *Journal of Business Research*, 34: 1–9.

Swimberghe, Krist, Flurry, Laura and Parker, Janna (2011) Consumer religiosity: Consequences for consumer activism in the United States, *Journal of Business Ethics*, 103(3): 453–67.

Ter Haar, Gerrie and Ellis, Stephen (2006) The role of religion in development: Towards a new relationship between the European Union and Africa, *European Journal of Development Research*, 18(3): 351–67.

Vitell, Scott (2009) The role of religiosity in business and consumer ethics: A review of the literature, *Journal of Business Ethics*, 90: 155–67.

Vitell, Scott and Hunt, Shelby (1990) The general theory of marketing ethics: A partial test of the model, in Jagdish N. Sheth (Ed.), *Research in Marketing* (pp. 237–65). Greenwich, CT: JAI.

Vroom, Hendrik (2006) *A Spectrum of Worldviews: An Introduction to Philosophy of Religion in a Pluralistic World*. Amsterdam: Rodopi.

Weber, Max (1930) *The Protestant Ethic and Spirit of Capitalism*. New York: Charles Scribner's Sons (German original 1904–5).

Wu, Jianlin, Zhu, Ning and Dai, Qi (2010) Consumer ethnocentrism, product attitudes and purchase intentions of domestic products in China, International Conference on Engineering and Business Management: 2262–5.

Wursten, H. and Fadrhonc, T. (2012) International marketing and culture, *International*, 1(9).

Zaman, Asad (2018) An Islamic approach to inequality and poverty, *JKAU: Islamic Economics*, 31(1): 69–92.

3. A critical examination of the nexus of groups, religion and consumer behaviour: A focus on developing countries

Gift Donga, Richard Shambare and Mohamed Djemilou

INTRODUCTION

The purpose of this chapter is to discuss the role played by social groups and, in particular, religion in shaping individual consumers' behaviour. Religion is a fundamental aspect of consumers' lives. Since all consumers, even atheists, belong to one religion or another, it can be argued that all consumers are effectively religious beings. Since religion is so central to people's lives and their sense making of life, it therefore follows that to understand consumers, one needs to first understand their religion. Clearly, the pervasiveness of religion in consumer decision making makes it a worthwhile topic for study for marketers.

Religion is the oldest institution of organised social structures (Bruneau, 2012). And the reason why religion is so important to marketing is that it is one of the key factors that shape, influence, and regulate human behaviour and consumer behaviour (Shambare and Donga, 2019b). The latter is in line with Delener's (1994) stance on religion. Delener proposes six factors that help to explain why religion is the framework for decoding and explaining consumer behaviour. These are:

1. Religion is a foundation of meaning and purpose for life.
2. Religion defines the manner, tools, and techniques for doing things.
3. Religion helps people to cope with and understand life events.
4. Religion is a means through which people deal with challenges in life.
5. Religion acts as a motivator for human behaviour.
6. Religion is stable and observable.

Having said that, it is important to note that people's understanding and appreciation of religion is not the same; as such, to different people, religion evokes a wide array of reactions. Equally, the literature also provides numerous definitions for religion. The lack of a universal definition seems to have been a challenge in early consumer behaviour studies, as pinning research to a single concept or construct was elusive. Researchers employed several approaches to overcome this obstacle. One strategy was to not dwell too much on definitional issues; another was to use proxy variables. Consumers' religious affiliation as well as their religiosity are common examples of variables used when referring to religion. For instance, Choi (2010) found religiosity and religious affiliation as major drivers for consumer product and store-switching behaviour among consumers. In a different study, Patel (2012) stressed that being able to identify how the behaviour of consumers is affected by their religious affiliation and religiosity is critical to the success of marketers, especially for those who operate in multi-religious countries. Although religiosity and religious affiliation are important variables as far as religion is concerned, a holistic perspective of religion with respect to the consumer behaviour of groups of consumers and individuals is crucial. It is, therefore, opportune for this chapter to (a) conceptualise religion as a construct and (b) examine how religion influences consumer behaviour.

This chapter further argues that because consumers are religious beings, religion not only influences spirituality but it also governs virtually all aspects of human life. Central to this chapter is the aspect of consumer behaviour, specifically the role played by religion in shaping consumer behaviour among social groups. To present this argument, the chapter focuses on consumers in developing countries to demonstrate how religion acts as both a cause and effect of culture, which in turn influences a variety of consumer behaviours.

The remainder of the chapter is structured as follows. The following section conceptualises religion and demonstrates how it is the basic framework for consumer behaviour at both the group and individual levels. Thereafter, some retailers' consideration on segmenting and targeting are presented. Lastly, ethics and religious marketing conclude the chapter.

CONCEPTUALISING RELIGION FROM A MARKETING PERSPECTIVE

At the very least, religion is 'a community of people unified by common beliefs, rituals, and values of life, life processes, and the supernatural' (Mathras et al., 2016: 231). So, when a group of people live according to the dictates of an identifiable set of shared beliefs and congregate in pursuit of these values, essentially what emerges is a religion. Therefore, religion is the 'social bridge' that connects people; it helps them socialise and helps people not only to identify themselves, but also to connect with those of a likeminded nature.

Why Religion?

For marketers, it is not religion per se that is important, but what religion represents to consumers. Specifically, consumers' quest for identity formation arouses marketers' interests. Because consumers are social beings that value positive identity and image creation, marketers invented the word 'self-concept' to describe the processes through which consumers go about creating their identities. Self-concept denotes the 'totality of the individual's thoughts and feelings having reference to himself as an object' (Sirgy, 1982: 289). In other words, how consumers view themselves and also how they like to be viewed by others within their communities. The question of identity speaks directly to the concept of belongingness, which is also articulated in Maslow's Hierarchy of Needs, as constituting social needs. This is where religion comes in. Religion, therefore, serves as the community through which consumers express their unique identities as well as shared values (Delener, 1994; Mathras et al., 2016; Shambare and Donga, 2019b).

Be that as it may, the connection between religion and consumer behaviour is not always a straightforward one to many people. While religious connections are commonplace in everyday life, they are rather benign and often overlooked. To illustrate this, go through the exercise in Box 3.1 and see which questions you can answer.

BOX 3.1. REASONING TOGETHER EXERCISE

How many questions can you answer?

1. How is it that the delicacy of choice for Thanksgiving in North America is a turkey?
2. Why are red clothes a taboo during rainy seasons in certain parts of southern Africa?
3. Why did Zimbabwe's former president Mugabe's mother name her son Robert Gabriel? Even more interesting, why name her other sons Albert, Michael, and David?
4. How many Japanese go by the name Mohamed?
5. How come Chinese cuisine offers several dishes that would never be considered edible in the United Kingdom?
6. Is it just fashion that Tiger Woods almost always wears solid coloured clothes, mostly red in colour?
7. Why does a weekend always fall on Saturday and Sunday?

8.   Why is it that every other Afrikaner male in South Africa goes by the
      name Johan?

Studying the answers in Box 3.1 reveals the pervasiveness of religion. It is,
therefore, our argument that most, if not all, consumer behaviours begin with
religion, or at the very least, are traceable to one form of faith or another.
Therefore, to understand consumers or consumer behaviour, marketers' eyes
ought to be trained on their subjects' religion. But, what exactly does religion
mean in marketing?

Defining Religion

There are many definitions of religion in the literature. Within the context of
consumer behaviour, the multiple definitions introduce at least two problems:
which definition should be used and how should it be used in consumer
behaviour studies. This definitional challenge seems to have been addressed
by Mathras et al. (2016). These authors seem to resolve on the comprehensive
definition by Schimdt et al. (1999: 108), which considers religion as a 'system
of meaning embodied in a pattern of life, a community of faith, and a worldview that articulates a view of the sacred and of what ultimately matters'.
From the latter, Mathras et al. (2016) go on to operationalise this definition
within consumer behaviour studies. Of note, the four central elements of
religion – beliefs, rituals, values, and community – as proposed in the latter
study are, therefore, considered to be the central pillars of religion. From these,
Shambare and Donga (2019b) extend these pillars and articulate religion as the
constant and continuous interplay of the four pillars of social life. Figure 3.1
depicts the diagrammatical representation of this interplay of the elements of
religion, as they relate to marketing and consumer behaviour.
    Figure 3.1 depicts the association between religion, its various constituent
elements and culture, which in turn predicts consumer behaviour. Having
addressed this, the chapter now turns to the interdependence of culture and
religion and how these shape societies and consumption.

THE INTERDEPENDENCE OF CULTURE AND
RELIGION IN DEVELOPING COUNTRIES AND HOW
THEY SHAPE SOCIETIES

Religion is a function or an extension of culture, such that where you see religion, culture is also present. Thus, culture and religion are not opposites, but
complementing social elements (Shambare and Donga, 2019a). Dalela (2017)
states that the day-to-day practice of religion involves societies whose cultural

A critical examination of the nexus of groups, religion and consumer behaviour   49

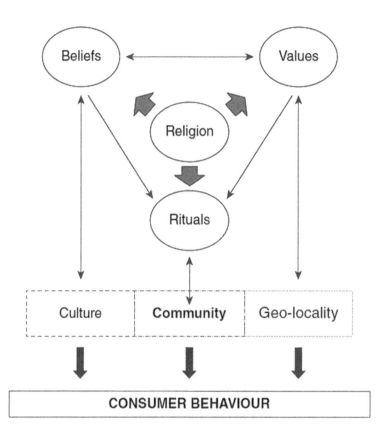

Source: Shambare and Donga (2019b).

Figure 3.1   The four elements of religion

norms must be compatible with the tenets of the religion and if there is a misfit between culture and religion, then most likely the religion would be changed rather than the culture. Within a culture are religious beliefs and values that highly determine which segment of society (family, friends, social classes) we happen to have been exposed to.

It has often been argued by researchers that in order to achieve a perspective on consumer behaviour, there is a need to conduct research in specific cultural settings so that similarities and differences among cultures can be found and compared (Yau, 1988; cited in Essoo, 2001). These researchers warn that transplantation of models derived from different cultural backgrounds can be extremely dangerous because people in different cultures have different views and choices are made because of very complex social influences or situations. Adding to this premise, with special attention to the developing countries context, cultural influence on religion can be considered crucial when it comes to understanding the needs and behaviours of social groups. As such, the developing nations perspective provides the ideal blend of cultural and religious groups among which consumer behaviour research can be carried out. According to Nasse et al. (2019), the marked influence of religion in all spheres of life in most developing nations also makes them a suitable setting for the study of the influence of religion on behaviour. As mentioned earlier in the introduction section, in most developing nations, collectivistic cultures are dominant and heavily intertwined with religion. To understand this notion in detail the next section reviews how when compared to individualistic cultures, collectivistic cultures and religion mutually influence each other and their interaction in stimulating social groups' behaviour.

Collectivistic Cultures versus Individualist Cultures

If someone asked you to finish the sentence, 'I am ___', what sorts of things would you include in your responses? Would you focus on your personality traits? Your job title? Or your relationships to others? As opined by Hoper (2015), psychologists have found that someone's cultural background can affect what sorts of things they choose to write down in an exercise like this. Although there are numerous ways in which culture can be defined, one of the cultural differences most studied by psychologists has been the difference between individualistic and collectivistic cultures (Bui and Farrington, 2019; Kolstad and Horpestad, 2009). People from individualistic cultures are more likely to have an independent view of themselves (they see themselves as separate from others, define themselves based on their personal traits, and see their characteristics as relatively stable and unchanging). On the other hand, people from collectivistic cultures are more likely to have an interdependent view of themselves (they see themselves as connected to others, define them-selves in terms of relationships with others, and see their characteristics as more likely to change across different contexts). Going back to the example at the beginning of this section, people from individualistic cultures are more likely to mention personal traits when finishing the sentence 'I am…', while people from collectivistic cultures are more likely to list relationships and group memberships.

   Collectivism which largely shapes religious beliefs and norms in developing nations stresses the importance of social interactions, while individualism is focused on the rights and concerns of each person (Hoper, 2015). A few common traits of collectivistic cultures as given by Kendra (2019) include:

- Social rules focus on promoting selflessness and putting the community needs ahead of individual needs.
- Working as a group and supporting others is essential.
- People are encouraged to do what's best for society.
- Families and communities have a central role.
- Greater emphasis on common goals over individual pursuits.

Typically, most African nations are collectivistic and constitute the greatest proportion of developing societies that put greater emphasis on solidarity of the community. For instance, the common cultural reference which shapes the African Tradition Religion is the saying, 'I am because we are: I exist because the community exists' (Brown, 1999: 235). As this reference suggests, the typical African's socialisation with others includes the acceptance of obligations to the community. The individual is to understand himself or herself as an integral part of the whole and play his or her appropriate role in the society. The above-stated cultural differences are pervasive and can influence many aspects of how society functions. For instance, how people shop, dress, learn, and conduct business can all be influenced by whether they are from a collectivist or individualist culture. Consumers who live in a collectivist culture, for example, might strive to sacrifice their own happiness for the greater good of the group. Those from individualistic cultures, on the other hand, may feel that their own well-being and goals carry greater weight.

Jakelic (2016) posits that, following their societal structures, religion in most developing nations is culturally specific, historically embedded, and defined in part by the presence of some religious other. They shape identities that distinguish their members from other religious groups, identities that members are often willing to die for. One does not choose to belong to these religious traditions; one is born into them. From the preceding discussion, it can be argued that the effect of religion on consumer choice behaviour among social groups is likely to be stronger in developing nations when compared to developed nations which are mostly individualistic. Furthermore, researchers have observed that while in developing nations religious faith is becoming more and more popular, in most developed nations it has been dwindling (Austin, 2017; Barber, 2012), thus, causing its impact on consumer behaviour, more specifically among social groups, to weaken.

Why Are Developed Societies Becoming Less Religious?

This is not to say consumers in most developed nations are not religious at all; they are according to Jakelic (2016) profoundly modern in character where citizens are mostly individualistic in their locus of experience and many often have religious beliefs but without necessarily belonging to a specific religious group. Barber (2011: 318) also mentioned that, 'with greater control over the external environment due to economic development and technological advances, religious belief is predicted to decline'. According to the author, if religion is primarily an adaptation to psychological uncertainty, then religiosity would be projected to decline in developed societies that enjoy greater economic security due to increased ability to prevail over the hostile forces of nature (e.g. predators, hunger, inclement weather, disease). In support of this postulation, in a cross-national analysis of frequency of prayer in 55 countries, Rees (2009) established that prayer was less frequent in developed nations with greater material security, including gross domestic product, and more unbiased income distribution.

The reasons causing religion to lose ground in developed nations can also be summarised in market terms (Barber, 2012). First, with advanced science, and government precautionary measures and smaller families, there is a reduction in people's fears and uncertainties and hence less of a market for religion. At the same time many alternative products are being offered, such as psychotropic medicines and electronic entertainment that do not require strict conformity to religious values and beliefs (Austin, 2017). This implies that as far as purchasing behaviour is concerned, religion is likely to exert lesser influence in developed nations. For instance, in developed societies, when people experience psychological difficulties they turn to their doctor, psychologist, or psychiatrist. They want a scientific fix and prefer consuming the real chemical medicines administered by physicians to the metaphorical opiates offered by religion (Barber, 2011).

The preceding discussion provides further impetus and lays fertile ground for focusing more of this chapter's attention on developing nations which are mostly characterised by collectivistic societies (Malhotra et al., 1994; Stolarski et al., 2015) where religiosity and social group influence seem to be high. Furthermore, from the discussion it appears that the literature provides strong evidence of a link between religion and behaviour. The influence is both on the cognitive and conative aspects of attitude. In other words, the influence of religion affects the psychological disposition of the individual as well as his physical actions. If religion has an influence on cognitive behaviour, the question that arises is whether this influence can be extended to consumer choice behaviour, which forms the focal point of this study. Before discussing this in detail, the next section highlights the generic influence of religion on behaviour in developed nations that is caused by their collectivist cultural background. As mentioned earlier, it is that influence which in turn is poised to impact on group dynamics of culture, family, reference groups, and social class in shaping consumption patterns among consumers in developing nations

INFLUENCE OF RELIGION ON SOCIAL GROUP BEHAVIOUR

The influence of religion on the value systems of social groups and the effect of these value systems on behaviour cannot be underestimated (Delener, 1989). Generally, religion has a big impact on a person's relationship with social groups. By nature, human beings are social and learn from observation rather than depending entirely on instinct, thus almost all aspects of human psychology and behaviour are socially influenced. Social networks found in religious groups in particular also play an important role in compelling people to conform to group behaviour. Marketing literature (e.g., Lindridge, 2005; Mathras et al., 2016; Shambare and Donga, 2019b) concur that religion constitutes an important element of society in most cultures, greatly influencing behaviour, which in turn affects purchasing decisions. Following this logic, religion could turn out to be a viable criterion for grouping markets. Formal study of religious beliefs and values should therefore improve understanding of the pressure exerted on consumption behaviour to the norms and expectations within social groups. In this chapter, we put forward that religion's role in shaping social groups is as a result of three influences on behaviour: (1) social affiliation, (2) conformity, and (3) self-concept clarity.

Social Affiliation

Social affiliation motivation, as defined by Van Cappellen et al. (2017: 24), is 'a concern with establishing, maintaining, or restoring positive interactions with another person or group. Social affiliation is characterised by a desire to interact and by pleasure in being with others and is one of human beings' basic and universal motivations'. According to Welch et al. (2006), religion as a subset of culture promotes first and foremost a fundamental motivation for social affiliation, which in turn may create a good foundation for group submission and conformity. Furthermore, beyond individual beliefs, social affiliation is a significant feature of religion that has imperative consequences for social group members' affiliation needs and their capacity to feel good and do good. Research has shown that in collectivistic societies, religious involvement is linked to having larger social group ties as well as greater frequency of contact and greater intimacy with members of the social network (Hook et al., 2009; Van Cappellen et al., 2017). Therefore, it is this motivation to socially affiliate which even influences what products or services members in a social group choose to consume or refrain from consuming.

Conformity

Religious identity also influences the motivation to either stand out or fit in with the rest of the group. For instance, in one experiment (Kendra, 2019), participants from American and Japanese societies were asked to select a pen. Most of the pens were the same colour, with a few options in different colours. Most American participants chose the rarer coloured pens. The Japanese participants, on the other hand, were much more likely to choose the most common coloured pen, even though they preferred the minority pens. One reason for this may have been because, coming from a collectivistic culture, the Japanese participants instinctively valued interpersonal harmony above personal preference and thus chose the inoffensive behaviour of leaving the rarer pens for others who might want them. This typical example also applies to consumer choice behaviour where religious affiliation shapes consumers to conform to specific purchasing patterns consisting of mutually shared assumptions, norms, values, standards for perceiving, believing, evaluating, and communicating.

Self-Concept Clarity

Religion influences how people behave, as well as their self-concept clarity which arises when an individual uses a social group's religious values, norms, and behaviours as a guide for his or her own actions. Campbell (1990, cited in Błażek and Besta, 2012: 948) defines self-concept clarity as 'the extent to which the contents of one's self-beliefs are clearly and confidently defined, internally consistent, and temporally stable'. Within social groups, an individual's religiosity often shapes his/her interactions with others and it is through those interactions where self-concept clarity is generated based on the perceptions and responses from others. Thus, religion provides the value system around which groups in particular have coalesced, and in which their members have identified themselves (Mokhlis, 2009). There is substantial evidence (Błażek and Besta, 2012) that people's religiosity is related to positive mental and subjective well-being. On the other hand, the psychologic trait of self-concept clarity has been shown to be linked to self-esteem, perceived meaning in life, and other positive mental outcomes. Within the consumer behaviour spectrum, researchers have found that consumers' decisions regarding products or services are also guided by self-concept clarity (Toth, 2014). It is suggested that consumers will choose products or services whose images are compatible with their own as well as those that are likely to result in positive appraisal from others. As such, religion plays a pivotal role in setting purchasing behaviour which is considered moral and ideal for creating positive social self-image.

Having discussed the influence of religion on social group behaviour, the focus now shifts to how this behaviour in turn shapes purchasing decision-making processes on specific group dynamics of culture, family, reference groups, and social class among consumers in developing nations.

RELIGIOUS COMMUNITIES AND GROUP-ORIENTED CONSUMPTION DECISIONS

As mentioned earlier, religion offers a system of values and beliefs around which communities gather. When people share mutual religious doctrine, they develop a shared identity as well as a sense of companionship. Therefore, affiliation to a specific religious group assists people in creating a sense of social as well as self-identity (Shambare and Donga, 2019b). Over time, shared identity and beliefs develop into a unique culture which determines how communities conduct their day-to-day activities including purchasing.

Research has shown that the strength of religious identity has a significant effect on consumer purchasing behaviour (Wright, 2015) and that the higher their strength of identification with a particular religious community the greater their propensity to purchase products associated with their religion. Hence, religion as a subset of culture (Marsiglia, 2010) is a macro-level perspective of a population whereas religious communities are a micro-level perspective of specific clusters of individuals within the religion. Within these clusters decisions are made. This is especially important for consumer-oriented marketing because religious beliefs and values form the lens through which consumers view advertising messages and products. Shambare and Donga (2019b) caution that, in order for marketers to develop effective marketing strategies for a specific culture, an intimate understanding yet comprehensive knowledge of how shopping behaviour of consumers is constantly affected by their religious values is apparently warranted. Next is a detailed discussion of the role of religion in shaping consumption within family, cultural, reference, and social class groups.

The Role of Religion in Shaping Consumption within Family Groups

Schiffman and Kanuk (2007: 326) define family as 'two or more persons related by blood, marriage or adoption who reside together'. A family creates first perceptions about brands or products and consumer habits (Khan, 2006). For example, the consumers who have created brand perceptions when they were young can carry out these same brand selections in their adult life without even recognising that their family influenced these selections. A consumer's family is one of the most significant factors which shapes purchasing patterns by influencing attitudes and behaviours. One way to understand the family's impact on consumer behaviour is to identify the decision maker for a purchase. A decision maker for a purchase can be a husband, a wife, or even a child, and sometimes decisions are made in collaboration. Often, the decision maker changes based on the type of purchase or the size of the purchase. A new refrigerator, for example, is likely to be a joint decision, while a week's groceries might be selected by a single member of the family.

Decision-making processes within family groups often follow specific patterns for those who strongly identify themselves with a certain religious faith as societal and group-specific beliefs that are consistent with moral conscience are highly regarded. As such, there is greater need for consumer research to establish the role that religion plays in shaping consumption within family groups. Unlike in the developed nations contexts which are mainly characterised by nuclear families, consumer decision-making processes among family groups in most developing countries are likely to be complex due to the extended nature of their families (Marsiglia, 2010). There are several salient reasons to this effect, the crucial one being that joint decision making is prevalent in multi-person households. Assael (2008) states that joint decision making is mainly influenced by the different role specifications for household members in the decision-making process. In an extended household, the family composition may consist of grandparents, aunts, uncles, and cousins, thereby further escalating the number of possible decision makers and increasing the chance of conflict in decision making (Childers, 1992). Religion therefore plays a very crucial role in reducing the complexity associated with family groups' consumer decision making in developing nations' purchasing patterns.

Religion facilitates harmony among family group members' decision-making processes by fostering reputable practices and facilitating a series of norms and values for social behaviour. These religious social norms and values may place some family members at the centre of decision making over others whilst in some cases amicably allowing mutual joint decision making. For instance, in a study which was carried out on two developing countries, Abduk Razak (2007) reported that religiosity appeared to influence family decision making in the purchase of major durable goods. The study established that Catholic families often focus on a rigid and authoritarian structure characterised by male dominance which results in husbands being the major influence in making purchase decisions. In Jewish households, however, family structure seems to be more democratic and there is greater emphasis on understanding other family members' view (*Shalom*), thereby making decisions for major durable goods to be taken jointly between husbands and their wives.

The Effect of Religion in Shaping Consumption within Cultural Groups

Religion has a profound impact on consumer behaviour within cultural groups. Religion and culture are closely related, they go hand in hand; in fact, they are according to Shambare and Donga (2019b) like the two sides to the same coin: where you see one, the other is not too far off. Therefore, religion and culture are not opposites, but they complement one another. Hofstede (1984: 21) defines culture as, 'The collective programming of the mind which distinguishes the members of one human group from another'. It is also the set of basic values, perceptions, wants, and behaviours learned by a member of society from family and other important institutions (Kotler et al., 2016). The elements of culture consist of mutually shared operating procedures, unstated assumptions, tools, norms, values, and habits about a particular cultural group. The element of value may be considered to include the concept of individuality, independence, achievement, and self-fulfilment. These elements are further shaped by the cultural dimension of religion and as such it becomes imperative for this section to assess the effects of religion in shaping consumption within cultural groups, particularly those found in developing nations.

Research has shown that religiosity exhibited within a particular culture has a significant effect on consumer purchasing behaviour and that the higher the religiosity the greater their propensity to purchase products associated with their cultural and religious values (Chattaraman and Lennon, 2008). Evidence further indicates that the longer consumers are in a host country the more likely the consumer will adopt cultural as well as religious values specific to the host country. This acculturation becomes complex when the consumer is in close contact with other unique ethnic cultures resulting in a cross-cultural amalgam (Marsiglia, 2010). Many cultures in developing countries, however, promote collectivistic societies based on a concept of protecting the livelihood of ethnic, racial, religious groups, or those who share a common language (Sijuwade, 2006). Therefore, this means that despite the probable consumer decision-making complexities within a cross-cultural amalgam for developing nations who are largely collectivistic, religion plays a pivotal role in mitigating against such complexities through instituting societal norms and structures that unify the decision-making process. In collectivistic societies, to view individuals as members of cultural groups is to view the individual as a product of a system of beliefs (Brown, 1999). These beliefs are both cultural and religious and in turn highly shape consumption patterns.

The South African culture, for instance, is extremely complex as it is made up of a variety of subcultures and communities, each with their own language, traditions, distinct culinary and dress styles, and religions. It is made up of a variety of cultures and traditions, stemming from the Malay, Indian, Koisan, Bantu (Nguni), Dutch, French, etc. The South African culture is also unique in that it encompasses features from both Afrocentric and Eurocentric cultural values. As such, the above-mentioned cultures are linked to different religions and religious practices, such as the Abrahamic religions (Christianity, Judaism, and Islam), Hinduism, Buddhism, and African Tradition Religions, which each have a profound impact on the consumption among cultural groups. For instance, Malay and Indian Muslims' consumption during the Muslim festive season (*Eid*) or the fasting period of *Ramadan* is guided by the Islamic religion. Similarly, *Diwali* and the Christmas festive seasons will also affect consumption within Hindu and Christian groups, respectively. Both the Diwali and Christmas celebrations, for instance, can most accurately be characterised as consumption festivals, communal experiences that rally consumers into spending overdrive. Although, religiously, the individuals are commanded to uphold their faith, conspicuous overconsumption has become a noticeable occurrence in all aspects of the respective festivals, especially in the purchase of foodstuffs, apparel, and leisure activities. During these periods, even the commercial and media landscapes are transformed and directed toward urging individuals towards worldly and profane experiences. Resisting this cultural pressure becomes difficult, household spending rises dramatically, and hedonic desires are felt more strongly than ever (Touzani and Hirschman, 2008).

Religion, Cultural Groups, and Food Consumption Practices

It is important to note that the major religious influences on consumer choice behaviour across cultural groups relate to food (Shambare and Donga, 2019b). In the case of food preferences, violating religious edicts (e.g. beef for Hindus), food taboos, and respect for cultural values determine the food choices within communities bound by certain cultural traditions (Monin and Szczurek, 2014). As a result, according to Shipman and Durmus (2017), food can be considered one of the easiest points of entry into a community to understand and evaluate cultural traditions as everybody wants to eat and gather together, but different cultural groups and different societies have different choices of food due to religion, beliefs, and ethnic behaviours. Eating is a daily reaffirmation of one's cultural identity (Kittler et al., 2012). Therefore, it can be stated that food choices, food culture, and food consumption habits can significantly reveal insight into a culture. While not all religions have specific guidelines regarding diet, Table 3.1 summarises food cultures imposed on consumption by some prolific religions found in most developing nations.

As portrayed in Table 3.1, Buddhists adhere to vegetarian diets, as these are seen as instrumental in improving quality of life. The lack of meat among many Buddhists' diet is in line with their beliefs around preserving life, including the lives of animals. Christians appear to have the most liberal diet,

Table 3.1   Influence of religious values on food consumption

Type of religion	Practice or restriction	Value rational
Buddhism	– Meat is not recommended, vegetarian diet is desired	– Earthly natural foods are regarded as highly pure
	– Moderation in all foods	– Monks refrain from all solid food after noon
	– Monks are required to fast	
Christianity	– Meat is restricted on certain days	– Holy days are observed, including fasting and restrictions to intensify spiritual progress
	– Fasting is selective	
Hinduism	– Beef is forbidden	– Cows cannot be eaten as they are sacred, however, products of the 'sacred' cow are considered pure and are preferred
	– All other meat and fish are restricted or avoided	
	– Alcohol should not be consumed	
	– Several fasting days	– Fasting stimulates spiritual development
Islam	– Refrain from eating pork and certain birds	– Food consumption is for good health
	– Alcohol is illegal	– Failure to eat appropriately reduces spiritual awareness
	– Coffee/tea/stimulants are not recommended	– Evil elements are cleansed through fasting
	– Fasting during specific periods	

Source: Shambare and Donga (2019b).

save for a few denominations such as the Seventh Day Adventists who seem to promote the vegetarian lifestyle (Tukamushaba and Musinguzi, 2018). In the case of Muslims, food consumption is highly aligned to the prescripts of the halal (permissible) dietary laws. Food, to Muslims, is a means to achieving and maintaining healthy lives. Accordingly, food is not supposed to be abused as a recreation tool, which means that excess indulgence of stimulants, for example tea, coffee, or alcohol, is not recommended in Islam (Shambare and Donga, 2019b). Another important consideration among Muslims over and above halal food is that the food must be prepared in an absolutely spotless environment, so much so that even halal ingredients can be considered to be *haram* (i.e. forbidden) if the food preparation environment is unsanitary or if it is contaminated with prohibited (*haram*) items. As a result, Muslim consumers could easily become unhappy and sometimes call for a massive boycott of any food outlets they perceive to be lacking in hygiene because of the value they attach to cleanliness.

The preceding discussion confirms that religiosity and culture play an important part in influencing several aspects related to consumer behaviour. In support, Mokhlis (2006; cited in Shambare and Donga, 2019b) posits that religiosity shapes cultural groups' conduct in life, their search for information, a buying risk aversion, perceptions related to advertising, buying behaviour, and designated concepts of retail behaviour. Therefore, there is sufficient evidence confirming the utility of religiosity in determining the behaviour of consumers within specific cultural settings. The need for continual interaction among societies might explain the rapid growth in community-based religions such as Islam and Christianity in developing nations. The expectation, on the part of adherents, is that unlike individual-based religions, community-based religions offer adequate social networks, support, a sense of belonging, and an opportunity for people to practise and express their culture (Mathras et al., 2016). In this way, religion affords people the opportunity to express both their personal and cultural beliefs, which is a public affirmation that they are not excluded from mainstream society. Religiosity, thus, acts as both a proxy for culture and a means through which it is expressed.

Reference Groups, Religion, and Consumer Behaviour

The Greek philosopher Aristotle famously asserted that humans are by nature social animals who are bound to live in groups (Asikaogu, 2018). This is certainly true and needs no better understanding than through the concept of reference groups. These groups which a person belongs to have a profound effect on the behaviour, attitudes, and beliefs of that particular individual. Therefore, an individual will refer to a certain extent to these groups with regards to the social acceptability of the dress code, type of speech, values, beliefs, attitudes, behaviour, as well as the consumption of given products and services (Engel et al., 1990). Reference groups can clearly be defined as 'a set of people with whom individual consumers compare themselves in developing their own attitudes and behaviour' (Noel, 2009: 16). Reference groups have a significant impact on consumption of products and services. They convey information to an individual about which products and services they should or should not be consuming. This is especially true for individuals who consider themselves to be very similar to their peers or reference groups (Kotler and Keller, 2012; Kotler and Armstrong, 2018). There are two kinds of reference groups: primary and secondary groups. Primary groups interact regularly and informally and are formed by family, friends, neighbours, and co-workers. Secondary groups interact occasionally and formally and are formed by trade unions, professional associations, and members of socio-cultural societies

(Schiffman and Kanuk, 2007). Reference groups' influence on consumer decision making is according to Nayeem (2012) likely to be strongest in collectivist cultures which are associated with strong interdependent ties and greater product visibility to other consumers. As such, in line with the earlier discussion, developing countries are mainly collectivistic, implying that individuals are much more likely to assimilate the same consumption patterns developed within their religious groups. There are three main types of influences caused by reference groups which can also be linked to religion: (1) value-expressive influence, (2) normative influence, and (3) informational influence.

Value-Expressive Influence

How religiosity affects reference group influence is unclear from previous research and there is a need for further studies on this phenomenon. According to Lindridge (2005), high religiosity and its inference of community suggest reference group usage would also be high, owing to a greater sense of belonging and therefore a need to involve others. Reference group-related factors include the extent to which a group is regarded as strongly knowledgeable about the norms and values of a particular religion and strictly adhering to them. Rather than engage in anti-confirmative activities, religion strongly fosters consumers to adapt their behaviours to religious-specific norms defined by their group identity in a conscious and rational process relating to a meaningful sense of identity. Thus, the need to conform to specific religious values and beliefs can affect the degree of influence that the reference group is able to exert. For instance, endorsement of a famous halal fast food is likely to be perceived as more credible coming from a famous chef with strong beliefs in the Islamic religion than a chef who is not knowledgeable and not adhering to Islamic values and beliefs. Due to the fact that the Islamic religion has a regulatory framework regarding the necessary standards to be observed and implemented by the food industries in processing their food products, it stresses the value for safety, hygiene, and wholesomeness in food preparation which creates an excellent platform for healthy and safe food (Mutsikiwa and Basera, 2012).

Normative Influence

The other important type of reference group influence in which religion can affect consumption is referred to as normative influence. Normative influence is the pressure exerted to conform to the norms and expectations of the group. Conformity in this case is important for social acceptance (Shambare and Donga, 2019b). Religion serves as one of the most enduring sources of core values for consumers, which influences consumption motives, even at a subconscious level (Mathras et al., 2016). For example, explicit references to materialism and pride-based consumption and status consumption are made in religious scripture (Geiger-Oneto and Minton, 2019), which suggests that a consumer's religious background provides insight into motives for and responses to the consumption of luxury products. Specifically, in developing nations most of the scripture advocates against materialism and prideful consumption, with pride even being one of Catholicism's seven deadly sins (Geiger-Oneto and Minton, 2019). The Franciscan Catholic priests, for example, are known for their humble dedication to a Christian life of virtue and hence act as a reference group for those consumers with strong beliefs and values linked to the Franciscan doctrine which is centred on the ideals of poverty and charity. Thus, in order for those consumers to conform to such doctrine, they strive for a modest life and by all means avoid materialism and the purchase of luxury products and services.

Informational Influence

The last important reference group influence is termed informational influence and occurs when the group provides the consumers with information that enables them to make a decision. Informational influence is based on the desire to make informed decisions and optimise the choice. Kelman (1961; cited in Yang et al., 2007) suggested that an individual would accept an influence that improves one's knowledge and ability to cope with the environment. The informational influence only functions when the individual regards the behaviour and value of reference group members as potentially useful infor-mation and takes them into consideration (Yang et al., 2007). For instance, the majority of religions have faith leaders who constitute a group of people with significant influence on other people's thoughts, emotions, and behaviours (Heward-Mills et al., 2018). As an integral member of the community, faith leaders are uniquely positioned to promote behaviour change. Hence, due to the high regards placed on faith leaders by other religious followers they can be considered opinion leaders who pose high informational reference influence on individuals' behaviour. In developing countries, which are characterised by high social embeddedness, religious leaders' informational influence on consumption decisions is likely to be stronger especially when adherents are uncertain about the correct interpretation of reality and/or the correct behaviour in a given context and therefore look to their leaders for guidance. For instance, in Indonesia, religious leaders are important resources for many religiously observant Muslims in decisions regarding particularly the consumption of medicines, including vaccines, as they are believed to be manufactured using animal-derived products (Padmawati et al., 2019). As espoused by Herbison (2015), realising the informational influence that faith leaders have on con-sumption, a Queensland University of Technology PhD marketing candidate suggested that companies should consult religious leaders before releasing new products and services to avoid lack of adoption among religious groups.

Religion and Consumption across Social Class Groups

Almost every society has some form of social class structure. Social classes are 'society's relatively permanent and ordered divisions whose members share similar values, interests and behaviours' (Kotler et al., 2016: 241). The social class segments the market on income criteria and standards of living. The concept of social class implies that some people have more power, wealth, and opportunity than others (Noel, 2009: 16). Consequently, a major influence on one's purchasing habits and consumer behaviour is the social class in which one finds him or herself. Social class is considered an external influence on consumer behaviour because it is not a function of feelings or knowledge. Social class is often hard to define; in fact, many people dispute the existence of social classes in the United States (Barr, 2014). Usually, however, people are grouped in social classes according to income, wealth, education, or type of occupation. Perhaps the simplest model to define social class and which is highly applicable to developing countries is a three-tiered approach that includes the rich, the middle class, and the poor. Other models have as many as a dozen levels. People in the same social class tend to have similar attitudes, live in similar neighbourhoods, dress alike, and shop at the same type of store (Abdolmaleki et al., 2016).

Shambare and Donga (2019a) distinguish three main categories of social classes which can be found in developing nations, namely: the upper class, the middle class and the lower class. These classes could be further subdivided into the following subclasses (see Figure 3.2):

- *Upper class*: this is divided into the upper-upper class and the lower-upper class.
  - The upper-upper class consists of individuals who predominantly acquire their wealth and status by means of inheritance (such as members of royal families or chieftaincies).
  - The lower-upper class consists mostly of individuals that were not born rich and attained their wealth and status based on their professional and/or business ventures. This class is also termed *nouveau riche* (newly rich) and includes people such as business owners, industrialists, entrepreneurs, corporate executives, lawyers, doctors, professors, etc.
- *Middle class*: this is divided into the upper-middle class and the middle class.

- • The upper-middle class is mostly constituted of qualified professionals with university qualifications, such as teachers, nurses, social workers, etc.
- • The middle class has the largest number of people and is constituted of white-collar workers such as bank tellers, accountants, etc. It is important to mention that some highly skilled blue-collar workers such as electricians, plumbers, and mechanics would also be considered in this class.
- • *Lower class*: this is divided into the working class, the lower class, and the lower-lower class.
  - • In the working-class group, workers may not require a particular qualification, and are often paid average salaries and wages. This sub-category comprises individuals referred to as blue-collar workers such as plant or factory workers.
  - • Lower-class consumers are living just above the poverty line and are struggling to make ends meet, they are unemployed or seasonally employed most of the time.
  - • The lower-lower-class group comprises the most vulnerable and finan-cially deprived individuals of society. People in this category are very poor and rely on government grants and welfare to meet their daily needs.

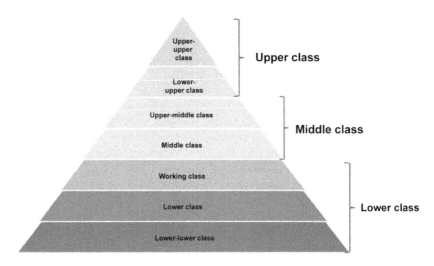

Source: Shambare and Donga (2019a).

Figure 3.2   Hierarchical structure of social classes

It is important to note that social class membership is not fixed as individuals can move from one class to another. Movement from a lower to a higher social class, for instance from middle to upper, is known as upward social mobility and is more desirable than downward social mobility.

It is important to note that the virtual absence of social class in the sociology of religion is almost as mysterious as it is telling. McKinnon (2017) notes that there has been a dearth of discussion about class in the sociology of religion, just as class analysis has been markedly inattentive to the role of religion in the formation of classes and class subjectivities. As a result, this poses a greater challenge when applying the interaction between religion and social class to consumer behaviour research as we are often stuck with relying on indicators which might not actually measure social class. Nevertheless, the little available literature forms the conceptual infrastructure and provides indispensable starting points for the analysis of social class, religion, and their relation to consumer behaviour. MacLaren (2019) argues that social class is not directly correlated to religiosity but is associated with individuals' religious affiliations and practices. This affiliation has more to do with how religion is practised than with the degree of religiosity. Members of lower classes, for instance, tend to be affiliated with the more fundamentalist religions and sect-like groups whilst members of the middle class and upper class tend to belong to more formal religious congregations.

Lower Class, Religion, and Consumption

In one of the earliest books which tried to link religion and social class titled *Social Sources of Denominationalism*, Niebuhr (1929) noted that people from the lower class are likely to be attracted to religious affiliations that strongly adhere to dogmas and strict doctrinal interpretation. As such, the lower class may have less room than the middle or upper classes to look outside of religion when making decisions. In most developing countries, the gap between the rich and the poor is very wide and those falling under the lower-class category are considered economically alienated people. Therefore, religion provides a form of comfort to which they can turn to alleviate their deprivation—hence Marx's famous dictum that religion is 'the opium of the people' (Rogers and Konieczny, 2018: 74). Due to their strict doctrinal interpretation of religious beliefs and values, consumers within the lower social class may have an important bearing upon the purchasing behaviour of its members. For instance, the acceptance of being born into a lower class and the expectation and willingness to behave in accordance with the norms of that class indicates a certain fatalism or inability to change things (Bailey and Sood, 1993). Furthermore, by focusing on the eternal rather than the temporal, it is expected that the lower-class consumers are docile, passive, and less motivated to consume luxury goods.

This could mean that minimum effort would be made by devout consumers in the lower class to search for information, acquire new products, and request quality service.

Middle Class, Religion, and Consumption

In contrast to the lower class, the middle-class members of society tend towards more modern religious affiliations. According to DeBrouse (2017), the concept of religious theodicy explains that people adopt beliefs that coincide with their status in life. Wealthier classes lean toward beliefs that justify their economic situations, while the lower classes lean toward those that promise wealth in the hereafter. Pew Research Centre (2009) found that in developing countries, unlike the lower class members, members of the middle class assign more importance to democratic institutions and individual liberties, consider religion less central to their lives, and hold more liberal social values. This pattern is true across a number of developing countries and a variety of faiths. In the survey conducted by Pew Research Centre (2009), for instance, one third of the middle class in predominantly Catholic Mexico said religion is very important to them, while about half (48 per cent) of the low-class Mexicans express this opinion. Similar gaps exist in largely Hindu India (middle class – 60 per cent very important; lower income – 72 per cent). In Malaysia, which is majority Muslim but has significant Buddhist, Christian, and Hindu minorities, 60 per cent of the middle class said religion is very important to them compared with 86 per cent of those with lower incomes. As such, religious beliefs and values for consumers within the middle social class may have less bearing upon the purchasing behaviour of its members when compared to those in the lower class. Nevertheless, due to greater chances for social mobility (either up to the upper class or down to the lower class), consumers within the middle class (Leventoğlu, 2014) are likely to be influenced by both traditional and modern religions. Therefore, their consumption is likely to be a blend of both non-luxurious and luxurious products depending on an individual's religious affiliation.

Upper Class, Religion, and Consumption

Previous Pew Global Attitudes research (Ciftci and Tezcür, 2016) has shown a link between wealth and religious affiliation at the country level – as a country's overall wealth increases, its level of religious affiliation generally declines. What this analysis illustrates is that within countries, wealthier individuals (i.e. upper social class) often are the least affiliated to a certain religion, implying that religion has minimum influence on consumption when compared to the lower and middle classes. Consumers from the upper class in developing countries tend to be more satisfied with their lives and less insecure and therefore lean toward beliefs that justify their economic situation. For instance, an increasingly defining feature of religion in developing nations especially in Africa is the subscription to the 'prosperity gospel'. This belief holds that financial success and physical health are always the will of God (Zulu, 2019). Moreover, this belief maintains that those with positive thoughts and words – plus big donations to the church – will receive an increase in material wealth in return. This has resulted in a number of individuals from the upper class preferring to affiliate with such doctrines and even the urgency for becoming wealthier and being recognised as such by other members of society has increased. This in turn is resulting in an increase in consumption of luxury products among upper-class consumers with some even openly and ostentatiously displaying their luxury possessions, such as very expensive and exclusive luxury cars.

RELIGION AND ETHICAL MARKETING

A greater part of the chapter has been largely consumer-centric in how religion as a subset of culture influences consumer decision making within social groups. It is however essential to also briefly look at the business side by determining the linkage between religion and ethical marketing. It appears that researchers (e.g. Emerson and Mckinney, 2010) have rediscovered spirituality and religion with renewed interest in integrating this aspect of life into business. Furthermore, partly in response to the ethical failures that have plagued business in recent years, there has been a great deal of interest in the relationship among religion, spirituality, psychology, and business (Emerson and Mckinney, 2010).

Certainly, current interest in spirituality and religion is hot among not only the consumers but also among all marketing participants. For instance, slightly more than a decade ago, the role of ethical failures in contributing to the global financial crisis of 2008–2009 demonstrated that the viability of the entire global economic system might require adherence to certain religious values by market participants in order to observe basic ethical standards. The financial crisis of 2008 was the result of numerous market inefficiencies, bad practices, and a lack of transparency in the financial sector (Cassey, 2013) as participants were engaging in behaviour that put the financial system on the brink of collapse. In order to uphold basic ethical standards, market participants may need to look or lean on their religion to deal with business ethical failures. Harkless, Jr. (2013) stresses that the way in which marketing players practise their businesses or the rules they follow, their ethics, and guidelines can be attributed to their religion. The global financial crisis of 2008 reinforces the vitality of religious faith in shaping behaviour to both consumers and firms as religion

Table 3.2   Unethical business practices and religion

| | Unethical business practices | |
	Customer abuse	Defrauding customers
Examples	– Emotional and physical abuse directed at a customer – Dismissal of genuine customer complaints	– Misleading advertisements – Unfair pricing – Short-changing – Selling of inferior products or services
Christianity	A soft answer turns away wrath, but a harsh word stirs up anger	Better is a little with righteousness than great revenues with injustice
Islam	Whoever believes in Allah should do good to others	And, do not cloak (and confuse) the truth with falsehood
Hinduism	You need to show compassion to all living beings	Nothing is higher than the Law of Righteousness
Buddhism	With gentleness overcome anger	Tell no lies and deceive no one
Judaism	For the anger of man does not produce the righteousness of God	No man who practises deceit shall dwell in my house

is constituted of moral teachings and in various ways indicates disapproval of unethical actions. Therefore, it is logical to assume that religious consumer groups would be less tolerant of unethical behaviour exhibited in firms.

Whether it is a big firm or a small business, the stakes of outperforming the competition are always high. This cut-throat struggle for survival and emerging as a winner attracts a lot of unscrupulous tendencies that have unfortunately become a part of the system (Khanna, 2018). The urge to rule the market has made businesses selfish and all-consuming, and the obligation to operate responsibly has been neglected. The lines between acceptable and unacceptable behaviour have blurred over the years, and the focus has shifted from the consumers to gaining higher profits and margins. Table 3.2 depicts some of the common religious morals which dictate to businesses how they can ensure adherence to ethical marketing from production to the moment when a product or service is delivered to the consumer.

Guided by religion, consumer groups are increasingly choosing to purchase from firms they believe make ethical, socially responsible decisions that do not conflict with their religious values and beliefs. Their buying process is becoming less about what is convenient and cheap and more about what is considered moral and honourable. By businesses being ethically aware and responsible, a positive rapport with the target religious market, especially those with higher levels of religiosity, is created and encourages relationships built on trust. Consequently, it makes sense for marketers to align their strategies with consumers' religious values and beliefs. In the next section, how marketers can effectively target social groups on the basis of their religion is highlighted.

THE POTENTIAL OF RELIGION AS THE BASIS FOR MARKET TARGETING AND STRATEGIES WITHIN SOCIAL GROUPS

McDaniel and Burnett (1990: 102) noted that unlike other human values, religion 'tends to be stable over a fairly long period of time and many of the elements of religiosity are observable'. From a marketing point of view, the stability of religion underlying consumer behaviour implies the potential of religion as the ground for market targeting and strategies within social groups (Abduk Razak, 2007). This is because much information about typical consumers is in a state of fluctuation, that is, the relevancy of certain social group characteristics might change depending on the time and situation. Marketers cannot depend merely on the implications related to consumers' basic demography such as income, level of education, age, and employment status, as these characteristics change over time and from one generation to the next, thus hampering market targeting to its full potential (Abduk Razak, 2007). As such, the capability of identifying how the behaviour of consumers within social groups is affected by their religiosity factors is critical to the success of marketers, especially for those who operate in countries dominant in religious faith such as those which fall under the developing nations category. This section therefore breaks down insightful strategies in which marketers' campaigns can successfully target social groups by incorporating their underlining religious values and norms.

Regarding *family groups*, marketers need to seek for a niche within a given market. Marketing should not be seen as a quick-fix solution for current problems, but rather entailing sensitivity in meeting the needs and wants of the consumers served (Delener, 1994). Specifically, in advertising, promotion, and direct sales the importance of the decision maker's religiosity in family groups must be considered. If his/her role in the decision-making process is ignored or treated as unimportant the sale of that product or service may be lost. In general, marketing and consumer behaviour researchers have been concerned with the relative influence of husbands and wives in various decisions because of the implications their role differentiation may have for product planning, advertising content, and media, as well as the choice of distribution channels.

With reference to *cultural groups*, cultural characteristics are largely country-dependent and research has shown that consumers within a specific culture tend to interpret and react to marketing information differently from other cultures, which means marketers should use culturally matched advertisements to induce consumers to act. For instance, consumers in countries like India are high in collectivism and react to advertisements differently than consumers in countries like the United States or England where there is a high degree of individualism.

Concerning *reference groups*, having knowledge about their target religious community in terms of their beliefs, values, aspirations, and needs necessitates marketers and retailers to associate their products with appropriate groups and to use the right people to represent them. Therefore, marketers can classify and properly represent target consumers in marketing campaigns by precisely reflecting the religious beliefs, values, and general conduct of their associative reference groups. For example, the Muslim religious communities are very proud of the two-time African footballer of the year Mo Salah who is known for his strong adherence to Islamic religion. Mo Salah thus can be considered an important aspirational reference whom Islamic companies may consider giving exclusive endorsement for commercial adverts targeted at Islamic consumers.

Every society possesses some form of *social class* which is important to the marketers because the buying behaviour of people in a given social class is approximately similar. In this way marketing activities could be tailored according to different social classes. Here we should note that social class is not only determined by income but other factors also, such as wealth, education, occupation, and even religion. However, according to Thompson (2018), the relationship between social class and religion is not yet straightforward and is hampered by a lack of suitable data, and as such there is a need for global marketers to collaborate with sociologists and conduct extensive research on the phenomenon. McKinnon (2017) espoused that this approach has the potential to provide important insights, including breaking new ground in identifying the affinity of different religious groups with different social class categories and how it affects consumer choice behaviour.

A number of markets are made up of different religious groups. Knowledge of the purchasing behaviour of these religious groups will provide valuable information to marketers willing to develop marketing strategies targeted at a specific religious group. The marketing mix elements might have to be reviewed in the light of possible religious influences. Branding, pricing, promotion, and distribution strategies might have to take into consideration the influence of beliefs and practices of certain religions as compared to others. In addition, marketers might also consider including consumers' religiosity as a legitimate segmentation variable for marketing their products and services. If larger market segments can be identified on the basis of religious value profiles, marketing strategists could develop programmes that would enhance the important values of consumers in each religious social group.

For a brand, it is important to understand and take into account the religious factors inherent to each religious group or to each situation in order to adapt its product and marketing strategy. McDonald's is a brilliant example of adaptation to the specificities of each religious group and market. Well aware of the importance to have an offer with specific products to meet the needs and tastes of consumers from different cultures, the fast food giant has, for example, carefully adapted food items according to local traditions and religions. For example, in Middle Eastern Arab countries, McDonald's consumers can get McArabia (grilled halal chicken with Arabic spices and bread), while also on offer is a new menu for vegetarians in India as some people do not consume meat. In addition to this they avoid beef as cow is sacred in Hinduism, the majority religion in India.

CONCLUSION

Religion is a major cultural factor that influences people's attitudes, values, and behaviours at both the individual and societal levels as evident in the chapter. Particularly we have observed that the religious effect on social groups' consumption behaviour plays a pivotal role mostly in developing nations, where collectivistic cultures are dominant and heavily intertwined with religion. In an attempt to holistically further this discourse, the chapter started with a discussion of the connection between religion and consumer behaviour. This was followed by an exploration of the interdependence of culture and religion in developing countries and how they shape societies. In this section, emphasis was given on the ground in which the developing nations' perspective provides the ideal blend of cultural and religious groups among which consumer behaviour research can be carried out. The discussion thus paved the way for the next section which centred on the chapter's main objective of determining the extent of the influence of religious affiliation and religiosity on social groups' consumer behaviour. Religious affiliation and religiosity's influence on group-oriented consumption behaviour was interrogated along four key social groups – family groups, cultural groups, reference groups, and social class groups – with illustrations cutting across the major religions found in most developing countries. In the penultimate section, the chapter delved into the business side by determining the linkage between religion and ethical marketing providing illustrations on some of the common religious morals which dictate to businesses on how they can ensure adherence to ethical marketing. The chapter wrapped up by presenting marketing implications as they relate to religion and social group-oriented consumption decisions.

REFERENCES

Abdolmaleki, H., Mirzazadeh, Z., and Alidoust Ghahfarokhhi, E. (2016). The role played by socio-cultural factors in sports consumer behavior. *Annals of Applied Sport Science*, 4(3), 17–25.

Abduk Razak, K. (2007). Religiosity and shopping orientation: a comparative study of Malaysia and Thailand consumers. *Journal of Global Business Management*, 3(2).

Asikaogu, J. (2018). A critical review of Aristotle's view on human sociality. *International Journal of Humanities, Social Sciences and Work Place Ergonomics in Africa*, 11(4/5), 37–48.

Assael, H. (2008). *Consumer Behavior: A Strategic Approach*. New Delhi: Dreamtech Press.

Austin, M. W. (2017). Can atheism replace religion? Available at: www.huffpost.com/entry/can-atheism-replace-relig_b_8556076 (Accessed on: 18 January 2020).

Bailey, J. M. and Sood, J. (1993). The effects of religious affiliation on consumer behavior: A preliminary investigation. *Journal of Managerial Issues*, 328–52.

Barber, N. (2011). A cross-national test of the uncertainty hypothesis of religious belief. *Cross-Cultural Research*, 45(3), 318–33.

Barber, N. (2012). Why atheism replaces religion in developed countries. Available at: www.huffpost.com/entry/why-atheism-to-replace- (Accessed on: 12 January 2020).

Barr, D. A. (2014). *Health Disparities in the United States: Social Class, Race, Ethnicity, and Health*. Baltimore, MD: Johns Hopkins University Press.

Błażek, M. and Besta, T. (2012). Self-concept clarity and religious orientations: prediction of purpose in life and self-esteem. *Journal of Religion and Health*, 51(3), 947–60.

Brown, K. (1999). Globalization and cultural conflict in developing countries: the South African example. *Indiana Journal of Global Legal Studies*, 225–56.

Bruneau, T. C. (2012). *The Church in Brazil: The Politics of Religion*, Vol. 56. Austin, TX: University of Texas Press.

Bui, L. and Farrington, D. P. (2019). Culture. In *Crime in Japan* (pp. 23–49). Cham: Palgrave Macmillan.

Cassey, M. J. (2013). Without stronger transparency, more financial crises loom. Available at: https://cpj.org/2014/02/attacks-on-the-press-transparency-finance.php (Accessed on: 14 January 2020).

Chattaraman, V. and Lennon, S. J. (2008). Ethnic identity, consumption of cultural apparel, and self-perceptions of ethnic consumers. *Journal of Fashion Marketing and Management: An International Journal*, 12(4), 518–31.

Childers, T. R. (1992). The influence of familial and peer-based reference groups on consumer decisions. *Journal of Consumer Research*, 19, 198–211.

Choi, Y. (2010). Religion, religiosity, and South Korean consumer switching behaviors. *Journal of Consumer Behaviour*, 9(3), 157–71.

Ciftci, S. and Tezcür, G. M. (2016). Soft power, religion, and anti-Americanism in the Middle East. *Foreign Policy Analysis*, 12(3), 374–94.

Dalela, A. (2017). How culture influences religion. Available at: www.ashishdalela.com/2017/03/04/how-culture-influences-religion/ (Accessed on: 19 January 2020).

DeBrouse, R. (2017). How does social class shape religious affiliation? Available at: https://classroom.synonym.com/how-does-social-class-shape-religious-affiliation-12087342.html (Accessed on: 14 January 2020).

Delener, N. (1989). Religious differences in cognitions concerning external information search and media usage. *Proceedings of the Southern Marketing Association*, 64–8.

Delener, N. (1994). Religious contrasts in consumer decision behaviour patterns: their dimensions and marketing implications. *European Journal of Marketing*, 28(5), 36–53.

Emerson, T. L. and Mckinney, J. A. (2010). Importance of religious beliefs to ethical attitudes in business. *Journal of Religion and Business Ethics*, 1(2), 5.

Engel, J. F., Blackwell, R. D., and Miniard, P. W. (1990). *Consumer Behavior*, 6th ed. Hinsdale, IL: Dryden Press.

Essoo, N. (2001). A study of cultural influences on consumer behaviour in a small island economy: religious influences on purchasing behaviour in Mauritius. Doctoral dissertation, University of Warwick.

Geiger-Oneto, S. and Minton, E. A. (2019). How religiosity influences the consumption of luxury goods: exploration of the moral halo effect. *European Journal of Marketing*, 53(12), 2530–55.

Harkless, Jr., G. (2013). Business – entrepreneurs share how religion has influenced their leadership and business practices. Available at: https://rescue.ceoblognation .com/2013/02/19/religion-and-business/ (Accessed on: 29 May 2020).

Herbison, M. (2015). Religion's impact on consumer behaviour: QUT study. Available at: www.marketingmag.com.au/news-c/religions-impact-consumer-behaviour-qut -study/ (Accessed on: 20 September 2020).

Heward-Mills, N. L., Atuhaire, C., Spoors, C., Pemunta, N. V., Priebe, G., and Cumber, S. N. (2018). The role of faith leaders in influencing health behaviour: a qualitative exploration on the views of Black African Christians in Leeds, United Kingdom. *Pan African Medical Journal*, 30.

Hofstede, G. (1984). *Culture's Consequences: International Differences in Work-Related Values*, Vol. 5. London: Sage.

Hook, J. N., Worthington, Jr., E. L., and Utsey, S. O. (2009). Collectivism, forgiveness, and social harmony. *Counseling Psychologist*, 37(6), 821–47.

Hoper, E. (2015). Individualist or collectivist? How culture influences behavior. Available at: https://healthypsych.com/individualist-or-collectivist-how-culture -influences-behavior/ (Accessed on: 6 January 2020).

Jakelic, S. (2016). *Collectivistic Religions: Religion, Choice, and Identity in Late Modernity*. London: Routledge.

Kendra, C. (2019). Understanding collectivist cultures: how culture can influence behavior. Available at: www.verywellmind.com/what-are-collectivistic-cultures -2794962 (Accessed on: 15 January 2020).

Khan, M. (2006). *Consumer Behaviour and Advertising Management*. New Delhi: New Age International.

Khanna, M. (2018). 5 extremely common but very distasteful unethical business practices. Available at: www.smallbusinessbonfire.com/unethical-business-practices/ (Accessed on: 22 January 2020).

Kittler, P. G., Sucher, K. P., and Nelms, M. N. (2012). *Food and Culture*, 6th ed. Belmont, CA: Wadsworth.

Kolstad, A. and Horpestad, S. (2009). Self-construal in Chile and Norway: implications for cultural differences in individualism and collectivism. *Journal of Cross-Cultural Psychology*, 40(2), 275–81.

Kotler, P. and Armstrong, G. (2018). *Principles of Marketing*. Harlow: Pearson.

Kotler, P. and Keller, K. L. (2012). *Marketing Management*, 14th ed. Upper Saddle River, NJ: Prentice Hall.

Kotler, P., Armstrong, G., Saunders, J., and Wong, V. (2016). *Principles of Marketing*, 16th ed. Harlow: Pearson.

Leventoğlu, B. (2014). Social mobility, middle class, and political transitions. *Journal of Conflict Resolution*, 58(5), 825–64.

Lindridge, A. (2005). Religiosity and the construction of a cultural-consumption identity. *Journal of Consumer Marketing*, 22(3), 142–51.

MacLaren, A. A. (2019). *Religion and Social Class: The Disruption Years in Aberdeen*. London: Routledge.

Malhotra, N. K., Ulgado, F. M., Agarwal, J., and Baalbaki, I. B. (1994). International services marketing: a comparative evaluation of the dimensions of service quality between developed and developing countries. *International Marketing Review*, 11(2), 5–15.

Marsiglia, A. J. (2010). Cultural effect on consumer behaviour. Available at: http://lead -inspire.com/Papers-Articles/Leadership-Management/Cultural%20Effects%20on %20Consumer%20Behavior%20Paper%20122610.pdf (Accessed on: 19 January 2020).

Mathras, D., Cohen, A. B., Mandel, N., and Mick, D. G. (2016). The effects of religion on consumer behavior: A conceptual framework and research agenda. *Journal of Consumer Psychology*, 26(2), 298–311.

McDaniel, S. W. and Burnett, J. J. (1990). Consumer religiosity and retail store evaluative criteria. *Journal of the Academy of Marketing Science*, 18(2), 102–12.

McKinnon, A. (2017). Religion and social class: theory and method after Bourdieu. *Sociological Research Online*, 22(1), 1–13.

Mokhlis, S. (2009). Religious differences in some selected aspects of consumer behaviour: a Malaysian study. *Journal of International Management Studies*, 4(1), 67–76.

Monin, B. and Szczurek, L. M. (2014). Food cultures. In A. B. Cohen (ed.), *Culture Reexamined: Broadening Our Understanding of Social and Evolutionary Influences* (pp. 155–90). Washington, DC: American Psychological Association.

Mutsikiwa, M. and Basera, C. H. (2012). The influence of socio-cultural variables on consumers' perception of halal food products: a case of Masvingo Urban, Zimbabwe. *International Journal of Business and Management*, 7(20), 112.

Nasse, T. B., Ouédraogo, A., and Sall, F. D. (2019). Religiosity and consumer behavior in developing countries: an exploratory study on Muslims in the context of Burkina Faso. *African Journal of Business Management*, 13(4), 116–27.

Nayeem, T. (2012). Cultural influences on consumer behaviour. *International Journal of Business and Management*, 7(21), 78.

Niebuhr, H. R. (1929). *The Social Sources of Denominationalism*. New York: Holt.

Noel, H. (2009). *Basic Marketing Consumer Behaviour*. Lausanne: AVA Publishing.

Padmawati, R. S., Heywood, A., Sitaresmi, M. N., Atthobari, J., MacIntyre, C. R., Soenarto, Y., and Seale, H. (2019). Religious and community leaders' acceptance of rotavirus vaccine introduction in Yogyakarta, Indonesia: a qualitative study. *BMC Public Health*, 19(1), 368.

Patel, M. (2012). Influence of religion on shopping behaviour of consumers: an exploratory study. *Abhinav National Monthly Refereed Journal of Research in Commerce and Management*, 1(5), 68–78.

Pew Research Centre (2009). The global middle class. Available at: www.pewresearch .org/global/2009/02/12/the-global-middle-class/ (Accessed on: 17 January 2020).

Rogers, M. and Konieczny, M. E. (2018). Does religion always help the poor? Variations in religion and social class in the west and societies in the global south. *Palgrave Communications*, 4(1), 73.

Rees, J., (2009). *The Dynamics of Religion in International Relations*. Unpublished PhD Thesis (University of New South Wales, Australia).

Schiffman, L. G. and Kanuk L. L. (2007). *Consumer Behavior*, 9th ed. Upper Saddle River, NJ: Prentice Hall.

Schmidt, R., Sager, G. C., Carney, G., Jackson, J. J., Zanca, K., Muller, A., and Jackson, J. (1999). *Patterns of Religion*. Belmont, CA: Wadsworth Publishing.

Shambare, R. and Donga, G. (2019a). The influence of social class and reference groups on the diffusion of innovations. In: Janine Loedolff (ed.), *Consumer Behaviour: South African Psychology and Marketing Applications*, 2nd ed. Johannesburg: Oxford University Press.

Shambare, R. and Donga, G. (2019b). Religion and consumer behaviour. In A. Gbadamosi (ed.), *Contemporary Issues in Marketing: Principles and Practice*. New York: Sage.

Shipman, D. and Durmus, B. (2017). The effect of culture on food consumption: a case of special religious days in Turkey. *Journal of Food Research*, 6(2), 92–8.

Sijuwade, P. O. (2006). Globalization and cultural conflict in developing countries: the South African example. *The Anthropologist*, 8(2), 125–37.

Sirgy, M. J. (1982). Self-concept in consumer behavior: a critical review. *Journal of Consumer Research*, 9(3), 287–300.

Stolarski, M., Jasielska, D., and Zajenkowski, M. (2015). Are all smart nations happier? Country aggregate IQ predicts happiness, but the relationship is moderated by individualism–collectivism. *Intelligence*, 50, 153–8.

Thompson, K. (2018). The relationship between religion and social class. Available at: https://revisesociology.com/2018/10/03/the-relationship-between-religion-and -social-class/ (Accessed on: 20 September 2020).

Toth, M. (2014). The role of self-concept in consumer behavior. Masters thesis, Western Washington University.

Touzani, M. and Hirschman, E. C. (2008). Cultural syncretism and Ramadan obser- vance: consumer research visits Islam. *ACR North American Advances*, 35.

Tukamushaba, R. K. and Musinguzi, D. (2018). Faith, religion and young consumer behaviour. In A. Gbadamosi (ed.), *Young Consumer Behaviour: A Research Companion* (pp. 334–6). New York: Routledge.

Van Cappellen, P., Fredrickson, B. L., Saroglou, V., and Corneille, O. (2017). Religiosity and the motivation for social affiliation. *Personality and Individual Differences*, 113, 24–31.

Welch, M. R., Tittle, C. R., and Grasmick, H. G. (2006). Christian religiosity, self-control and social conformity. *Social Forces*, 84(3), 1605–23.

Wright, H. (2015). YBMs: religious identity and consumption among young British Muslims. *International Journal of Market Research*, 57(1), 151–64.

Yang, J., He, X., and Lee, H. (2007). Social reference group influence on mobile phone purchasing behaviour: a cross-nation comparative study. *International Journal of Mobile Communications*, 5(3), 319–38.

Zulu, A. (2019). The 'prosperity gospel' means exploitation. Available at: https:// mg.co.za/article/2019-02-22-00-theprosperity-gospelmeans-exploitation/ (Accessed on: 21 January 2020).

4. Exploring the role of religion in consumer decision-making processes: Perspectives on developing nations

Ayantunji Gbadamosi, Kathy-Ann Fletcher, Kareem Sani, Roshan Panditharathna and David J. Bamber

INTRODUCTION

Be it in Paris, Pakistan, or Peru; wherever a consumer is based, the discourse of his/her consumption remains thought provoking. Similarly, whether one believes in Judaism, Jainism, or is a member of a Jehovah's Witness religious group, one of the enduring topics on consumer behaviour that spans over several decades is the consumer decision-making process. From the early seminal scholarship work of Dewey (1910), Engel et al. (1978), Assael (1998), the contribution of Blackwell et al. (2005), and more contemporary perspectives such as Martínez et al. (2020) and Roseta et al. (2020), it remains a topic of key relevance to our day-to-day endeavours. The notion indicates that whether you are interested in luxury products/brands such as Lamborghini or Gucci, or a house in a choice location, the arrangement begins at a stage and follows a process. Correspondingly, for the decision to purchase trifling items like cookies, bottles of water, or table salt the experience follows a process. Given that consumption is mainly explained around meeting needs, the explication of consumption transcends transactions involving physical products as in these stated examples to include services such as those offered by hairdressers, tutors, and banks to mention but a few. Moreover, it is relevant to indicate that this consumer decision-making process covers several other contexts including online marketing and consumption activities. This is particularly noteworthy in terms of the surge in the use of digital technologies in the past couple of years. In fact, the radical changes associated with the Covid-19 pandemic makes such modelling a worthwhile research endeavour. By and large, all consumption activities are goal-oriented driven by the need of the consumer to crave value in all transactions in various ways. Hence, the process in its conventional form has five stages: need recognition, search for information, evaluation of alternatives, purchase act, and post-purchase evaluation. With this background narrative, it is understandable why the topic has attracted so much attention in the literature. Meanwhile, in a way that extends the current understanding, this chapter presents a meticulous discussion of these stages in relation to religion in developing nations. Accordingly, examples and illustrations are drawn from developing nations using religion as the thread that knits the discourse together. Hence, this chapter begins with an overview of the consumer decision-making process followed by need recognition. The discussion of the information search stage in relation to religion as a key influencing factor and linked to consumption in developing countries is presented next. The evaluation of alternatives and the purchase act are presented just before the final stage of post-purchase evaluation.

AN OVERVIEW OF CONSUMER DECISION-MAKING PROCESSES

The consumption decision-making process is an important aspect of consumer behaviour, and marketing scholars have attempted to understand how consumption decisions are made for effective marketing strategies (Lovelock and Wirtz, 2011; Kim et al., 2018). Consumer decision making refers to the process whereby consumers evaluate and compare various brands based on their needs, and eventually purchase the chosen brand among the available options (Panwar et al., 2019). Understanding consumer expectations and the dynamics of their decision-making process is important in order to create a better value that satisfies customers' needs more than the competitors do (Alzaydi et al., 2018). Behavioural decision theory has been one of the most dominants areas of research in marketing over the past decades. Behavioural decision theorists identify several situations in which consumers make rational choices during the decision-making process (e.g. Simon, 1959; Howard and Sheth, 1969; Sheth et al., 1991). These studies emphasise that consumer behaviour is valuable, and the context of the decision-making process is very important. It is therefore crucial for marketers to understand how the effects of consumer decision making manifest in the marketplace. To understand the concept, the five-stage traditional method of the consumer decision-making process has been widely accepted by various scholars in the field of marketing (Stankevich, 2017), and is also used to explore the concept in this book. The five-stage traditional model of decision-making theory explains that consumers pass through five phases during product or service purchases (Kotler et al., 2018). It is critical for marketers to understand these various stages of the decision-making process, and to ensure effective communication between them and the consumers, to influence purchase decisions.

Variations in Consumer Decision-Making Processes

Customer purchase decisions are not usually straight-forward, they are subject to so many influences, depending on the situation and the customer. Solomon et al. (2006) criticise the traditional decision-making process of product selection, as it is observed that the selection process does not always move in an exact order. The authors argue that the traditional model is only applicable in a rational situation, whereas individuals may occasionally behave irrationally. This shows that consumers may not always follow through the five-stage sequence during purchase decisions as they may at times involve impulse buying, leading to unplanned purchases. Besides, consumers often skip some of the purchase decision stages, especially when it involves repeated purchases or a familiar brand. For example, a college student purchasing a favourite soft drink would recognise the need (thirst) and then make a purchase decision, without going through the information search and evaluation stages (Panwar et al., 2019). Furthermore, Jha and Prasad (2014) affirm that purchase decision-making processes vary, depending on consumer belief, product utilities, urgency, and the intensity of consumers' needs and wants for a product. Consequently, purchase decisions for low-priced and frequently purchased products are usually faster, involving a quick search and purchase, without engaging in external searches or alternative evaluations (Stankevich, 2017). As a response, marketers need to maintain high levels of brand awareness through reminder advertisement campaigns, periodic promotions, and prominent shelf positions in stores. However, for new brands or those with a low market share, marketers need to devise means of getting consumers' attention, by interrupting their routine choice processes and getting them to consider new or alternative products in the market.

These variations in consumer decision-making processes are usually as a result of certain factors, ranging from service-related issues to religious considerations (del Rio et al., 2018). Accordingly, some customers may use religiosity as a criterion in their decision-making process, while others may focus on the price and quality of the products or services. Customer decision-making processes can also change from time to time, depending on the products involved and the situation (del Rio et al., 2018). For example, when a disposable income increases, price may no longer be the major criterion in decision making, and may be replaced by religious considerations. Thus, consumers that are very religious will consider their religious acceptability of a product's consumption before making purchase decisions. Hence, how the individuals view themselves in terms of their religious faith influences their consumption of certain products or services. In developing countries, religiosity also plays a dominant role in consumer purchase decisions (Figure 4.1). Therefore, it is important for marketers to understand various factors influencing the consumer decision-making process, with the aim of having a better understanding of the process and how and when is the best time to interrupt it with a promotion. The five-stage traditional model of the decision-making process identifies need/problem recognition as the first stage of the model.

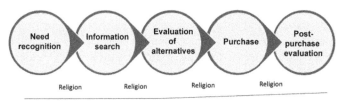

Figure 4.1   Consumer decision-making processes in developing countries: the impact of religion

IDENTIFICATION OF NEED/PROBLEM

The consumer decision-making process usually begins with need/problem recognition when the consumer realises that certain products or services are required to satisfy a need, and marketers always try to meet these needs at a profit. Need/problem recognition is when consumers realise that they need something (Pride and Ferrell, 2019). Two factors have been found to influence needs in the literature. An internal stimulus which can occur immediately due to a very basic impulse and an external stimulus which can occur when an individual is affected by outside influence (Wasan, 2018). By recognising an unfulfilled need and identifying a product or service to satisfy it, the consumers on their own parts have created a want. The marketers often try to understand these needs and help the customers to attain the desired status by providing products or services to satisfy the identified needs. This is usually achieved by monitoring these trends in the market and engaging in advertisement and sales promotions to influence consumers' purchase decision-making processes once these needs/wants are established (Stankevich, 2017). At times, marketers may also help to recognise the consumers' problem/need or the circumstances that trigger a need/want to influence purchase decision making. Consequently, scholars and marketers alike have tried to identify different types of needs and their unique impacts on the consumer decision-making process.

Types of Needs (Maslow's Hierarchy of Needs)

Marketing is the understanding of different types of needs. Reactive marketing is meant to understand and satisfy customers' expressed needs, while proactive marketing is aimed at understanding the customer's latent needs (Kotler, 1999). So many theories have been propounded to explain the different types of needs in the literature. However, this book adopts the classic pyramid of needs conceived by Abraham Maslow, known as Maslow's Hierarchy of Needs, to explore the various types and impacts of religiosity on needs. Maslow's (1943) assertion is that even though everyone is unique, all humans have certain common needs. The author arranges these needs in hierarchical order, according to the level of importance, and presents five basic levels of human needs, ranking from lower-level biogenic to higher-level psychogenic needs.

Although Maslow's theory has been widely accepted in the literature, it has also been criticised by scholars for its shortcomings. For example, Zikmund and d'Amico (1996) argue that consumers may not always follow the hierarchy in the quest to satisfy their various needs; instead, they may seek to satisfy both lower-level and higher-level needs simultaneously. Therefore, the hierarchy cannot be applied universally to every individual. In some environments like Anglo-Saxon culture, people in the setting value self-actualisation and individuality above all else, while the Japanese and Germans are mostly motivated by a need for personal security and conformity. People in countries like France, Portugal, Spain, and Latin American and Asian countries are highly motivated by the need for security and belonging (Kotler et al., 1999). Moreover, Maslow's theory has not been empirically tested extensively, so it is difficult to measure individuals' acceptable level of satisfaction of need before the next higher need is triggered (Schiffman and Kanuk, 2000). Despite these criticisms, Maslow's hierarchy seems to provide a useful insight into the different types of needs for this book. This is because it represents the universality and comprehensiveness of almost all the human needs. Therefore, Maslow's theory provides a basis for exploring the impacts of religion on different levels of customer needs and on consumer behaviour in general. Maslow's hierarchy of needs includes psychological, safety, love and social, self-esteem, and self-actualisation needs (Maslow, 1943).

Psychological and safety needs in Maslow's theory are considered as biological needs for human survival, where individuals provide the basics to satisfy those needs and then move to satisfy the next level of needs (Maslow, 1962). Examples of physiological needs include food, water, air, shelter, clothing, and sex and individuals consume these items to satisfy their psychological needs (Lussier, 2019). But religious beliefs have impacts on the purchase decision-making process for this category of needs, as various religions permit and prohibit the consumption of certain foods and diets to their followers. For example, Judaism permits the consumption of items that are considered kosher (e.g. goats, sheep) and prohibits items that are not kosher (e.g. rabbits, pork) (Shih et al., 2019), whereas Christianity seems not to be so restrictive about food. Muslims also follow certain standards such as halal (permissible), which includes how animals are slaughtered and the types of products acceptable for consumption. There is a huge market for halal products in Christian countries like France. The 4.5 million Muslims in France, which is about 7.5 per cent of the total population, consume 300,000 tons of meat products every year through 3,000 independent butcheries and chain supermarkets for a total sale of 3 billion euros (Assadi, 2003).

Safety and security needs refer to both the actual need for physical safety and the need to feel secure from threatening events or the environment (Lussier, 2019). It is protection from elements, security and law and order, stability, and freedom from fear. For example, health and the availability of health care are important safety concerns. Savings accounts, insurance policies, education, and vocational training are all means by which individuals satisfy safety needs (Lussier, 2019). Different religions also affect the way health care is provided. For example, Judaism and Islam prohibit touching when treating patients of the opposite sex unless medically necessary. Additionally, dietary requirements in Islam also apply to medical injections and tests when admitting, screening, or treating patients. So, alcohol-free medications are preferred (Shih et al., 2019). In contrast, Christianity mostly does not have any restriction or special traditions regarding medical care, but frowns at the consumption of items that are considered harmful to health like illegal drugs and tobacco. Consuming any of these drugs and alcohol in excess is also considered a sin for the Catholic religion (Assadi, 2003).

Social needs or love and belonging needs is third in Maslow's hierarchy of needs after psychological and safety needs. It includes mainly love, affection, belonging, and acceptance and relies on the idea that people seek warm and satisfying human relationships with others in an environment (Khoa, 2020). To satisfy social needs certain personal care products like cosmetics, mouthwash and shaving cream are used. Social needs are also met through moments of social gatherings and religious beliefs which have impacts on individuals' social activities. Jews observe two religious holidays, Rosh Hashanah and Yom Kippur, known as the 'High Holidays'. Rosh Hashanah is commonly known as the Jewish New Year. No work is permitted on Rosh Hashanah and much of the day is spent in the synagogue (Shih et al., 2019). Christians' weekly Sunday worships as well as special religious events like Good Friday, Easter Monday, Christmas, and New Year festive periods constitute part of their social lives, which impact on their social needs. In Islam, Friday Jum'ah, and the two Eids observed annually are the days for collective worship, which also influence their social needs (Assadi, 2003).

Egoistic or esteem needs is the fourth level of Maslow's pyramid. These can take either inward (self-esteem), outward (peer recognitions), or both orientations (Khoa, 2020). Inwardly directed ego needs indicate an individual's need for self-esteem, self-acceptance, success, independence, and personal satisfaction. Outwardly directed ego needs include the needs for status, reputation, prestige, and recognition from others. Individuals fulfil their egoistic needs by consuming high-tech products such as computers or sound systems, and luxury products such as big cars (Khoa, 2020). Religion also influences egoistic needs of individuals. For example, Islam teaches the consumer to show moderation in spending and consumption, with an emphasis on maintaining a balance between personal needs and those of society and between the provisions of this world and those of the life to come (Assadi, 2003). Another product an individual can use to satisfy their egoistic needs is music, because it is valued both by the social group (peer recognition) and by one's self (self-esteem) (Shih et al., 2019). In Judaism, there are no restrictions as to the type of music that one can listen to. In Christianity, music is allowed too. During mass almost all of the time there is a choir or at least a person playing the organ or piano and congregational singing. Music can vary according to the country. In Islam, there are certain types of prohibited music and songs. Islam prohibits any song that promotes immorality without any acceptable goal at the religious level, and is therefore considered a distraction (Assadi, 2003).

Self-actualisation or self-fulfilment needs is the highest level of needs, according to Maslow's theory, and refers to the idea of realising one's potential and seeking personal growth, to become everything one is capable of becoming (Lussier, 2019). Religious beliefs equally have impacts on self-actualisation needs. For example, spiritual devotions can be considered part of the self-actualisation process. Accordingly, Jews and Muslims are not allowed to have images or statues of God, therefore there is no market for that. On the contrary, Christianity permits followers to have images or statues of God, resulting in a huge demand for these kinds of products (e.g. crosses, images, pictures, and statues) (Assadi, 2003).

In conclusion, the impacts of different religious regulations on various types of needs are evident in the literature. However, this should not be generalised as individuals' behaviour based on religion differs, depending on the religion and the degree of observance. For example, traditional Muslims adhere more strictly to the rules, such as prohibiting the use of alcohol, dating, and sexual relationships, than liberal Muslims who remain reluctant in following literally such practices. This indicates that religious influences on customers' decision-making processes vary depending on the degree of observance. Therefore, religiosity or the degree to which beliefs in specific religious values and ideals are held and practised by an individual influence the various types of customer needs and the decision-making process.

CONSUMERS' NEEDS, DECISION-MAKING PROCESSES, AND RELIGIONS IN DEVELOPING NATIONS

Overview of the Various Religions in the World

Religion has been part of human civilisation and has played a vital role over the centuries. Despite the recent increase in secularisation in some parts of the world, religion still plays an important role influencing the formation of beliefs, values, and social normative systems in every society (Heiman et al., 2019). Some of the most popular religions in the world are Christianity, Islam, Judaism, and Hinduism. It has been predicted that two thirds of the world's population will be Christians and Muslims by the year 2070 (Hasan Bukhari et al., 2019). As at 2019, Muslims comprise 26 per cent of the world's population, accounting for over 1.9 billion of the world (Islam and Chandrasekaran, 2020). This is a huge market and global firms should provide products and services that are in compliance with their faith. For example, halal products and services are estimated to have a value exceeding $2.1 trillion (Heiman et al., 2019). Today, the global halal food market is worth more than $632 billion annually, which represents over 16 per cent of all food consumption worldwide (Islam and Chandrasekaran, 2020). This shows that religion continues to play a dominant role in human affairs. Consequently, global firms have started focusing their attention on faith-based marketing as another important path towards understanding and satisfying needs across the globe. Accordingly, organisations like KFC, McDonald's, Nando's, Pizza Express, and Subway are beginning to introduce faith-compliant foods in some countries in order to attract that segment of the market. In 2016, Bloomberg declared halal food 'a $20 billion hit' in the United States, with 7,600 outlets serving it to both Muslims and non-Muslims (Wilkins et al., 2019). The faith-based product concept applies to all products and services including food, banking, insurance, fashion, tourism, pharmaceuticals, and entertainment.

Religiosity and Consumer Needs

Religion is that aspect of human norms, beliefs, and rules which shapes individuals' activities, including consumption and the type of products/services consumers will need and purchase (Nazihah and Arifin, 2020). This indicates that various religions have their own distinct laws and guidelines, prescribing how and by whom food consumed by followers must be processed and handled to meet their needs. Muslims follow halal laws and Jews have kosher laws. Kosher laws are derived from the Bible (Old Testament), while halal regulations are derived from the Quran. The halal, kosher, Hinduism, and Mormonism regulations prohibit the consumption of certain products/services. For example, Islam prohibits the consumption of alcohol and certain foods like pork. Kosher prohibits the simultaneous consumption of dairy and meat products and require that they be cooked using different utensils. Mormonism restricts the consumption of alcohol, coffee, and tea, while the veneration of the cow among the Hindus excludes them from consuming beef (Heiman et al., 2019).

At the centre of religion is religious obligation, often referred to as religiosity, and this is defined by Hasan Bukhari et al. (2019) as: 'The degree to which a person uses or adheres to his or her religious values, beliefs and practices and uses them in daily living'. It is the underlining holy or transcendent principles and practices which guide human behaviour, including consumption. Consequently, differences in religion have resulted in differences in consumers' preferences and needs. Three categories of measurements of religiosity are introduced in the literature, namely: subjective measures (e.g. self-assessment of strength of affiliation), behavioural measures (e.g. church or mosque attendance), and quasi-institutional measures (e.g. respect given to religious authority) (Heiman et al., 2019). Subjective measures are individual differences in terms of their level of affiliation to their religion. So, individuals with strong affiliations to their religion tend to be more obedient to the rules and regulations guiding their faith and will make purchase decisions in accordance with their religious requirements more than those with weak affiliations. Behavioural measures of religiosity are individuals' commitment level to their faith. Those who are more committed will tend to strictly observe their religious doctrine in every facet of their lives, unlike those who are not, who may not be committed; and this influences their purchase decision-making processes. Quasi-institutional measures are individuals' level of respect for the religious authority. Those who tend to respect religious authorities will be more obedient to their directives on consumption of certain products and services than those who are not, which also has an impact on consumer purchase decision-making processes (Heiman et al., 2019). Therefore, Bomhoff and Siah (2019) conclude that the influence of religiosity in consumption decision-making processes depends on the level of commitment and the extent of adherence to the religious rules and guidelines.

Religiosity and Consumption Decision-Making Processes

It is well acknowledged that religions and being religious (religiosity) influence consumers' product selection and decision-making process. Building on this logic, Wilkins et al. (2019) suggest that individuals with stronger beliefs tend to be more influenced by their faiths in their consumption decision-making processes. Thus, religiosity influences various aspects of consumers' lifestyle including decision making and consumption choices (Hasan Bukhari et al., 2019). The application of religiosity in explaining consumer decision-making processes is vital for firms' success in any industry. This is necessary as highly religious individuals often evaluate life activities through religious values and, thus, will incorporate religion into much of their activities, including consumption decisions (Sevim et al., 2016). However, the level of adherence to the doctrine of the religions depends on individuals' level of religiosity, which determines the level of influences on consumption decision-making processes. According to Mehkar et al. (2018), those who are more committed to their religion are more likely to be influenced by their faiths in decision-making processes than those who are not committed. It is therefore imperative in faith-based marketing to understand the religious affiliations of the target market, in order to provide products and services that could influence purchase decisions (Lysonski and Durvasula, 2013). This is considered essential since religiosity is an expression of individuals' beliefs, which guide consumption decision-making processes (Hasan Bukhari et al., 2019).

Religiosity and Consumption in Developing Countries

Several religions affect the general lifestyles of individuals in developing countries; notable among these religions are Christianity, Islam, Judaism, and Hinduism, although unlike in the Islamic world, there are not many restrictions as to what should be consumed in the Christian world (Churchill et al., 2019). However, certain spiritual views guide Christian activities across the globe, including the developing countries. Therefore, it can be concluded that religiosity influences consumption decision making in most developing countries. Unfortunately, most of the religiously compliant products in the developing world are traditionally offered by smaller, independently owned retailers and restaurants. However, in recent years, various religions have started compelling large corporate organisations to produce mainstream brands in compliance with their faiths. Accordingly, leading food manufacturers such as Nestlé, Unilever, and McDonald's are now offering faith-based products in many developing countries to satisfy those segments of the market (Wilkins et al., 2019). For example, McDonald's started producing vegetarian foods for the Indian market in 1996 and India became the first country in McDonald's system in developing countries where non-beef and non-pork products are served (Fischer, 2019). The company developed more than 70 per cent of the menu locally, completely segregating vegetarian and non-vegetarian products from the food-processing plants to the point of serving the customers (Fischer, 2016).

The halal perspective

In Islam, there are lots of restrictions guiding Muslim activities in the developing countries, including consumption. The Muslim doctrine prescribes halal products and services for its followers (Islam and Chandrasekaran, 2020). Although the word 'halal' is mostly used in the context of acceptable products or services, in real terms it connotes anything that is permissible or lawful according to the Quran (Nawawi et al., 2019). The opposite of halal is haram, which means unlawful or forbidden. Prohibited items like pork and alcohol are known as 'haram', while permissible items are regarded as 'halal', usually by approved certification agencies (Wilkins et al., 2019). For a product and service to gain halal certification, certain criteria and procedural standards must be met throughout the production process, including slaughtering, storage, preparation, display, and overall hygiene (Nawawi et al., 2019). Muslims are also more traditional and tend to prefer fresh to frozen products as compared to other religions like Judaism (Nazihah and Arifin, 2020). Muslims also prefer food prepared at home than food from outside, to ensure compliance with their religious faith (Heiman et al., 2019).

The kosher (halacha) perspective

In the case of Judaism, the religion is mostly associated with Jews all over the world and their laws known as 'kosher' are derived from the Old Testament Bible. Kosher law ultimately applies a system of religious teachings that give directives on the types of products that can be consumed by the people of the Jewish faith. The system is built on several verses from the Bible, rabbinic biblical exegesis, and ordinances; as presented in the Talmud (the written record of the oral law as redacted in the fifth century) and the writings and decisions of rabbinic authorities (Fischer, 2018). Kosher law concepts are centred on certain acceptable plants and species of animals. Other important aspects are rennin, gelatine, lactose, sodium caseinate (a protein produced from casein in skimmed milk), vitamins, eggs, grape products, fruits, vegetables, and Passover (a major Jewish festival) items (Regenstein and Regenstein, 1979). Like the halal doctrine, there are several prohibitions in kashrut and kosher law (halacha), such as a ban on pork and the mixing of milk and meat (Fischer, 2016). Kosher laws also provide guidance on production and procedures, including ingredient suppliers, factories, marketing, technical services, quality assurance, legal, and regulatory affairs. Like halal, kosher products are also labelled for easy identification in the market (Fischer, 2016). According to Churchill et al. (2019), developing countries are the most religious in the world, which affects their consumption decision-making processes.

Consequently, marketers must understand the level of religiosity of their target markets in the developing world so as to influence their purchase decisions, by providing products and services in line with their religious beliefs.

The Hindu vegetarianism perspective
The Hindu concept of vegetarianism is mostly practised in the developing country of India and is an integral part of Hinduism, grounded on the concept of ahimsa (non-injury to all living creatures) (Simoons, 1994). To Hindus, consumption is closely related to bodily substance, health, well-being, purity/pollution, as well as to caste, class, gender, and kinship (Kroeze, 2012). In India, there are contentious issues around Hindu product recommendations and practices among divergent class and caste groups. The country has recently found itself fundamentally reshaping and standardising conventional forms of vegetarianism: the 'Hinduisation' (the promotion of Hinduism) of society and state, as an increasing number of companies, such as McDonald's, are beginning to take advantage of these new developments to satisfy the rising demand for vegetarian food, which has led to the emergence of a new Hindu middle class of about 300 million consumers (Fischer, 2019). This in recent years has resulted in a global market for vegetarian food products. Compared to halal and kosher, Hindu vegetarianism is not under strict regulations, but seems to follow many of the consumption patterns in different parts of the world.

From the various analyses presented so far in this book, it is evident that religion permeates every aspect of our lives (Navarro-Prado et al., 2017). For example, halal emphasises purity in substance and prescribes the consumption of products closest to their natural state (Izberk-Bilgin and Nakata, 2016). Even non-Muslims understand that halal is concerned with food safety issues and environmentally friendly production methods (Islam and Chandrasekaran, 2020). Therefore, halal products may be considered by consumers who prefer food that is free of pesticides, preservatives, and antibiotics and which has not been genetically modified. Thus, marketers may position halal products as the safe and healthy option for every consumer, rather than as simply a product aimed at Muslims. This is evident in many countries, as non-Muslim consumers in countries such as China, India, Russia, and the Philippines buy halal products/services on the assumption that the products are fresh, natural, and safe; with the belief that religious Muslims are more likely to be honest (Golnaz et al., 2010). In Moscow, Golnaz et al. (2010) estimate that sales of halal foods doubled between 2004 and 2008 by $25 million (from $45 million to $70 million), with the expectation that the trend will continue. Izberk-Bilgin and Nakata (2016), in their own study, estimate the potential of the global halal market to the tune of $2.1 trillion. Apart from Russia, the growing purchasing powers of Arab Americans and other American Muslims, including non-Arab Americans and non-Muslims who are interested in halal products, have boosted the sales and consumption of the products in the United States as well. Consequently, prominent multinational companies like Walmart, Nestlé, McDonald's, and even the marketing agency Ogilvy and Mather have introduced halal-compliant products to this fast expanding market segment. However, smaller halal-compliant ethnic food stores were in existence prior to 2008, providing halal products to consumers in many developed and developing countries (Roodbar, 2018). In view of the enormous impacts of religion on consumers, marketers in developing countries should understand the religious affiliations of their target consumers, to influence their consumption decision-making processes.

INFORMATION SEARCH, RELIGION, AND CONSUMPTION DYNAMICS IN DEVELOPING COUNTRIES

Information Search within the Decision-Making Model

Although the stages begin with need recognition, it could also be argued that information search within the consumer decision-making model is the first step towards solving a problem. Ikoja-Odongo and Mostert (2006: 148) note information search's problem-solving capabilities by defining it as 'a purposive search to satisfy a certain goal'. This goal is to find the solution to the need identified in the problem definition stage of the decision-making model. Van Staden and van Aardt (2011) speak of various methods of seeking and different sources of information in the process of information search. Internal search speaks to using one's previous knowledge, memories, and experience to gain information about solving a problem. External search makes the space for environmental factors to have an influence in supplying information (van Staden and van Aardt, 2011). These external sources include various forms of media, reference groups (such as friends, family, and associated groups) as well as institutions in one's society (i.e. school, government, organisations). An essential feature in many cultures that is both a reference group and an institution is that of religious affiliation. One's church, temple, synagogue, mosque, or other sacred congregation acts as an institution guiding the opinions, attitudes, and perceptions of its members on various issues within the wider society (Hwang, 2018; Choi, 2010). This includes what products to purchase to satisfy a need or indeed even if purchase is a necessary act to meet needs. Also, one's membership within that congregation presents one with a set of relationships with fellow individuals and a group of belonging who then act as trustworthy sources of information (Choi et al., 2010; Leon and Shoham, 2018).

Extant literature has explored in-depth various decision-making styles indi- viduals use to choose between competing alternatives. Since consumers are in a state of information overload on the available options, they have to adopt certain decision-making processes to make their choices (Mehta and Dixit, 2016). The Consumer Styles Inventory (CSI) is one such model that identifies methods of consumer decision making. Developed by Sprotles and Kendall (1986), this model identifies eight decision-making styles which speak to the consumer personality (Lysonki et al., 1996). These styles were then compared by various researchers including Sprotles and Kendall (1986), Mehta and Dixit (2016), and Lysonski et al. (1996) across developed versus developing countries to varying results. While Sprotles and Kendall (1986) determined that the model was more relevant to developed countries, Mehta and Dixit (2016) noted that the changing retail landscape in India, which was the subject of their study, has changed dramatically. In accounting for the differences seen between developed and developing countries regarding decision making, culture has been identified as a modifying factor (Arli and Pekerti, 2017). For example, Mehta and Dixit (2016) argue that time consciousness and price con- sciousness are greater drivers for Indian consumers than for German consum- ers. In this example, the socio-cultural, political, and economic circumstances within which the consumer exists influences their decision making and within that process their search for and evaluation of relevant information sources. The differences in culture also make developing a universal instrument for defining consumer decision making a problematic endeavour (Lysonski et al., 1996).

Various factors influence information search. These include product type, location, economy (national and personal), education, religion, and culture (van Staden and van Aardt, 2011; D'Haene et al., 2019). Information, which is data within an individual's environment (Ikoja-Odongo and Mostert, 2006), supports the complex process of decision making. The influences mentioned above support the simplification of the process for the individual. These can be categorised as either marketing-related or non-marketing-controlled (van Staden and van Aardt, 2011). Therefore, the company has a definitive role to play in ensuring that the information gathered in the search phase is com- pelling, clear, and of good quality. Culture will influence what is determined to be quality information (Filieri et al., 2018). For instance, in Germany consumers generally require comparative facts between options and in the United States individuals require convincing content (Mehta and Dixit, 2016). Ultimately, companies need to treat their marketing communications and cus- tomer interactions as reliable and trustworthy sources of customer education about their products' suitability to solving the consumers' need. This also applies in markets located in developing or emerging economies. As religion is a strong influence on some consumers in these marketplaces, in relation to information search and the overall consumer decision-making process, companies need to be aware of its role, including choosing the appropriate spokesperson. In discussing fast-moving consumer goods in India, Sardana et al. (2018) demonstrated that the purchase process was positively influenced by information shared by favoured spiritual or religious gurus as well as price and product features. Therefore, it is important to understand not only how religion influences individuals' reaction to information, the information source, but also how it boosts the level of trust awarded to source and content (Choi et al., 2010; Muhamad et al., 2016). For instance, Yousaf and Malik (2013) argued that Islam was important in determining the reaction of individuals in Malaysia to advertising appeals.

Religion's Influence on Information Search

The role of religion within the process of information search is growing in interest to researchers (Muhamad et al., 2016; Rana and Paul, 2017). Religion's influence is multidimensional. Within the context of the consumer decision-making process as adapted by Darley et al. (2010), religion touches each category. Religious members are a reference group with its own sub-culture that influences the decisions of its membership and builds that impact and trust by providing a sense of belonging and identification via shared values. Additionally, religion is a motivating factor within the wider situational influences such as socio-cultural, political, and economic features in some societies. Choi (2010) notes that in South Korea, religion is a major influence on education, media, and aspects of the wider society. On the individual facet of motivating factors on consumer decision making, religion is a belief structure that supports the elements of personality, perceptions, motivations, and attitudes that guide individuals' search processes. Religion, which represents the unified system of beliefs and practices related to sacred things (Lawan and Zanna, 2013), supports individual motivations in consumption patterns. These motivations include commitment to beliefs and practices, religious affiliation, extent of religious knowledge, social issues, and religious motivation. Decision is implicit and explicit, with religion exerting an influence over both aspects. The internal process of memory, experience, and religious knowledge develops implicit biases towards or against certain sources of information as well as ways that information is presented. Van Staden and van Aardt (2011) showed that regarding fashion in South Africa, internal sources of information are more important than other sources. This has implications since religion influences the perceptions of individuals, with Arli and Tjiptono (2014) noting the power of religion in shaping the orientation of people in Indonesia. Ignoring the influence of religion and its regulations or affiliations is one way that marketers make potentially devastating mistakes in the development of their marketing mix in developing or emerging economies.

Lawan and Zanna identify culture as an essential facet within the motivation of consumer behaviour and argue that religion can be considered an element of culture. They define culture as a 'complex whole which includes knowledge, belief, art, law, morals, customs and any other capabilities and habits acquired by humans as members of society' (Lawan and Zanna, 2013, p. 519). However Arli and Pekerti (2017) argue that cultural differences can overshadow the role of religion in consumer behaviour, citing the examples of Indonesia and Australia, when examining the differences in moral ideologies and ethical beliefs among religious and non-religious consumers. The practice of religion supports the development of cultural traditions (Min and Kim, 2005), guides the acceptance of shared values in a community (Mathras et al., 2016), and dictates the rejection of specific conditions (Pace, 2013; Lindridge, 2009) such as materialism or excessive consumption for the process of identity creation. Arli and Pekerti (2017) revealed that religious consumers were more idealistic with stronger ethical beliefs towards negative consumer behaviours. While this idealism was not extended to specific ethical behaviours such as eco-conservation, a proliferation within a culture of individuals who share passionate views towards certain concepts, e.g. media and consumption practices based on religious affiliation and regulation, supports the development of certain dynamics of consumption within the country. Such a strong influence is due to religion being woven into diverse aspects of daily life (Choi, 2010; Arli and Pekerti, 2017) including market-related responses. D'Haene et al. (2019) show that values are important in consumer decisions and factor in information-seeking behaviour. They spoke directly to the role religious regulations play in the Muslim and Orthodox Christian communities in Ethiopia and their approach to finding information regarding meat and dairy products. Religion and culture create the shared values that develop approaches to information search. Choi et al. (2010) argue that religion influences the selection and reaction to information sources. They state that the religious community trust members of the same religious group more and show less trust for media and sales personnel than non-religious individuals.

Religion, Marketing Mix, and Consumption Dynamics

The influence of religion has an effect on both the marketer and the consumer in the exchange relationship. Religion supports the development of pre-purchase search criteria (Labuschagne et al., 2012) on the part of the consumer, which then guides the marketer to wisely create product labels as clear sources of external information. Koen et al. (2018) argue that marketers need to simplify food labelling. For example, by listing ingredients and production process to assist religious consumers in the search for information about products that abide by their religious affiliation. The culture of the country affects the dynamics including the decision process and buying process, i.e. who has a role in the decision making within a household and how that decision is then actioned based on specific aspects of family or household relationships. For instance, Mulkeen and Kakay (2017) show that family (in collaboration with a collectivist culture and religion) acts as a tool of socialisation in Sierra Leone, influencing the consumption habits, including meals, of its population. Culture plays a distinct role along with religion. However, other elements cannot be ignored for the way they guide consumer information-seeking behaviour. Facets such as health and regulations will influence information search. Kempen et al. (2011) showed how consumers in certain countries rely on information about nutritional value, personal benefits, health attributes, and product quality, in addition to culture to guide their information-seeking behaviour. Furthermore, Koen et al. (2018) noted that the law influences the types of information provided to support information seeking, using the example of South African food labelling regulations post-2010. As such religion and culture add levels of high involvement to the information search behaviour and wider consumption process of goods within sectors considered widely by academia and industry to be low risk. Van der Colff et al. (2016) argue that food shopping, for example, can be high involvement, due to the need for appropriate information to guide the decision making. As such religious influence can make it complicated for marketers to determine what information is needed even within a single market. Van der Colff et al. (2016) note that there are differences within South Africa itself as one country on the basis of culture and Choi et al. (2010) noted the religious diversity of South Korea. Therefore, marketers need to understand not only diversity across developing countries but also within these emerging economies, to avoid painting all religious consumers with the same marketing mix.

EVALUATION OF ALTERNATIVES WITH REFERENCE TO RELIGION: PERSPECTIVES ON DEVELOPING NATIONS

Extant research agrees that alternative evaluation is a crucial phase of the consumption process. Engel et al. (1978) identify various influences on alternative evaluations such as culture, reference group, and family in addition to the individual's beliefs, attitudes, and intentions. Religious principles are one such influence (Souiden et al., 2018), shaping attitudes and behaviours of individuals, including consumption patterns (Hwang, 2018). Religious values affect the process judging the merit of alternatives. Alternative evaluation is a seminal part of the consumption process, as it has been implicitly or explicitly included within a majority of decision-making models (Bettman, 1982; Panwar et al., 2019). Sequential delineations of the consumer decision-making process place alternative evaluation as the crucial step before making a choice (Shocker et al., 1991; Shim et al., 2018). However, some discussions of the consumption process argue that choice and alternative evaluation may be undertaken simultaneously (Bettman, 1982; Stankevich, 2017). Individuals set choice criteria (Vieira et al., 2018) such as price, quality perceptions, and brand self-identity match (Stokburger-Sauer et al., 2012; Tavana et al., 2017; Voramontri and Klieb, 2018). Religion is an identity (Hwang, 2018; Benjamin et al., 2016), a community of belonging (Agarwala et al., 2019), and a means of self-expression (Khan et al., 2017). The impact is, therefore, contextual to several factors, i.e. product category, specific religion or denomination, the society or country, and the individual's own level of adherence to religious regulations (Choi et al., 2013). These are important considerations for companies, assisting in product development, pricing, and marketing communications strategies (Tsai and Hsiao, 2004; Moraes et al., 2019; Mihaela, 2015).

Religion, Culture, and the Evaluation of Alternatives

Consumer research has investigated the influence of the external environment on consumers' evaluation of alternatives (Azizi and Makkizadeh, 2012; Broilo et al., 2016). Religion's influence spreads wide in developing countries, touching laws, rituals and traditions, and consumer behaviour (Hasan, 2017a; Auf et al., 2018). Religion influences the type of products considered. For example, Seventh Day Adventists won't eat pork because it is forbidden in the Old Testament of the Bible, while Muslims need to ensure their meat products are killed in accordance with halal instructions (Islam and Chandrasekaran, 2019; Cleveland et al., 2013). In circumstances like these, alternative evaluation supports religious consumers to make sure that products meet their beliefs and values.

Cleveland et al. (2013) noted that in Lebanon, religion (Christianity and Islam) plays a significant role in consumer evaluations within the context of globalisation and its colonial history. Such a relationship between colonial history and religion is evident in other former and current colonised states. Mathras et al. (2016) and Lindridge (2009) similarly placed religion in relation to other factors in discussing the influence on individuals' behaviour. Mathras et al. (2016) discussed religion and its differences to aspects such as culture and personality. These three aspects – religion, culture, and personality – work in relation with each other to influence people's attitudes, values, and behaviours, e.g. consumption patterns. From a different perspective, Lindridge (2009) investigated the role of religion and acculturation in relation to the consumption choices made by individuals within a host country, examining whether those choices reflect a measure of assimilation or integration into the host culture. The relation between religion and acculturation is also applicable within developing countries that seek to develop their status as emerging economies in a globalised world by consuming similar products as the developed world. Meanwhile, Sandıkcı (2018) note that the acculturation is such that middle-class Muslims in developing countries want the same access to middle-class services as anywhere else in the world, even if these services are adjusted according to Muslim standards.

Identity Congruence

Religion has a diverse influence on the process of alternative evaluation. One of these influences is its role in identity creation, which is powerful in developing countries (Haynes, 2009). Religion guides individuals' engagement with their society in a number of spheres, e.g. political, social, and consumption (Mokhlis, 2009). Individuals set consumption priorities according to identity goals (Shrum et al., 2013). Prominent institutions within the individuals' frame of reference often guide those priorities. This process of socialisation includes schools, universities, the media, friends, celebrities, and in some communities, religion and religious institutions (McAlexander et al., 2014). Religious socialisation is essential to alternative evaluation, guiding individuals to evaluate options that will help them conform to their religious rules (Karataş and Sandıkcı, 2013). Hasan (2017b) argues that religious socialisation within developing countries is particularly strong, shaping morals and values. Therefore, religion plays a crucial role in consumer–brand inter-relations and positive brand evaluations. Butt et al. (2017) showed that the strength of an individual's religious identity in Malaysia and Pakistan predicted choice behaviour as well as brand equity.

Religion is a form of social identity as developed by Tajfel and Turner (1979). Religions' social identity centres on a shared belief in deity(ies), shared practices and rituals, and adherence to the terms of belonging to that religion. However, Cohen et al. (2005) note that this social identity is likely weaker in religions that are themselves individualistic. In places where religion and collective identity are hallmarks of the society, religion is a major influencer of social identity (Fam et al., 2004). Mathras et al. (2016) note that religion creates a community that supports members socially. This social support creates the affective and cognitive bonds that shape a sense of social identity and gives power to the group to impact consumption evaluations. Rauf et al. (2019) showed how the social order developed by the religious community in Pakistan strengthened their role in assisting members in choosing the brands or products that support their moral sensitivities, while guiding marketers in terms of the appropriate form of marketing content or campaigns.

Value Congruence

Haynes (2009) argued that religious identity has collective influence on identity due to the emergence of shared values. Tuškej et al. (2013) and Kwon et
al. (2017) are among researchers that link value congruence between brand
and consumer within the decision-making process. Religion creates the terms
of some aspects of individuals' value system (Al-Hyari et al., 2012), therefore, companies include religious messages or symbols in their marketing
communications as a means of building religious congruence between their
brand(s) and their customer base (Alhouti et al., 2015). There are other factors,
however, that moderate the influence of religious congruence in assessing the
suitability of several options. Kalliny et al. (2019) reveal culture/nationality as
one of those moderating factors, showing that in certain developing countries,
where religion is important, religious congruence is essential to the success
of brands and their marketing communications. In their study in Indonesia on
Islamic banking, Wahyuni and Fitriani (2017) noted that the congruence led
to levels of brand loyalty while boosting the positive attitude of customers and
strengthening the brand–customer emotional bond.

Regulation Adherence

Religious regulations and individual adherence influence consumer behaviour
(Fam et al., 2004; Muhamad and Mizerski, 2010). Adherence is a potential
signal of commitment (Muhamad and Mizerski, 2010). Therefore, in some
communities, conspicuous consumption displays religious adherence. Mirkhah
and Karami (2019) support the link between religious commitment and purchase of self-expressive brand products in the Iranian marketplace. In a similar
vein, Baazeem et al. (2016) note the changes of behaviours for sabbaths for
Jews and Seventh Day Adventists, while Martin (2016) outlines the role religious holidays play in the formation of consumer behaviour. The role religion
plays in crafting the social and cultural environments of customers (Assadi,
2003) means that companies need to accommodate for these in marketing
communications and product development in order to be more positively evaluated by potential customers. Regulations support everyday buying behaviour
(Assadi, 2003; Floren et al., 2019), hence integrating religion into everyday
consumption ethics (Sandıkcı, 2020). For example, Islamic rules speak to the
approach to spending and managing money (Assadi, 2003; Alam et al., 2011).
Ultimately, individual motives impact the effect of religious adherence on
consumer behaviour. Muhamad and Mizerski (2010) noted that those with
extrinsic motivations are trendier and more brand conscious than those who are
intrinsically motivated and therefore more conservative and traditional. Such
supports the work of Assadi (2003) who argues that more traditional Muslims

adhere more strictly to the associated regulations. Ultimately, the variance in levels of religious adherence to regulations means that companies must avoid a 'one-size-fits-all' marketing communications approach.

PURCHASES IN DEVELOPING NATIONS: THE PLACE OF RELIGION AND RELIGIOSITY

Religion is emphasised as an important cultural influence in the marketplace and that needs to be recognised and researched in the marketing sphere (Mittelstaedt, 2002; Muhamad and Mizerski, 2010). Scholars, and indeed practitioners, should 'understand the effects of religion on the kinds of issues they face in business and, more important, how these issues are defined, informed, and regulated by religion' (Mittelstaedt, 2002, p. 6). Here, Christianity, Buddhism, and Islam are used to indicate how customers act on purchases and how post-purchase behaviour may be influenced from their religious background. Once customers go through the process of need recognition, information search, and evaluation of alternatives, they purchase the product or service and then react on what they feel and think once they consume in a post-purchase behaviour phase. Kotler et al. (2009) claim that the final buying decision may be influenced by two major reasons: customer wishes and situational factors (Kotler et al., 2009). In this sense, the buyers' final product purchases are shaped by religion in terms of devotees' feedback and the seasonal aspect of religion. As per the conceptualisation of Mathras et al. (2016), it could be argued that purchase and post-purchase behaviour is shaped by religious beliefs, religious rituals, religious values, and the customer's religious community.

Religious Beliefs on Purchase Behaviour

Religious beliefs are beliefs that induce worship or worship-related activities (Carter, 2014). These beliefs largely decide what customers should buy. The major groups of Christians, including Anglicans, Catholics, Lutherans, Methodists, and various Orthodox groups, avoid eating meat on a certain day of the week and while fasting during the Easter period (Vitz, 1991). Moreover, some Catholic groups allow having a manageable level alcohol, while Latter Day Saints, Seventh Day Adventists, Baptists, Methodists, and Pentecostals ban having alcohol (Domenico and Hanley, 2006). However, for any person the uptake of such practices will be dependent on the adherence to the stated rubrics of their particular religion and indeed the intensity of their surrounding religious communities.

The Buddhist perspective of buying a product entails being mindful of consumption (Alsop, 2002). Buddhism suppresses the use of luxury products and brands that the modern market so often promotes. Buddha preached living a simple life and the way of enlightenment. Therefore, devoted Buddhists buy products that may satisfy their needs but not to impress others. However, concerning Muslims' beliefs, the Quran states: 'Those who are extravagant are the brothers of Shaitan (devil)' (17: 27). Muslims are not allowed to buy haram products, such as pork and pork products (ham, sausages, or bacon), non-certified meat and poultry, or any product prepared with alcohol or animal fats. However, food products which are halal are those which are allowed. Moreover, Islam discourages consumerism that consumes or buys things that exceed their level of requirement (Gagne, 2020). Thus, a main concern for Muslims is to ensure that food products which are purchased and used are 'halal'. A parallel is drawn in Judaism with the kosher construct: kosher foods conform to the Jewish dietary regulations of kashrut, that originated from the scripture (Leviticus and Deuteronomy). Meanwhile, Buddhists usually follow a lacto-vegetarian diet, meaning that they may consume dairy products, but their diet dismisses eggs, poultry, fish, and meat from their consumption. However, some Buddhists consume meat and use animal products if the animals are not slaughtered specifically for those uses. So, the evaluation of product purchase and consumption is dependent on the devotee's sect allegiance; similar complexities exist with all major religions as they each have multiple sectarian divisions. Whilst regarding the certain religious strictures placed on product and service purchases and purchase evaluations, non-religious requirements, such as product or service 'quality', remain. For example, halal kebabs may be purchased, with the customer relying on the 'halal branding' of the product, and customers may trust in the retailer but then may reject future purchases as the taste or quality does not fit with the consumers' taste and quality expectations: a product may indeed be halal but that does not necessarily imply the product tastes good and is of good quality. However, vast opportunities exist for marketeers to cross-market products to people from religions to which the original product or service has been designed: for example, Islamic banking has received much attention in practice and in the literature for Islamic banking and its virtues have been well acclaimed over 'Western banking', yet by and large this has not been marketed to non-Muslims.

Religious Rituals and Purchase Behaviour

Rook defines rituals as 'a type of expressive, symbolic activity constructed of multiple behaviours that occur in a fixed, episodic sequence, and that tend to be repeated over time' (1985, p. 252). Religious rituals are largely shaped by seasons such as Christmas for Christians, Poya Day for Buddhist devotees and Eid for Islamic followers. Christmas is one of the global feasts that commemorate the birth of Jesus Christ (Batinga et al., 2017). Many Christians and non-Christians celebrate Christmas symbolically without understanding a true sense of its meaning; at least in part because of promotional drives and the marketing of consumerism and materialism surrounding 'Christmas' (Batinga et al., 2017). In this sense, Santa Claus is considered as a god of materialism where the biggest target market is young children who expect gifts and rewards. Church attendance is very high on Christmas Eve compared with other religious days in the year, while scholars argue that Christmas Day has moved from churches to department stores (Miller, 1995). The preparation, marketing, and promoting of Christmas does not start in December, it starts at least from September, especially in the Philippines. Nevertheless, devotee Christians in the Philippines formally mark Christmas by attending nine consecutive morning masses that take place on Christmas Day. Moreover, Christmas celebrations in the Philippines continue to the first Sunday in January when the Feast of the Three Kings is celebrated (SBS, 2014). In this context, Christmas can be considered one of the main events that increases sales and consumption (Batinga et al., 2017).

Poya Day is a national holiday which takes place every month in Sri Lanka. Every Poya Day is meat free and calls on devotees to practise the 'Eight Precepts' or 'Ten Precepts' at temples. In May, Buddhists commemorate the festival of Vesak Poya Day which commemorates the birth, enlightenment, and death of Buddha. Throughout Poya Day, devotees must refrain from intox- icating drinks and drugs, eating at the forbidden time (after noon), dancing, singing, music, going to see entertainment, wearing garlands, using perfume, beautifying the body with cosmetics, and lying on a high or luxurious sleeping place (Access to Insight, 2013). Therefore, marketers need to find alternative ways of approaching such devotees. As Buddhist devotees avoid eating meat and have a preference to be vegetarians, the demand of vegetarian options rises at this time, in Sri Lanka. Bakery products tend not to be readily available during Poya Day in the suburbs of Colombo due to the fact that most of the bakery staff return to their homes 'up country'.

For Islamic followers, the feast of Ramadan is one of the highly celebrated events in their holy calendar. All medically fit individuals are called to fast and refrain from having food or water, 'while the sun is shining'. They have special food habits during Ramadan and claim high demands for dates and sweet drinks (Klein, 2020). In Muslim countries both in developed and developing nations, most businesses and restaurants remain closed during the day during Ramadan.

Religious Values and Purchase Behaviour

Values 'provide normative guidance to adherents about what is desirable to consume, how much to consume, and when to consume it' (Mathras et al., 2016, p. 6). Depending on religious values, individual consumption and buying behaviour can be varied. Doran and Natale (2011) claim that Buddhist devotees tend to buy more fair-trade products than any other religion. However, it is also noted that Christians buy more environmentally friendly products than any other religion. Religion thus shapes how people trade, when they trade, and where trade occurs and most religious traditions prohibit, discourage, encourage, or obligate the trade of certain products in the marketplace (Mittelstaedt, 2002, p. 6).

Advertising can take people's minds from want to need by convincing them that the target purchases will bring ultimate satisfaction (Christman, 2015). Jewellery commercials are especially good at this by associating jewellery with happiness, joy, and love. The actors in the commercials portray the idea that buying a special bracelet or diamond will fix a relationship or rekindle their love for each other. Advertising no longer describes the qualities and virtues of a product, such as the cut and clarity of a diamond, but instead creates visions of the ways in which their product can transform the lives of the consumer (Christman, 2015). The advertising focuses not just on the object but the satisfaction that the object will bring. When primary sources of satisfaction such as love and meaning are not met, then we as humans try to replace them with secondary sources of satisfaction. Constantly pursuing these secondary sources of satisfaction will never truly satisfy a consumer as they are just shadows of the primary sources. As advertisers promise love and happiness, perhaps universal values that are closely related to certain religious values, even though the product they are selling does not necessarily deliver those emotions, consumers are often left disappointed. This is a good thing for advertisers and businesses because it means they can sell and upsell their new products (Christman, 2015). This is not to forget that certain products may be directly connected to specific religious groups such as silver crucifixes connect to Christians and wedding rings that may be used in religious ceremonies in different ways by different religions. Some retailers acknowledge this, such as Baunat (www.baunat.com), a Belgian jeweller, which states:

> The hand you wear your wedding ring and engagement ring on is different for each religion. In Christianity, the wedding ring is worn on the right hand while the engagement ring is worn on the left side. Wearing both rings on the left side comes from Roman traditions: Traditional Western religions, Traditional Middle Eastern religions and Traditional Eastern religions, and there are many traditions associated with wearing engagement and wedding rings. These traditions often depend on culture and place. Religion plays a big role in this even if some do not practise it. Which hand does your most symbolic jewellery belong to? Or rather, should you wear your wedding ring on the right or left if you want to respect both tradition and social convention?

The Ten Commandments set out a value system for Christian followers to comply with. Under the fourth commandment, God orders his followers to keep the Sabbath day holy. This means that Christian devotees must refrain from working, instead engaging in a spiritual connection with God. In reality, the Ten Commandments can be fulfilled completely, however, many devotees attend churches and spend the day with God's wishes. Such behaviours are highly sensitive for business and marketing activities. The common activity allowed on the Sabbath day is that individuals can eat outside with friends and family. This is where many commercial establishments provide packages for families or friends to eat out or engage with some recreational activities. In this sense, the Sabbath day has become a lucrative day for business organisations.

From the perspective of Buddhism, religious values are prime expectations. Buddhist followers act and behave based on the value system given under the remit of Buddhism. Within their value system, every Buddhist should obey five moral precepts. The five precepts encourage devotees to engage in ethical consumption that shapes how business organisations may cater for them. One of the five precepts is that the individual must refrain from having alcohol or alcohol-related products. For Buddhists, the five precepts are not compulsory as the Ten Commandments of God are supposed to be for Christians; however, the precepts show the road map to achieve enlightenment or *Nirvana*. When it comes to Eastern cultures where Buddhism has been widely accepted, the five precepts are widely practised.

From the Islamic point of view, religious values are highly influential for Islamic followers who expect to win Jannah when they depart from this world. To realise Jannah, sharia law is practised and that decides what they are allowed to do or not. Islamic devotees should not use banking services from ordinary banks which give interests on savings, as bank interest is prohibited under sharia law. As a result, many sharia-friendly banking institutions and products are available in the marketplace. Several foreign banks operating in India, like Citibank, Standard Chartered Bank, and HSBC, now operate interest-free windows in some of the West Asian countries, Europe, and the United States (Shahid and Raj, 2019). There are popular Islamic banking products such as QardHasan and Halal Activities. QardHasan is a loan-based product that does not charge any interest. The borrower is ordered to pay the amount borrowed originally at the beginning of the contract. Deposited funds would not support haram business activities such as 'gambling, pork products, weapons, defence, alcohol, pornography and any speculative activities' (Shahid and Raj, 2019, p. 249). Therefore, the consumption of the products and services are based on the values that are given by the religion.

Religious Community and Purchase Behaviour

Religion 'is an element of culture that pervades every aspect of society and permeates the life of individuals whether one is a believer or a non-believer' (Khraim, 2010, p. 166). Religious communities may affect consumer behaviour because member involvement shapes the religion's cultural dimensions (Mathras et al., 2016). Belonging to a religious group helps the individual to create a sense of self and social identity through a history that is shared with past, present, and future members (Cohen et al., 2005; Saroglou, 2011). Religious communities also help by providing social support to members (Mathras et al., 2016).

Christians are called to not just think about their own individual desires but to think about how what they consume affects others (Christman, 2015). It has been argued that 'God intended that humans were created to act in a way that should not cross over the line into consumerism and materialism' (Christman, 2015, p. 7). This becomes most obvious in the Philippines, where religion is an integral part of daily life and penetrates all areas of society. The mutual Christian tradition and Christian rites are the basis for cooperation in the community and represent a 'moral reason' for existence. Social connections outside the family are usually grounded on common membership in Christian communities. The importance of religion becomes obvious, considering that 68 per cent of the Philippines population take part in a Catholic service every week. Churches run a number of educational institutions, including several universities (Hefele and Dittrich, 2011). Also, in South Korea an important part of Christian life happens within communities; many Koreans find a job or their partner through the mediation of community members. Korean Christians engage themselves within their own community, whereas social exchanges with the rest of society remain restricted. Christian communities in Buddhist-dominated states in South East Asia show a lot of willingness to engage in social projects in order to contribute to general public life. In Mongolia, with only a very small number of Christians, their strong social engagement has contributed to a positive image of Christianity. From the business point of view, some countries do not allow Christians to engage certain ventures such as in China and Christian communities are severely restricted in running educational institutes (Hefele and Dittrich, 2011).

In the Buddhist philosophy, the ultimate ideal of human happiness is to reach Nirvana and salvation through the extinction of desire. Thus, acquiring material objects to extend the self is to chain oneself to the vicious circle of illusive consumption. There is nothing absolute in this world; everything is in continuous flux and is relative, conditioned and impermanent. Thus, to avoid suffering, individuals should not attach to the selfless and should share what they have with others (Wattanasuwan and Elliott, 1999). In Sri Lanka,

Vesak Poya Day is an opportunity for businesses to provide the necessities and promote their brands to the community. This is because many business owners sponsor the building of huge illuminating 'thoranas' in the main cities of Sri Lanka. Also, businesses donate funds to set up food stalls during the Vesak week that provide free drinks, foods, or ice cream for commuters. By means of such activities, they try to create a name in society that is evaluated positively by religious consumers. Some of the businesses even sell 'Vesak kuudu', colourful lanterns, to busy families who cannot make their own during the Vesak week.

From the Islamic point of view, devotees engage various community activities to uplift individuals who need much support. Especially, individuals who feel socially excluded are given priority to be sustained in the competitive world. Muslim communities are therefore often marginalised simply because they are poor and suffer similar disadvantages to other poor communities (Perry and El-Hassan, 2008). As bank interest is haram in Islamic, if customers receive any interest for their deposit, they must donate the interest to the neediest person. As many Islamic devotees are price-sensitive, many business organisations will have to decide on the competitive prices for their products. Moreover, marketers know that religious communities may buy products or services with the minimum information available, however, certainly with their own religious strictures in mind.

A further illustration of how religion is linked to consumption is shown in Table 4.1, which provides some sort of classification of products that are religion-oriented compared to those that could be considered to be in the conventional category. This takes a cue from previous scholarship on consumer involvement that illustrates high- and low-involvement product categories (Vaughn, 1986; Ratchford, 1987; Gbadamosi, 2013).

The diversity of designs of the flags of countries reflects the complex nature of our topic: 64 countries have religious symbols on their flags (www.pewresearch.org/fact-tank), which leaves 131 that do not; 31 have Christian symbols (many with various forms of crosses), 21 have Islamic symbols (many with various forms of the crescent moon), 12 have other religions depicted including one with a Judaic symbol (Israel which shows the Star of David). A metaphor for that marketing complexity may be seen in the Sri Lankan flag (Table 4.2) which represents several elements of ethnicity, value systems, and religion. What the 'flag' of any customer is and what that flag contains are moot points for marketers to consider and they have been introduced to some extent in this chapter. How those intertwined notions of ethnicity, values, thoughts, and practices may be applied to understand customers' evaluations of products and services, including tangible and intangible attributes, still remain for other researchers to investigate.

Table 4.1   *Classification of goods and services*

High and rational involvement	Conventional	Banking, credit cards, insurance
		Furniture and appliances
		Computers and software
		Home improvements
	Explicitly religious	Religious buildings, fixtures, and fittings
		Religious books
		Music and musical instruments used in religious services
		Religious prayer services
		Religious buildings
High and emotional involvement	Conventional	Club membership
		Fashion apparel
		Sports luxury vehicles
		Travel and vacation services
	Explicitly religious	Pilgrimage destinations
		Zakat, church offerings
		Involvement in religious events, retreats
		Incense
		Funeral services
Low and rational involvement	Conventional	Essential diet items
		Essential clothing
		Health, beauty, and hygiene products
		Office supplies
		Maintenance and repair services
	Explicitly religious	Religious school uniform
		Religious apparel
		Wine and bread used in religious services

	Conventional	Alcoholic beverages
		Soft beverages
		Games and toys
		Sporting goods
		Sports venues
Low and emotional involvement		
	Explicitly religious connection	Holy water and relics purchased at pilgrimage sites
		Flowers and offerings used in religious devotions
		Parties associated with significant (personal) religious events

Table 4.2   *Religious, ethical, and ethnic symbolism within the Sri Lankan flag*

Symbol	Meaning
Lion	The Sinhalese ethnicity and the strength of the nation
Bo leaves	The four Buddhist virtues of loving kindness, compassion, sympathetic joy, and equanimity
Sword of lion	The sovereignty of the nation
Curly hair on lion's head	Religious observance, wisdom, and meditation
Eight hairs on lion's tail	The noble eightfold path
Beard of lion	Purity of words
Handle of sword	The elements of water, fire, air, and earth
Nose of lion	Intelligence
Two front paws of lion	Purity in handling wealth
Orange stripe	The Tamil ethnicity
Green stripe	The Moor ethnicity
Saffron border	Buddhism and unity among the people
Maroon background	The Sinhala ethnicity

Source: Lankalibrary (2020).

POST-PURCHASE EVALUATION

Unlike the evaluation at the third stage of the process discussed above, the associated decision has taken place before the post-purchase evaluation. So, it is about gauging the 'experience–expectation' link to know whether there is a perfect match or if there is a gap between the two ends. If the outcome shows a match, or the consumers' experience surpasses expectation, then they will be deemed satisfied. Conversely, when their expectations fall short of the standard provided, we have the case of dissatisfaction. Given the scale of the impact that religion has on the earlier stages of the process, it is logical to expect that religious criteria will be core to the post-purchase evaluation. As demonstrated in the book, there are many religions in developing countries. The task of focusing on all of these towards satisfying the adherents will be extremely challenging for marketers. Hence, segmentation, targeting, and positioning will pave the way for effective value creation and delivery by marketers in relation to the targeted consumers of specific religious affiliations. Accordingly, the post-purchase evaluation of the targeted members may not be based on only the functional attributes of the products but also on the symbolic elements as this has been a long held postulation in the consumer behaviour literature (Levy, 1959; Sirgy and Johar, 1999; Gbadamosi, 2019a). It has been found that having an understanding of the intricacies of consumer behaviour will essentially involve understanding their degree of religiosity and product involvement (Yousaf and Malik, 2013). Accordingly, it was found that higher religious consumers are more influenced by social factors in their consumption decisions (Yousaf and Malik, 2013), hence social approval in relation to religious values will play a key role in how the product is evaluated afterwards. One of the main reasons why marketers are interested in post-purchase evaluation is the possible behaviour of the consumers after the experience.

Fundamentally, a satisfied consumer is expected to make a repeat purchase and could also become loyal to the offerings and brands of the organisation. On the other hand, a dissatisfied consumer is expected to switch to new offerings at the next purchase opportunity and engage in negative word-of-mouth communications. However, one of the complex issues around religion as a factor in post-purchase evaluation is that the decision to switch or vent frustration on the brand is not as straightforward as in the conventional thought in consumption and marketing. A clear example of this is that many religions emphasise forgiveness which is expected to overshadow the disappointment of the brand. Hence, they are not expected to react adversely to dissatisfaction or service failure. It is even more complicated if the providers are members of the religious circle as the consumer, where solidarity is markedly encouraged (Gbadamosi, 2019b). In this context, the notion of loving one another as emphasised in the Bible, I John 4: 7–8, and that of forgiveness explained in Matthew 18: 21–2, could play a part. A similar tone of forgiveness is emphasised in Islam as shown in the Quran, 42:30 (BBC, 2020). Meanwhile, in view of the prevailing competition in this day and age, marketers are expected to embrace the notion of relationship marketing where the focus of their transactions is to maintain long-term relationships with the customer rather than merely concentrating on the benefits associated with a single transaction which is short term in nature.

CONCLUSION

The consumer decision-making process is a fundamental aspect of consumer behaviour thought. It has undergone several analytical scholarship reviews over the years towards unravelling the appropriate version for different scenarios. A conventional model of this subject has a five-stage process that comprises need recognition, search for information, evaluation of alternative, purchase act (decision), and post-purchase evaluation. One of the criticisms of this model is that it is more applicable to scenarios involving rational decision making whereas there are other models of consumer behaviour that are not necessarily rational. For example, decisions involving low-involvement purchases as indicated in the literature (Krugman, 1977) do not necessarily align with this postulation. This is because decision cases like this tend to move faster with a quick search or no search at all. However, this conventional (rational) model has been widely applied, especially due to its wider and all-encompassing scope. Therefore the model could not only be applied to developing countries but also with relevance to religion as a key influencing factor as shown in Figure 4.1. Accordingly, we can explore the fact that consumers' needs for goods and services could be driven or influenced by religious values and rituals. At this stage of need recognition, the consumer spots the gap between the desired state and the status quo and is driven to fill this gap. One of the exciting aspects of consumer behaviour in recent times is the diverse nature of our needs as consumers of different levels of religiosity. Some of these could be basic, some could be security or social, while some are motivated to pursue the need for esteem and self-actualisation. Another valuable, interesting, and noteworthy scenario lies in how religion moderates each of these need categories. Therefore, it is understandable that some multinationals are adapting their market offerings to be fit for the religious needs of several consumers in developing countries. As consumers have a stronger belief in the ethos associated with their religion, they are less likely to be tolerant of market offerings that deviate from what the religion embraces. As there are various religions, so we have a plethora of religious values. This is why the business of tailoring market offerings to these needs will have to be strategic based on the segmentation, targeting, and positioning of the establishment. Meanwhile, the information search stage of the decision-making process is essential in that the consumers are able to explore all of the available data sources concerning how their needs could be met. The role of religion as the basis for a reference group that complements other sources of information cannot be ignored. This is because of the bond that exists among members (Gbadamosi, 2019b). Similarly, their evaluation of the alternatives is facilitated by religious beliefs which are closely linked to the identity of the adherents. Hence, a closer look at ensuring the rich mix of this with other marketing stimuli could be the 'game changer' for marketers operating in developing nations which is a context notably religious as indicated in the extant literature (Hasan, 2017b; Churchill et al., 2019). As evident, the stage of making the decision is inextricably linked to others, especially that of evaluation of alternatives. On the question of which alternative to accept, the consumer will be guided by a myriad of factors such as price, availability, marketing communications, and many others including religion. In some religions such as Islam, excessive consumption and pork meat is discouraged, while Buddhist devotees often show preference for being vegetarian. Other religions have other specifications which reflect at the stages of making the actual purchase. The post-purchase evaluation which ends the process often results in satisfaction, dissatisfaction, or some combination of the two. The disparity between the expectation of the consumers and their experience would yield dissatisfaction. Conversely, when the expectations are met, the consumers are satisfied. More often than not, expectations are developed around religious values in developing nations and the outcome of the decision-making process will be dependent on how these expectations are met.

REFERENCES

Access to Insight (2013) 'The eight precepts'. www.accesstoinsight.org/ptf/dhamma/sila/atthasila.html (Accessed 24 May 2020).

Agarwala, R., Mishra, P., and Singh, R. (2019) 'Religiosity and consumer behaviour: A summarizing review', *Journal of Management, Spirituality and Religion*, 16 (1), pp. 32–54.

Al-Hyari, K., Alnsour, M., Al-Weshah, G., and Haffar, M. (2012), 'Religious beliefs and consumer behaviour: From loyalty to boycotts', *Journal of Islamic Marketing*, 3 (2), pp. 155–74.

Alam, S.S., Mohd, R., and Hisham, B. (2011) 'Is religiosity an important determinant on Muslim consumer behaviour in Malaysia?', *Journal of Islamic Marketing*, 2 (1), pp. 83–96.

Alhouti, S., Musgrove, C.C.F., Butler, T.D., and D'Souza, G. (2015) 'Consumer reactions to retailers' religious affiliation: Roles of belief congruence, religiosity, and cue strength', *Journal of Marketing Theory and Practice*, 23 (1), pp. 75–93.

Alsop, P. (2002) 'Spending wisely'. https://tricycle.org/magazine/spending-wisely/ (Accessed 25 May 2020).

Alzaydi, Z.M., Al-Hajla, A., Nguyen, B., and Jayawardhena, C. (2018) 'A review of service quality and service delivery: Towards a customer co-production and customer-integration approach', *Business Process Management Journal*, 24 (1), pp. 295–328.

Arli, D. and Pekerti, A. (2017) 'Who is more ethical? Cross-cultural comparison of consumer ethics between religious and non-religious consumers', *Journal of Consumer Behaviour*, 16 (1), pp. 82–98.

Arli, D. and Tjiptono, F. (2014) 'The end of religion? Examining the role of religiousness, materialism, and long-term orientation on consumer ethics in Indonesia', *Journal of Business Ethics*, 123 (3), pp. 385–400.

Assadi, D. (2003) 'Do religions influence customer behavior? Confronting religious rules and marketing concepts', *Databases*, 22 (10), pp. 2–13.

Assael, H. (1998). *Consumer behavior and marketing action*. Cincinnati, OH: South-Western College Publishing.

Auf, M.A.A., Meddour, H., Saoula, O., and Majid, A.H.A. (2018) 'Consumer buying behaviour: The roles of price, motivation, perceived culture importance, and religious orientation', *Journal of Business and Retail Management Research*, 12 (4), pp. 177–86.

Azizi, S. and Makkizadeh, V. (2012) 'Consumer decision-making style: The case of Iranian young consumers', *Journal of Management Research*, 4 (2), pp. 88–111.

Baazeem, T., Mortimer, G., and Neale, L. (2016) 'Conceptualising the relationship between shopper religiosity, perceived risk and the role of moral potency', *Journal of Consumer Behaviour*, 15 (5), pp. 440–8.

Batinga, G.L., de Rezende Pinto, M., and Resende, S.P. (2017) 'Christmas, consumption and materialism: Discourse analysis of children's Christmas letters', *Revista Brasileira de Gestão de Negócios-RBGN*, 19 (66), pp. 557–73.

BBC (2020) 'Forgiveness: Islamic teaching about forgiveness', *BBC Bitesize*. www.bbc.co.uk/bitesize/guides/z98d3k7/revision/5 (Accessed 18 September 2020).

Benjamin, D.J., Choi, J.J., and Fisher, G. (2016) 'Religious identity and economic behavior', *Review of Economics and Statistics*, 98 (4), pp. 617–37.

Bettman, J.R. (1982) 'Functional analysis of the role of overall evaluation of alternatives in choice processes', *Advances in Consumer Research*, 9, pp. 87–93.

Blackwell, R.D., Miniard, P.W., and Engle, J.F. (2005) *Consumer Behavior*. Cincinnati, OH: South-Western College Publishing.

Bomhoff, E.J. and Siah, A.K.L. (2019). 'The relationship between income, religiosity and health: Their effects on life satisfaction', *Personality and Individual Differences*, 144, pp. 168–73.

Broilo, P., Espartel, L., and Basso, K. (2016) 'Pre-purchase information search: Too many sources to choose', *Journal of Research in Interactive Marketing*, 10 (3), pp. 193–211.

Butt, M., Rose, S., Wilkins, S., and Ul Haq, J. (2017) 'MNCs and religious influences in global markets: Drivers of consumer-based halal brand equity', *International Marketing Review*, 34 (6), pp. 885–908.

Carter, J. (2014) 'What is a religious belief?' www.thegospelcoalition.org/article/what-is-a-religious-belief/ (Accessed 23 May 2020).

Choi, Y. (2010) 'Religion, religiosity, and South Korean consumer switching behaviors', *Journal of Consumer Behaviour*, 9 (3), pp. 157–71.

Choi, Y., Kale, R., and Shin, J. (2010) 'Religiosity and consumers' use of product information source among Korean consumers: An exploratory research', *International Journal of Consumer Studies*, 34 (1), pp. 61–8.

Choi, Y., Paulraj, A., and Shin, J. (2013) 'Religion or religiosity: Which is the culprit for consumer switching behavior?', *Journal of International Consumer Marketing*, 25 (4), pp. 262–80.

Christman, A. (2015) *Consumerism and Christianity: An Analysis and Response from a Christian Perspective*. Doctoral dissertation, Malone University.

Churchill, S.A., Appau, S., and Farrell, L. (2019) 'Religiosity, income and wellbeing in developing countries', *Empirical Economics*, 56 (3), pp. 959–85.

Cleveland, M., Laroche, M., and Hallab, R. (2013) 'Globalization, culture, religion, and values: Comparing consumption patterns of Lebanese Muslims and Christians', *Journal of Business Research*, 66 (8), pp. 958–67.

Cohen, A.B., Hall, D.E., Koenig, H.G., and Meador, K.G. (2005) 'Social versus individual motivation: Implications for normative definitions of religious orientation', *Personality and Social Psychology Review*, 9 (1), pp. 48–61.

D'Haene, E., Desiere, S., D'Haese, M., Verbeke, W., and Schoors, K. (2019) 'Religion, food choices, and demand seasonality: Evidence from the Ethiopian milk market', *Foods*, 8 (5), pp. 167–88.

Darley, W.K., Blankson, C., and Luethge, D.J. (2010) 'Toward an integrated framework for online consumer behavior and decision making process: A review', *Psychology and Marketing*, 27 (2), pp. 94–116.

Del Rio Olivares, M.J., Wittkowski, K., Aspara, J., Falk, T. and Mattila, P. (2018) 'Relational Price Discounts: Consumers' Metacognitions and Nonlinear Effects of Initial Discounts on Customer Retention', Journal of Marketing, 82 (1), pp. 115–31.

Dewey, J. (1910) *How We Think*. Boston, MA: Heath.

Domenico, R.P. and Hanley, M.Y. (2006) *Encyclopaedia of Modern Christian Politics*. Westport, CT: Greenwood Publishing Group.

Doran, C.J. and Natale, S.M. (2011) 'ἐμπάθεια (Empatheia) and caritas: The role of religion in fair trade consumption', *Journal of Business Ethics*, 98 (1), pp. 1–15.

Engel, J.F., Kollat, D.T., and Blackwell, R.D. (1978) *Consumer Behavior*, 3rd ed. Hinsdale, IL: Dryden.

Fam, K., Waller, D., and Erdogan, B. (2004) 'The influence of religion on attitudes towards the advertising of controversial products', *European Journal of Marketing*, 38 (5/6), pp. 537–55.

Filieri, R., Hofacker, C.F., and Alguezaui, S. (2018) 'What makes information in online consumer reviews diagnostic over time? The role of review relevancy, factuality, currency, source credibility and ranking score', *Computers in Human Behavior*, 80, pp. 122–31.

Fischer, J. (2016) 'Markets, religion, regulation: Kosher, halal and Hindu vegetarianism in global perspective', *Geoforum*, 69, pp. 67–70.

Fischer, J. (2018) 'Kosher biotech: Between religion, regulation, and globalization', *Religion and Society*, 9 (1), pp. 52–67.

Fischer, J. (2019) ,Veg or non-veg? From bazaars to hypermarkets in India', *IJAPS*, 15 (1), pp. 1–32.

Floren, J., Rasul, T., and Gani, A. (2019) 'Islamic marketing and consumer behaviour: A systematic literature review', *Journal of Islamic Marketing*. https://doi.org/10 .1108/JIMA-05-2019-0100 (Accessed 14 March 2020).

Gagne, A. (2020) 'Eating according to religious practices: Kosher and halal'. www.gfs .com/en-us/ideas/eating-according-religious-practices-kosher-and-halal (Accessed 23 May 2020).

Gbadamosi. A. (2013) 'Consumer involvement and marketing in Africa: Some directions for future research', *International Journal of Consumer Studies*, 37 (2), pp. 234–42.

Gbadamosi, A. (2019a) 'Postmodernism, ethnicity, and celebrity culture in women's symbolic consumption', *International Journal of Market Research*, DOI: 10.1177/1470785319868363.

Gbadamosi, A. (2019b) 'Women entrepreneurship, religiosity, and value-co-creation with ethnic consumers: Revisiting the paradox', *Journal of Strategic Marketing*, 27 (4), pp. 303–16.

Golnaz, R., Zainalabidin, M., Mad Nasir, S., and Eddie Chiew, F.C. (2010) 'Non-Muslims' awareness of halal principles and related food products in Malaysia', *International Food Research Journal*, 17 (3), pp. 667–74.

Hasan, R. (2017a) 'Introduction: The nexus between religion and development', in *Religion and Development in the Global South*. Cham: Palgrave Macmillan, pp. 1–39.

Hasan, R. (2017b) 'Religion and cognitive development: Implications for the developing world', *Development*, 60 (3–4), pp. 201–5.

Hasan Bukhari, S.F., Woodside, F.M., Hassan, R., Latif Shaikh, A., Hussain, S., and Mazhar, W. (2019) 'Is religiosity an important consideration in Muslim consumer behaviour: Exploratory study in the context of western imported food in Pakistan', *Journal of Islamic Marketing*, https://doi.org/10.1108/JIMA-01-2018-0006

Haynes, J. (2009) 'Conflict, conflict resolution and peace-building: The role of religion in Mozambique, Nigeria and Cambodia', *Commonwealth and Comparative Politics*, 47 (1), pp. 52–75.

Hefele, P. and Dittrich, A. (2011) 'The situation of Christians in North East Asia and South East Asia', *KAS International Reports*, pp. 70–86.

Heiman, A., Gordon, B., and Zilberman, D. (2019) 'Food beliefs and food supply chains: The impact of religion and religiosity in Israel', *Food Policy*, 83, pp. 363–9.

Howard, J.A., and Sheth, J.N. (1969) 'A theory of buyer behaviour', *Journal of the American Statistical Association*. DOI: 10.2307/2284311.

Hwang, H. (2018) 'Do religion and religiosity affect consumers' intentions to adopt pro-environmental behaviours?' *International Journal of Consumer Studies*, 42 (6), pp. 664–74.

Ikoja-Odongo, R. and Mostert, J. (2006) 'Information seeking behaviour: A conceptual framework', *South African Journal of Libraries and Information Science*, 72 (3), pp. 145–58.

Islam, T. and Chandrasekaran, U. (2019) 'Religiosity, values and consumer behaviour: A study of young Indian Muslim consumers', *Journal of Consumer Marketing*, 36 (7), pp. 948–61.

Islam, T. and Chandrasekaran, U. (2020) 'Religiosity and consumer decision making styles of young Indian Muslim consumers', *Journal of Global Scholars of Marketing Science*, 30 (2), pp. 147–69. DOI: 10.1080/21639159.2019.1679031.

Izberk-Bilgin, E. and Nakata, C.C. (2016) 'A new look at faith-based marketing: The global halal market', *Business Horizons*, 59 (3), pp. 285–92.

Jha, K. and Prasad, R. (2014) 'Consumer buying decisions models: A descriptive study', *International Journal of Innovation and Applied Studies*, 6 (3), pp. 335–51.

Kalliny, M., Ghanem, S., Shaner, M., Boyle, B., and Mueller, B. (2019) 'Capitalizing on faith: A cross-cultural examination of consumer responses to the use of religious symbols in advertising', *Journal of Global Marketing*, pp. 1–19.

Karataş, M. and Sandıkcı, Ö. (2013) 'Religious communities and the marketplace: Learning and performing consumption in an Islamic network', *Marketing Theory*, 13 (4), pp. 465–84.

Kempen, E., Bosman, M., Bouwer, C., Klein, R., and van der Merwe, D. (2011) 'An exploration of the influence of food labels on South African consumers' purchasing behaviour', *International Journal of Consumer Studies*, 35 (1), pp. 69–78.

Khan, M., Asad, H., and Mehboob, I. (2017) 'Investigating the consumer behaviour for halal endorsed products: Case of an emerging Muslim market', *Journal of Islamic Marketing*, 8 (4), pp. 625–41.

Khoa, B.T. (2020). 'The antecedents of relationship marketing and customer loyalty: A case of the designed fashion product', *Journal of Asian Finance, Economics and Business*, 7 (2), pp. 195–204.

Khraim, H. (2010) 'Measuring religiosity in consumer research from Islamic perspective', *International Journal of Marketing Studies*, 2 (2), pp. 166–79.

Kim, S.E., Oh, Y., Lee, K.H., and Bae, J. (2018) 'Designing a business model for sustainable consumption: Toward the managing consumption habit', *International Textile and Apparel Association Annual Conference Proceedings*, 97. https://lib.dr.iastate.edu/itaa_proceedings/2018/posters/97

Klein, A. (2020) 'How is Ramadan celebrated?' https://people.howstuffworks.com/culture-traditions/holidays-other/ramadan2.htm (Accessed 23 May 2020).

Koen, N., Wentzel-Viljoen, E., and Blaauw, R. (2018) 'Price rather than nutrition information the main influencer of consumer food purchasing behaviour in South Africa: A qualitative study', *International Journal of Consumer Studies*, 42 (4), pp. 409–18.

Kotler, P. (1999) *Marketing Management: The Millennium Edition*, Vol. 199. Upper Saddle River, NJ: Prentice Hall.

Kotler, P., Armstrong, G., Saunders, J., and Wong, V. (1999) *Principles of Marketing*, 2nd ed. Harlow: Prentice Hall Europe.

Kotler, P., Keller, K.L., Koshy, A., and Jha, M. (2009) 'Creation customer value satisfaction and loyalty', *Marketing Management*, 13, pp. 120–5.

Kotler, P., Keller, K.L., Ang, S.H., Tan, C.T., and Leong, S.M. (2018) *Marketing Management: An Asian Perspective*. Harlow: Pearson.

Kroeze, I.J. (2012) 'How to eat: Vegetarianism, religion, and law', *TD: The Journal for Transdisciplinary Research in Southern Africa*, 8 (1), pp. 1–16.

Krugman, H.E. (1977) 'Memory without recall, exposure without perception', *Journal of Advertising Research*, 17 (4), pp. 7–12.

Kwon, S., Ha, S., and Kowal, C. (2017) 'How online self-customization creates identification: Antecedents and consequences of consumer-customized product identification and the role of product involvement', *Computers in Human Behavior*, 75, pp. 1–13.

Labuschagne, A., van Zyl, S., van der Merwe, D., and Kruger, A. (2012) 'Consumers' expectations of furniture labels during their pre-purchase information search: An explication of proposed furniture labelling specifications', *International Journal of Consumer Studies*, 36 (4), pp. 451–9.

Lankalibrary (2020) 'The national flag of Sri Lanka'. www.lankalibrary.com/pro/flag.html (Accessed 2 July 2020).

Lawan, L.A. and Zanna, R. (2013) 'Evaluation of socio-cultural factors influencing consumer buying behaviour of clothes in Borno State, Nigeria', *International Journal of Basic and Applied Science*, 1 (3), pp. 519–29.

Leon, N. and Shoham, H. (2018) 'Belonging without commitment: The Christocentric view and the traditionist perspective on modern religion', *Culture and Religion*, 19 (2), pp. 235–52.

Levy, S.J. (1959) 'Symbols for sale', *Harvard Business Review*, 37 (July–August), pp. 117–24.

Lindridge, A. (2009) 'Acculturation, religion and consumption in normative political ideology', *Advances in Consumer Research*, 36, pp. 16–19.

Lovelock, C. and Wirtz, J. (2011) *Services Marketing: People, Technology, Strategy*, 7th ed. Boston, MA: Prentice Hall.

Lussier, K. (2019). 'Of Maslow, motives, and managers: The hierarchy of needs in American business, 1960–1985', *Journal of the History of the Behavioural Sciences*, 55 (4), pp. 319–41.

Lysonski, S. and Durvasula, S. (2013) 'Consumer decision making styles in retailing: Evolution of mindsets and psychological impacts', *Journal of Consumer Marketing*, 30, pp. 75–87. https://doi.org/10.1108/07363761311290858

Lysonski, S., Durvasula, S., and Zotos, Y. (1996) 'Consumer decision-making styles: A multi-country investigation', *European Journal of Marketing*, 30 (12), pp. 10–21.

Martin, C.L. (2016) 'How nature, culture and legal calendars influence the calendrical timing of consumer behaviour', *Journal of Customer Behaviour*, 15 (4), pp. 337–68.

Martínez, P., Herrero, Á., and García-de lose Salmones, M.D.M. (2020) 'Determinants of eWOM on hospitality CSR issues. In Facebook we trust?', *Journal of Sustainable Tourism*, pp. 1–19.

Maslow, A.H. (1943) 'A theory of human motivation', *Psychological Review*, 50 (4), pp. 370–96.

Maslow, A.H. (1962) *Toward a Psychology of Being*. Princeton, NJ: D. Van Nostrand.

Mathras, D., Cohen, A.B., Mandel, N., and Mick, D.G. (2016) 'The effects of religion on consumer behavior: A conceptual framework and research agenda', *Journal of Consumer Psychology*, 26 (2), pp. 298–311.

McAlexander, J.H., Dufault, B.L., Martin, D.M., and Schouten, J.W. (2014) 'The marketization of religion: Field, capital, and consumer identity', *Journal of Consumer Research*, 41 (3), pp. 858–75.

Mehkar Sherwani, A.A., Ali, A. Hussain, S., and Gul Zadran, H. (2018) 'Determinants of Muslim consumers' Halal meat consumption: Applying and extending the theory of planned behavior', *Journal of Food Products Marketing*. DOI: 10.1080/10454446.2018.1450173.

Mehta, R. and Dixit, G. (2016) 'Consumer decision-making styles in developed and developing markets: A cross-country comparison', *Journal of Retailing and Consumer Services*, 33, pp. 202–8.

Mihaela, O.O.E. (2015) 'The influence of the integrated marketing communication on the consumer buying behaviour', *Procedia Economics and Finance*, 23, pp. 1446–50.

Miller, D. (1995) *Unwrapping Christmas*. Oxford: Oxford University Press.

Min, P.G. and Kim, D.Y. (2005) 'Intergenerational transmission of religion and culture: Korean Protestants in the US', *Sociology of Religion*, 66 (3), pp. 263–82.

Mirkhah, S. and Karami, N. (2019) 'Investigating the impact of religious commitment on purchase of self-expressive brand products', *Journal of Islamic Marketing*, 11 (2), pp. 320–43.

Mittelstaedt, J.D. (2002) 'A framework for understanding the relationships between religions and markets', *Journal of Macromarketing*, 22 (1), pp. 6–18.

Mokhlis, S. (2009) 'An investigation of consumer decision-making styles of young-adults in Malaysia', *International Journal of Business and Management*, 4 (4), pp. 140–8.

Moraes, M., Gountas, J., Gountas, S., and Sharma, P (2019) 'Celebrity influences on consumer decision making: New insights and research directions', *Journal of Marketing Management*, 35 (13–14), pp. 1159–92.

Muhamad, N. and Mizerski, D. (2010) 'The constructs mediating religions' influence on buyers and consumers', *Journal of Islamic Marketing*, 1 (2), pp. 124–35.

Muhamad, N., Leong, V.S., and Mizerski, D. (2016) 'Consumer knowledge and religious rulings on products', *Journal of Islamic Marketing*, 7 (1), pp. 74–94.

Mulkeen, J. and Kakay, S. (2017) 'A critical evaluation of the impact of religion on collectivist families' meal social interaction behaviour in Sierra Leone', *International Journal of Advanced Research*, 5 (1), pp. 2675–93.

Navarro-Prado, S., González-Jiménez, E., Perona, J.S., Montero-Alonso, M.A., López-Bueno, M., and Schmidt-RioValle, J. (2017) 'Need of improvement of diet and life habits among university student regardless of religion professed', *Appetite*, 114, pp. 6–14.

Nawawi, M.S.A.M., Abu-Hussin, M.F., Faid, M.S., Pauzi, N., Man, S., and Sabri, N.M. (2019) 'The emergence of halal food industry in non-Muslim countries: A case study of Thailand', *Journal of Islamic Marketing*, pp. 1759–833. DOI: 10.1108/JIMA-05-2018-0082.

Nazihah, A. and Arifin, B.S. (2020) 'The impact of food on Muslims' spiritual development', *Indonesian Journal of Halal Research*, 2 (1), pp. 27–32.

Pace, S. (2013) 'Does religion affect the materialism of consumers? An empirical investigation of Buddhist ethics and the resistance of the self', *Journal of Business Ethics*, 112 (1), pp. 25–46.

Panwar, D., Anand, S., Ali, F., and Singal, K. (2019) 'Consumer decision making process models and their applications to market strategy', *International Management Review*, 15 (1), pp. 36–44.

Perry, J. and El-Hassan, A.A. (2008) *A Guide to Engaging Muslim Communities*. Coventry: Chartered Institute of Housing.

Pride, W.M. and Ferrell, O.C. (2019) *Foundations of Marketing*, 8th ed. Boston, MA: Cengage Learning.

Rana, J. and Paul, J. (2017) 'Consumer behavior and purchase intention for organic food: A review and research agenda', *Journal of Retailing and Consumer Services*, 38, pp. 157–65.

Ratchford, B.T. (1987) 'New insights about the FCB grid', *Journal of Advertising Research*, 27 (4), pp. 24–38.

Rauf, A. A., Prasad, A., and Ahmed, A. (2019) 'How does religion discipline the consumer subject? Negotiating the paradoxical tension between consumer desire and the social order', *Journal of Marketing Management*, 35 (5–6), pp. 491–513.

Regenstein, J.M. and Regenstein, C.E. (1979) 'An introduction to the kosher dietary laws for food scientists and food processors', *Food Technology*, 33 (1), pp. 89–99.

Roodbar, S. (2018). *Spatial and Temporal Changes in Halal Food Sales and Consumption: A Case Study of the City of Dearborn, Michigan*. Thesis.

Rook, D.W. (1985) 'The ritual dimension of consumer behaviour', *Journal of Consumer Research*, 12 (3), pp. 251–64.

Roseta, P., Sousa, B.B., and Roseta, L. (2020) 'Determiners in the consumer's purchase decision process in ecotourism contexts: A Portuguese case study', *Geosciences*, 10 (6), p. 224.

Sandıkcı, Ö. (2018) 'Religion and the marketplace: Constructing the "new" Muslim consumer', *Religion*, 48 (3), pp. 453–73.

Sandıkcı, O. (2020) 'Religion and everyday consumption ethics: A moral economy approach', *Journal of Business Ethics*, pp. 1–17.

Sardana, D., Gupta, N., and Sharma, P. (2018) 'Spirituality and religiosity at the junction of consumerism: Exploring consumer preference for spiritual brands', *International Journal of Consumer Studies*, 42 (6), pp. 724–35.

Saroglou, V. (2011) 'Believing, bonding, behaving, and belonging: The big four religious dimensions and cultural variation', *Journal of Cross-Cultural Psychology*, 42 (8), pp. 1320–40.

SBS (2014) 'How do different Asian countries celebrate Christmas?' www.sbs.com .au/popasia/blog/2014/12/16/how-do-different-asian-countries-celebrate-christmas (Accessed 25 May 2020).

Schiffman, L.G. and Kanuk, L.L. (2000) *Consumer Behaviour*, 7th ed. Upper Saddle River, NJ: Prentice Hall.

Sevim, N., Eroglu Hall, E., and Abu-Rayya, H.M. (2016) 'The role of religion and acculturation in the consumer ethnocentrism of Turkish immigrants in Germany', *Religions*, 7 (3), p. 29.

Shahid, M. and Raj, J. (2019) 'Islamic banking in India: An overview', *ZENITH International Journal of Multidisciplinary Research*, 9 (6), pp. 246–52.

Sheth, J.N., Newman, B.I., and Gross, B.L. (1991) 'Why we buy what we buy: A theory of consumption values', *Journal of Business Research*, 22 (2), pp. 159–70.

Shih, C.Y., Huang, C.Y., Huang, M.L., Chen, C.M., Lin, C.C., and Tang, F.I. (2019) 'The association of sociodemographic factors and needs of haemodialysis patients according to Maslow's hierarchy of needs', *Journal of Clinical Nursing*, 28 (1–2), pp. 270–8.

Shim, D., Shin, J., and Kwak, S.Y. (2018) 'Modelling the consumer decision-making process to identify key drivers and bottlenecks in the adoption of environmentally friendly products', *Business Strategy and the Environment*, 27 (8), pp. 1409–21.

Shocker, A.D., Ben-Akiva, M., Boccara, B., and Nedungadi, P. (1991) 'Consideration set influences on consumer decision-making and choice: Issues, models, and suggestions', *Marketing Letters*, 2 (3), pp. 181–97.

Shrum, L.J., Wong, N., Arif, F., Chugani, S.K., Gunz, A., Lowrey, T.M., Nairn, A., Pandelaere, M., Ross, S.M., Ruvio, A., and Scott, K. (2013) 'Reconceptualizing materialism as identity goal pursuits: Functions, processes, and consequences', *Journal of Business Research*, 66 (8), pp. 1179–85.

Simon, H.A. (1959) 'Theories of decision-making in economics and behavioural science', *American Economics Review*, 49 (3).

Simoons, F.J. (1994) *Eat Not This Flesh: Food Avoidances from Prehistory to the Present*. Madison, WI: University of Wisconsin Press.

Sirgy, M.J. and Johar, J.S. (1999) 'Toward an integrated model of self-congruity and functional congruity', in Bernard Dubois, Tina M. Lowrey, L. J. Shrum, and Marc Vanhuele (eds), *European Advances in Consumer Research*, Vol. 4. Provo, UT: Association for Consumer Research, pp. 252–6.

Solomon, M., Bamossy, G., Askegaard, S., and Hogg, M.K. (2006) *Consumer Behaviour: A European Perspective*, 3rd ed. Upper Saddle River, NJ: Prentice Hall.

Souiden, N., Ladhari, R., and Zarrouk Amri, A. (2018) 'Is buying counterfeit sinful? Investigation of consumers' attitudes and purchase intentions of counterfeit products in a Muslim country', *International Journal of Consumer Studies*, 42 (6), pp. 687–703.

Sprotles, G.B. and Kendall, E.L. (1986) 'A methodology for profiling consumers' decision-making styles', *Journal of Consumer Affairs*, 20 (2), pp. 267–79.

Stankevich, A. (2017) 'Explaining the consumer decision-making process: Critical literature review', *Journal of International Business Research and Marketing*, 2 (6), pp. 7–14.

Stokburger-Sauer, N., Ratneshwar, S., and Sen, S. (2012) 'Drivers of consumer-brand identification', *International Journal of Research in Marketing*, 29, pp. 406–18.

Tajfel, H. and Turner, J.C. (1979) 'An integrative theory of intergroup conflict', in W. Austin and S. Worchel (eds), *The Social Psychology of Intergroup Relations*. Monterey, CA: Brooks/Cole, pp. 33–48.

Tavana, M., Di Caprio, D., and Santos-Arteaga, F.J. (2017) 'A multi-criteria perception-based strict-ordering algorithm for identifying the most-preferred choice among equally-evaluated alternatives', *Information Sciences*, 381, pp. 322–40.

Tsai, H.C. and Hsiao, S.W. (2004) 'Evaluation of alternatives for product customization using fuzzy logic', *Information Sciences*, 158, pp. 233–62.

Tuškej, U., Golob, U., and Podnar, K. (2013) 'The role of consumer–brand identification in building brand relationships', *Journal of Business Research*, 66 (1), pp. 53–9.

Van der Colff, N., Van der Merwe, D., Bosman, M., Erasmus, A., and Ellis, S. (2016) 'Consumers' prepurchase satisfaction with the attributes and information of food labels', *International Journal of Consumer Studies*, 40 (2), pp. 220–8.

van Staden, J. and van Aardt, A.M. (2011) 'Information seeking by female apparel consumers in South Africa during the fashion decision-making process', *International Journal of Consumer Studies*, 35 (1), pp. 35–49.

Vaughn, R. (1986) 'How advertising works: A planning model revisited', *Journal of Advertising Research*, 26, pp. 57–66.

Vieira, V., Santini, F., and Araujo, C. (2018) 'A meta-analytic review of hedonic and utilitarian shopping values', *Journal of Consumer Marketing*, 35 (4), pp. 426–37.

Vitz, E.B. (1991) *A Continual Feast: A Cookbook to Celebrate the Joys of Family and Faith throughout the Christian Year*. San Francisco, CA: Ignatius Press.

Voramontri, D. and Klieb, L. (2018) 'Impact of social media on consumer behaviour', *International Journal of Information and Decision Sciences*, 11 (3), pp. 1–25.

Wahyuni, S. and Fitriani, N. (2017) 'Brand religiosity aura and brand loyalty in Indonesia Islamic banking', *Journal of Islamic Marketing*, 8 (3), pp. 361–72.

Wasan, P. (2018) 'Predicting customer experience and discretionary behaviours of bank customers in India', *International Journal of Bank Marketing*, 36 (4), pp. 701–25.

Wattanasuwan, K. and Elliott, R. (1999) 'The Buddhist self and symbolic consumption: The consumption experience of the teenage dhammakaya Buddhists in Thailand', *Advances in Consumer Research*, 26 (1).

Wilkins, S., Butt, M.M., Shams, F., and Pérez, A. (2019) 'The acceptance of halal food in non-Muslim countries: Effects of religious identity, national identification, consumer ethnocentrism and consumer cosmopolitanism', *Journal of Islamic Marketing*, 10 (4), 1308–31.

Yousaf, S. and Malik, M.S. (2013) 'Evaluating the influences of religiosity and product involvement level on the consumers', *Journal of Islamic Marketing*, 4 (2), pp. 163–86.

Zikmund, W.G. and d'Amico, M. (1996) *Basic Marketing*. Eagan, MN: West Publishing Company.

5. Religiosity and global brand consumption as an agent of modernisation in developing economies

Rula M. Al-Abdulrazak

INTRODUCTION

Wrestling with the new geographies of space, and new borders such as the Republic of Ireland, the Republic of South Sudan, and the Czech Republic, is modernisation a product of capitalism, or an organic fruit of history? The last four decades witnessed an increasing number of so-called emerging economies vying for attention, such as the United Arab Emirates. 'Cities from zero' like Dubai (Basar 2006) are called 'instant cities' due to super-fast urbanisation (Bagaeen 2007). These cities present a specific formula for high-pace economic development that includes vision and the ability to attract investment, in a model of a state-controlled open market which is an unapologetic new-found economy. The rapid urbanisation of China is another example of the same formula. Eschewing participatory democracy in these new economies has resulted in a market-based populist culture of consumerism (Basar 2006), where consumer preferences converge (homogenisation of tastes) alongside a growing demand to consume (pluralisation of consumption). Other countries with growing economies and participatory democracy are India, Brazil, and South Africa, with growing appetites and purchasing power to brand consumption. These emerging markets are following the roots of well-established consumption culture in markets such as the United States (US), the United Kingdom (UK) and the European market, which progressed through a history of evolving capitalism.

The purchase of iconic global brands is considered a manifestation of the culture of consumption. They are the target of anti-consumerism and anti-materialism activists, such as journalist Naomi Klein (1999) the author of *No Logo*. *No Logo* criticised corporate dominance in a new branded world and evolved into a movement that challenged 'brand bullies' and increased awareness. The book became a point of reference not only for social justice and environmentalists but also for marketers and brand agents. *No Logo* became a brand in its own right and alerted other activists to the power of branding their entities and causes by applying the tools and rationale of corporate brand managers (e.g. Bob 2002, 2005). Schlosser (2002), the author of *Fast Food Nation*, is another investigative journalist who challenged corporate dominance through the phenomenon of fast food that spread from North America to the rest of the world and its effect on people's lives.

Communications and cultural studies scholars Melissa Aronczyk and Devon Powers (2010) edited *Blowing Up the Brand*, a collection of studies that critically examined the power of brands in an increasingly market-oriented culture. The book is an intervention into 'the' commodification phenomenon which became 'the way of life' that represents modernity; where the brand is the way to communicate effectively and efficiently any social, political or commercial aim. Holt (2004) examined the concept of the iconic brand, as a brand that imbeds itself in culture, champions cultural change and becomes an activist in a cultural movement. Brands in such a powerful position can influence or lead cultural change as they work with traditional socio-cultural activists, such as journalists, artists, creative writers and media. With this understanding, brand meaning can become part of cultural, sociological and philosophical enquiry, that both complements and complicates the commercial and managerial analysis of brand and brand decision making.

> [Brand] knowledge doesn't come from focus groups or ethnography or trend reports – the marketer's usual means for 'getting close to the customer'. Rather, it comes from a cultural historian's understanding of ideology as it waxes and wanes, a sociologist's charting of the topography of contradictions the ideology produces, and a literary critic's expedition into the culture that engages these contradictions. (Holt 2003: 49)

Brand Culture, an edited book by Jonathan Schroeder and Miriam Salzer Morling (2006), refers to brands as cultural, ideological and political objects. The editors identify cultural influences and implications of brands from two angles: first, brands infuse culture with meaning, and provide brand management with a profound influence on modern society. Second, in addition to brand identity and brand image, brand culture is an essential part of the brand theory, as it enhances our understanding of the branding process by providing the needed cultural, historical and political foundation to understand how brand meaning is formed in context.

Cultural codes, ideological discourse, consumers' background knowledge and rhetorical processes are some of the identified influences in branding, brand communication and the consumer–brand relationship. Basic cultural processes, including historical context, ethical concerns and consumer response, affect brand meaning (Schroeder and Morling 2006). Consumers form and perform identities and self-concepts in collaboration with brand culture (Borgerson and Schroeder 2002). Marketers and consumers cannot completely control the branding process, and the formation of brand meaning as cultural codes can have a major role to play. Marketing research is yet to comprehend the complexity of the branding process and formation of meaning, identity and image in a cultural context, and what the consequences of consuming the brand and forming brand meaning can be on society. This research gap can be due to the need for multidisciplinary research methods and theorisation due to its complexity (Holt 2003).

To enhance our understanding of the interaction between brands and cultures in the global market, this chapter defines the brand and studies brands' interactions with different cultures, by examining the brands' consumption in relation to specific cultural codes. The chapter raises an enquiry into the role global brands play in developing economies' consumerism and culture. As a major source of individuals' values and lifestyle, faith values and religious beliefs represented in religiosity, which is a key element of culture (Tyler 1870, cited by Avruch 1998; Spencer-Oatey 2008, 2012), is selected to examine the phenomenon of global brands' consumption in developing economies as a form of modernisation in recently modernised cities such as Dubai and Riyadh. The focus here is on the brand influence on social and economic developments of developing economy consumers.

Global brands aim to address the world from an ethnocentric perspective as they develop global strategies and minimise adaptations. They thus segment international markets in search of a global strategic segment interested in sharing the brand culture and values. This approach increases the brand power to influence international market consumers. Accordingly, this study explores global brands' interaction with consumers from developing economies. It utilises the narrative of modernisation theory and the dialectic discourse of postmodernism and the dependency theory to shed light on this global brand–consumer interaction. To clarify the narrative, religiosity and the value of modesty consumers may have are examined in relation to examples of global brand interactions in countries such as Saudi Arabia. Finally, a balancing act model is developed to illustrate the unbalanced interaction between a global brand and emergent market consumers in this narrative.

BRANDS, BRANDING AND BRAND MANAGEMENT

Brand

Marketers often consider brands as a psychological phenomenon which emerges from the perceptions of individual consumers. The collective nature of these perceptions is what can lead to a powerful brand (Holt 2006). Stephen Brown (2016) stated that a brand is a property in the sense that it is a vital asset of any business as per the space a brand occupies in consumers' minds. This conscious and subconscious mind share creates brand value; whereas cultural brands' value emerges from their culture share that is obtained through the collective perception of brand articulation and active engagement in culture. An example of cultural brands can be McDonald's as a brand embedded in the fast-food cultural movement in the US.

There are many potential definitions of the brand as per the examples in Table 5.1; however, there are shared understandings among these definitions, which can be grouped into six themes: meaning-oriented, object-oriented, ownership-oriented, competitiveness-orientated, communication-oriented and value-oriented (see Table 5.1 for examples). There are many claimed definitions of brand, which can lead to a vague understanding of the concept and can be themed in several ways. To clarify how this chapter's enquiry is grounded in brand theory, the *brand* is defined as consumers/stakeholders' perception of a distinctive idea and emotion associated with tangible and intangible features. Experiencing the brand leads to individual and social responses and forms individual and collective perceptions that create the brand value.

The object-oriented brand definitions focused mainly on products as the branded object dismissing the broader range of branded subjects such as places, people, non-profit organisations, corporations and ideas. Thus, a differentiation between a product and brand is necessary here (see Table 5.2 for clarification).

To understand the brand, it is also important to differentiate between the brand and the image and identity of the branded object or idea. There are several interpretations of the three concepts and how they interrelate. Brand meaning is formed through a projected identity and a perceived image of the branded object, subject or idea. Thus, it is helpful for this enquiry to define these concepts and their relationships. Identity is the way an object aims to be perceived (Al-Abdulrazak 2016). Image is the way the public perceives the object (Al-Abdulrazak 2016). A brand is what represents the essence of the identity of the branded object/subject. A brand is consumers' experience to form an image of the object/subject that is close to its projected identity. A brand is an illusion and a reality of the branded object/subject; as what is perceived, is what is real (Bonansea 1969, cited by Reid 2013).

Branding and Brand Management

Some of the reviewed definitions of a brand are definitions of the branding process. Process-oriented definitions were combined by a few marketers and academics such as Michael Beverland (2018). For example, '*branding* is

Table 5.1 Orientations of brand definitions

Classification	Definition	Author
Meaning-oriented	[A brand is] a repository of meanings fuelled by a combination of marketers' intention, consumers' interpretations, and numerous socio-cultural networks' associations.	Marie-Agnes Parmentier, cited in Beverland 2018
	Corporate brand is the core value that defines it and provides strategic direction to a firm's activities.	Ind 1997; De Chernatony 1999; Simões et al. 2005
Object-oriented	A brand is a product that provides functional benefits plus added values that some consumers value enough to buy.	John Philip Jones, cited in Beverland 2018
	A brand is a product but one that adds other dimensions that differentiate it in some way from other products designed to satisfy the same need.	Keller et al. 2012
Ownership-oriented	A brand is a label, designating ownership by a firm, which we experience, evaluate, have feelings towards and build associations with to perceive value.	Brakus et al. 2009
Competitiveness-oriented	A brand is a reason to choose.	Cheryl Burgess, cited in Beverland 2018
	A brand is a name, term, sign, symbol or design, or a combination of these, intended to identify the goods or services of one seller or group of sellers and to differentiate them from the competitors.	American Marketing Association n.d.
Communication-oriented	A brand is the intangible sum of the product's attributes, its name, packaging and price, its history, its reputation and the way it is advertised.	David Ogilvy 1911–99, cited in Beverland 2018
	A brand is a customer experience represented by a collection of images and ideas; often, it refers to a symbol such as a name, logo, slogan and design scheme.	American Marketing Association n.d.
Value-oriented	A brand is a cluster of values that enables a promise to be made about a unique and welcoming experience.	De Chernatony 2009

Table 5.2   Product and brand differentiation

Product	Brand
– Product is a *bundle of benefits* which consumers perceive to satisfy their need or solve their problem.	– A brand is a *perception (intangible)*
	– It is a result of consumers' experiences of
– Usually, the product is *tangible*, but it could include services.	– a company;
	– a product;
	– a service;
	– a place;
	– a person; or
	– an idea, etc.
– Tangibles can cost much more than they add value to consumers.	– Intangibles usually add much more value to consumers than they cost.

the art of aligning what you want people to think about your company with what people actually think about your company and vice-versa' (Jay Baer, cited in Beverland 2018: 8). Branding is the process by which a brand idea is formed, communicated and engaged with society to gain meaning. The perceived meaning can align with the original idea to some extent and differ in many others. The gained *brand meaning* is a shared production among all stakeholders. *Brand management* attempts to enhance the alignment between the gained brand meaning and the original brand idea, which management expects to be in favour of the brand value. Brand management goes beyond the branding process to evaluate the perceived brand meaning, monitor its value and update the brand experiences accordingly. Branding may initially emphasise functionally oriented values, which are then amplified with emotionally oriented values. As brand management sophistication increases, it drives a visionary promise that adds value to all stakeholders. And as the perceived brand meaning enhances brand preference, brand equity (as the financial value of the brand) increases and vice versa unless unforeseen circumstances interfere in the process. *Brand preferences* result from consumers' rational and non-rational choices following their cognition and emotions. Emotion can be a primary influence on the development of brand preferences and may precede cognition. Many important aspects of emotion are social. The meaning of emotion may be constructed by social interaction leading to an understanding of acceptable behaviour and value patterns; this explains cultural and sub-cultural differences in consumption. As emotions are socially and culturally constructed their influence on how consumers process brand communication and experience the brand can be rooted in culture, in particular consumers' non-rational preferences. The symbolic meaning of consumption also can be grounded in the self – or social – symbolism (Rosenbaum-Elliott et al. 2015) which is heavily influenced by culture.

Brand management involves identifying and developing brand plans, designing and implementing brand marketing programmes, measuring and interpreting brand performance and growing and sustaining brand equity (Keller et al. 2012). Such a rigid management process can easily slip into brand management from the management perspective rather than the consumer perspective. As the power of a brand lies in what resides in the minds and hearts of consumers, to refocus brand management teams' orientation towards the consumers and other stakeholders, Keller et al. (2012) suggested the customer-based brand equity (CBBE) model. *Brand equity* is a set of assets (and liabilities) linked to a brand's name that adds to (or subtracts from) the value provided by brand offerings to a firm and/or that firm's customers (Aaker 1996, 2002). The major assets of brand equity, as identified by Aaker, are brand awareness, perceived quality, brand associations and brand loyalty. CBBE suggests four stages to develop brand identity and meaning, followed by consumer response and the brand relationship they create. These stages correspond with the objectives of achieving brand awareness, creating points of parity and points of difference that stimulate positive reactions from consumers in terms of emotions and judgement, leading to brand loyalty. However, the effect of culture is not salient either in CBBE, or in the brand management process. CBBE focuses on individuals' perceptions rather than collective perception and does not clearly address the impact of socio-cultural contexts. In expanding a brand overseas, for example, marketers need to build brand equity by relying on specific knowledge about the experience and behaviours of those market segments, and without understanding the effect of influential cultural components such as faith and religion, their predictions of consumer behaviours and preferences can be misleading. It is not clear how religion can influence buying and consumption behaviour as the number of empirical studies in this area is rather small. However, studies suggest that consumer segmentation and targeting in multicultural and cross-cultural markets can increase the accuracy of its knowledge into consumer behaviour by considering faith and religious values (Mathras et al. 2015; Hollensen 2017). Including religion in customer persona analysis can help marketers understand the buying and consumption reasoning and emotions, such as the trade-off between pleasure and guilt, and consumer judgement when it comes to risk taking such as in gambling and investments.

BRANDS REPRESENTING MODERN LIFE IN DEVELOPING ECONOMIES

Modernisation Theory and Developing Economy

Modernisation theory is a Western theory that was populated in the US for political reasons. Its main goal was to overcome communism post-Second

World War and lead the rising 'third-world' nations (Wohlforth 1995; Abid 2004). Based on *the evolutionary theory*, modernisation is a phased lengthy process that can be achieved over a long period of time. It is a homogenising process where collective societies become individualistic yet represent a group of homogeneous people living within a system where their dreams and hopes are similar. Modernisation reflects Europeanisation or Americanisation as the model of a modern society. It is an irreversible process which suggests that whichever stage a country is stuck at it cannot reverse it even if it wanted. As soon as there is a demand for modernisation, or a process has started, it is difficult to take that back. The Middle East crisis in the 2010s started a revolution for reform which turned into conflicts around modern ideologies and power that trapped the region in a circle of endless battles. Finally, modernisation is a progressive process that should improve healthcare and increase income and productivity as it increases consumption.

The *economic approach* to understanding *modernisation* explains self-sustained growth of modernised societies. Rostow's (1964) take-off into self-sustained growth model based on an aeroplane metaphor suggests five stages for a society to move from traditional to high mass consumption society, which represented modernisation in this discourse. This model corresponds with the evolutionary theory as development is slow and takes decades. The five stages start with the traditional society, which is a collective society with limited resources and strong community ties and strong ties with its heritage. The second stage is when the traditional society is experiencing a cultural shift and a move towards individualism and market economy, and wants to have material wealth. This can be explained by Levy's (1953) trigger of wanting to modernise through contact points between non-modernised and modernised societies. These are the preconditions of the take-off stage and suggest political leadership that moves the country towards greater flexibility and openness in culture and economic diversification. The shift and want will lead to the third stage, where the society takes off. The take-off stage, however, requires a stimulus such as a significant technological advancement or political revolution. The stimulus preconditions the take-off. An evolving sense of individualism characterises it, an entrepreneurship approach to development as the country establishes a market economy that reflects a well-established want of material wealth where growth is the ideology, the policy and the development measure. The fourth stage is the technological maturity phase, where the society produces efficiently more than it consumes and, thus, it starts trading internationally and creating new markets to sustain its growth. At this stage, the community ties are weakened, and the economy is diversified in different sectors. More businesses are created, leading to urbanisation as employment gets concentrated in cities while the workforce gets specialised to serve the diversified economy, and public education with clear directions is offered. Finally, the phase of high mass consumption is where a modernised society is established with growing national income that is turning into a consumption society where it is cheaper to buy a new product than to repair one, with well-developed international trade. Welfare systems get established as community ties and collectivism diminish much further. At this stage, services expand dramatically as higher-income earners look for others to do more of their daily duties while they specialise in high-earning jobs. Although this model is also unidirectional countries can get stuck in the middle at the take-off stage when a political revolution leads to continuous unrest and a lack of resources and capital. Here Rostow suggests that modernised societies lend these non-modernised countries the capital needed and provide the knowledge and technology for financial benefits, for example, oil exploration technologies offered by brands such as Royal Dutch Shell (the Netherlands and the UK), Total (France) and ExxonMobil (the US), or medical technology brands such as Medtronic (the US), Philips (Netherlands), and GE Healthcare (the US). Both industries' leading brands are American brands that grew to become global brands.

From a *functionalist theory perspective*, modernisation is a systematic and transformative process, where shifts in society and culture occur following a specific stimulus. It is an immanent process – as soon as a change happens in one aspect of the community the rest follows. Usually, it starts with either education or political change. The functionalist theory led by the biologist Talcott Parsons (1967) argues that society is like a biological organism; it adjusts its temperature based on the environment it is in and the body's status, what is called 'homeostatic equilibrium'. Modernisation in this interpretation requires society to be *Adaptive* to the economic environment, work towards attaining specific *Goals* set by governments, *Integrate* institutional efforts to achieve the goals and maintain certain values in family and education, *Latency*. These are the four critical functions (AGIL) required of the society in this explanation of modernisation.

The functionalist theory interpretation of how modernisation works in non-modern societies suggests several pattern variables that distinguish traditional from modern society: affective versus affective neutrality; particularistic versus universalistic relationships; collective versus self-orientation; ascription versus achievement; and functionally diffused versus functionally specific society (Parsons and Shils 1951: 77). As such the *sociological approach* defines modernisation as the degree to which tools and sources of power are utilised (Levy 1953, 1966), where societies are on a continuum that progresses from non-modernised to modernised. For example, the US, Japan, and the UK are considered modernised, while China and India are progressing on the continuum as developing economies. The idea here is that modernisation occurs after the non-modernised country gets in contact with modernised countries.

The suggestion is that to start drinking soft drinks instead of tap water is modernisation, due to all the developments that come with it, so it is a trigger of modernisation. Latecomers to modernisation are to seek modernised countries' expertise and be aware of what to expect. However, they are in return expected to modernise at a faster pace dealing with a large scale of development at the same time, which may be constrained by resources and lead to disappointment.

From a *political* perspective, Coleman (1968) measures modernisation through a political restructuring, secularisation of political culture and enhanced capabilities of the political system through equal participation. He suggests that the ultimate measure of a modernised society is a political system that can handle a crisis in, for example, national identity and political legitimacy. Political systems that can survive such crises and ensure stability for growth have the sign of a modernised society.

Postmodernism

The Covid-19 pandemic challenges modern societies and economies designed by the Industrial Revolution in the West, and spread through mass product consumption across the world, followed by the shift of outsourcing manufacturing to the East. This pandemic is leading to a global economic crisis as it is challenging our mobility and forcing us to interact online in all aspects of life, due to closed airports, empty aeroplanes, hotels, restaurants, malls, offices and factories with reduced productivity as consumption shrank dramatically overnight. In the fashion industry Vogue Business reported in April 2020 that Galeria Karstadt Kaufhof, Germany's biggest department store retailer, for example, filed for administrative insolvency after losing more than €80 million in revenue per week, with a potential 28,000 job losses. Debenhams, a UK retail brand, appointed an administrator, with 22,000 jobs at risk across its 142 stores for the second time in a year. The US department store Neiman Marcus filed for bankruptcy. Small independent fashion designers, with brands worth under US$1 million, are the most at risk, and they represent around 40 per cent of the Council of Fashion Designers of America's 477 members. The year 2020 pushed many businesses to rethink their business model, and consumers may rethink their consumption habits and priorities, as some of them fight with their stuff for space in their tiny flats in some of the wealthiest cities across the world. Working, practising teaching and religious gatherings online while the sky becomes clearer and pollution drops significantly, giving other forms of life a better survival chance, may lead many consumers to question their consumption choices and rethink their lifestyles. Modernisation as we know it can be under threat and a change of form could be imminent following the 2020 Covid-19 pandemic.

The hypothesis that modernisation as a form of mass consumption leads to economic development does not necessarily reflect social development. Bhutan's use of the Happiness Index instead of gross domestic product to measure progress suggests that mass consumption is not an indication of happiness and mental health. The assumption that all societies are striving for harmony, stability and equilibrium as known in the Western form of modernisation and economic development ignores the painful and disruptive decades of suffering and unrest that people in less developed economies would have to endure for the promised modern lifestyle. Moreover, modernisation is not a process that countries may only enter voluntarily. Colonialism and postcolonialism play a significant role in imposing modernisation as Westernisation, Europeanisation or Americanisation. This can lead to the exploitation of non-industrial countries. A combination of capitalism and a form of democracy as the only desirable outcomes of progress is questioned by postmodernism and by the dependency theorists.

The continuous restructuring of institutions with the aim of integration to achieve modernisation can be disruptive and lead to losses in heritage and tacit knowledge and not necessarily achieve economic progress, while it can break the unity of communities. Uniformity of human society through a modernisation process that promotes individualism in many cases leads to inequality and injustice in income and life opportunities while devaluing the values of these societies, which had given them stability and happiness premodernisation.

These theories of modernisation do not consider the geographical locations, climate differences and natural resources, as they do not consider the historical evolution of a nation, its culture and values. The idea that the recommended modernisation process brings people together to work on a common goal is idealistic as every revolution faces a counter-revolution of those resisting change and rejecting the new ideologies. Furthermore, continuous economic growth is not necessarily the way forward as it is not environmentally friendly and can lead to a materialistic society where ownership matters more than relationships. Therefore, ethnocentric bias towards development in Western countries, as the European model, may not be the ideal model for every country. Many external factors of influence need to be considered, such as colonialism (see the dependency theory, Wallerstein 1967; Frank 1969).

In summary, linear theories that suggest modernisation as a progressive one-way, forward-looking process that assumes all nations would follow the same model are misleading. Development can take different shapes, can happen at different speeds and differ based on society's system of values and capabilities, education history and colonisation history, in addition to the geographical location and resources; plus, modernisation can be reversible. These theories are very descriptive and have a Western bias, as they describe West Europe and the US's development journey and do not address the willingness of other nations to follow the same approach. They do not address the influence of the West that drives many societies to want this style of modernisation, as suggested by Levy (1966). The Western influence is particularly evident in driving or hindering colonies' economic development and trade, as their resources were serving the colonising nation first. Western scholars such as Talcott Parsons (1967) were critical of the values of, what he considered, 'underdeveloped' countries. He suggested that being attached to customs, rituals and institutions hinders progress. He criticised the extended kinship and tribal systems found in many of these societies, as in his opinion they hinder the geographical and social mobility which is essential for country development as outlined in his functional fit theory. This includes religiosity that brings people together and can create strong kinship and social identity, which would influence all aspects of life, including daily consumptions. The impact of modernisation felt strongly across the world, and its impact on religions, is suggested to be seen in the falling of the number of worshippers in churches across Western societies and the appearance of cults and sub-sects that either aim to modernise religion or protect it leading to violence, such as in Pakistan (Menhas et al. 2015). In a case study analysis of South Korea as a developing economy, Kim (2002) suggests that globalised modern culture has deeply influenced a membership crisis in Korean Christianity since the 1960s. It can also be deduced from a theology study on the impact of modernism in Ethiopia (Girma 2018) that the impact of modernism is evident in self-political and social identity (state–church relations), which, in turn, affect brand consumption and decisions in favour of Western global brands that represent modernity.

Modernisation theory assumes that Western civilisation is technically and morally superior to other societies, implying that the values of the developing world have little value compared to those of the West. Meanwhile, *dependency* theorists argue that modernisation is not about helping the developing world as much as it is about making Western companies and countries richer, opening them up to exploit cheap natural resources and cheap labour (Ferraro 2008). On the other hand, many developed countries in the West show a high level of inequality, high crime rates, high suicide rates and health problems such as drug abuse. *Postmodernists* such as Heidegger, Lyotard and Derrida (Ferraris and Segre (1988) questioned the modernist belief in universalism in favour of relativism and identity. They questioned the narratives of societal and scientific progress in modernisation theory and emphasised the need to appreciate differences, rather than impose a forced unity. Postmodernism suggests that the world is a complicated place and that there are many ways to understand and enjoy the world.

Brand Consumption, Modernism and Postmodernism

In the modernist ethos, knowledge is a tool for improving the material conditions of human life, which is reflected in the branded products they buy as they become consumers. Human life is considered in terms of the here and now, what they buy and possess today and how these brands and possessions improve their lives. There is little reference to life after death, as was the case in the premodernist period. Thus, the progression of knowledge becomes linear, futuristic and goal-oriented (teleological) towards improving material conditions for a better life. In this logic brands' existence is a necessity to achieve a better human life, as well as improving the cognitive capacities of individual minds and enhancing their reasoning skills and abilities so they can make better judgements. The University of Oxford, Harvard University, Stanford University and the University of Cambridge are some of the top global brands to develop human minds and lives, while Google and Apple are at the top of the list of sought-after employers where a human can progress. Microsoft brand communications and mission focus on empowering people to progress with the embedded understanding that better life is achieved through progress. They communicate slogans such as 'your potential, our passion', and 'be what's next'. The social system accordingly expects to prepare its members to apply their knowledge to socially determined goals. Individuals become investments and society rewards them with more brands based on how well they perform in this rationalist enterprise, yet individualism is intended to prevail.

Consumer behaviour studies offer little attention to postmodernism (Firat and Venkatesh 1992; Sherry 1989). In an examination of the 'individual' and his or her relationship to the external world, Venkatesh (1992) identified three concepts that represent three periods of history in the West: premodernism, modernism and postmodernism. In premodernism the philosophical focus was on the concept of 'being', that is, the human existence in relationship to God and the Universe; while modernism shifts from the 'being' to 'knowing', that is, the human cognition as a subject and the external world as a rational social order of power. Postmodernism shifts further to the 'communicative' subject and a symbolic system of meaning. These shifts from a human being, to a knowing subject, to a communicative subject in a semiotic world reflect the market move from knowledge acquisition and production to a world of symbol and sign management, with the brand as the lead player.

Neo-liberalism criticises modernisation's emphasis on foreign aid, where those identified as developing economies need the help of developed economies to progress (Cammack 2001). This help mainly involves finance aid or borrowing and expertise in the modernism approach to development. However, the financial aid may not be employed where it is most beneficial or may not reach the target recipient due to greed and corruption, leading to inequality and elites maintaining power. Neo-liberalism perceives competition as the defining characteristic of human relations and defines citizens as consumers, whose democratic choices are exercised through market transactions (buying and selling), a process that is supposed to reward merit and punishes inefficiency. Thus, it maintains that the market delivers benefits that could not be achieved by modernism planning.

Dependency Theory Reacts to Modernism and Redefines Economic Development

While modernisation theory states that the development or underdevelopment of a country is a result of the internal conditions that differentiate its economy (resources and capabilities), the dependency theory argues that a country's development is a result of underdevelopment, and that underdevelopment is a result of development. The idea is that countries are classified as underdeveloped because of the existence of the countries that are classified as developed and vice versa. This understanding highlights the competitiveness as the extent of development of an economy cannot only be the result of its internal conditions. Countries' developments are ranked and categorised based on global comparative criteria set by the West which leads the supranational institutions developing these rankings, such as the United Nations, the World Bank and the World Trade Organization. The 2008 financial crisis that started in the US and spilt over to the rest of the global financial market, and the Covid-19 epidemic in 2020 that affected the world health and is leading to a worldwide economic crisis, have proven that the economic development of any country is to a great extent dependent on the economic status of other countries. The economy of any country market is conditioned by the development of and ties with other economies. Hence, the preference of Western global brands in developing economies, as shown in many studies that examined the dynamic between the brand and country-of-origin image.

Ajayi (2015) clarifies that the periphery economics and the internal social and political structure of the developing countries are conditioned by the dominant centres (developed or advanced countries), to reinforce the primary nature of the export community. Accordingly, internal and external structures of the world's economies are connected and form an elaborate pattern of structural underdevelopment. Nations in the 'third world' provide natural resources, cheap labour, a destination for obsolete technology and markets to the wealthy economies with which they would not have the standard of living they desire. This understanding led Ajayi (2015: 8) to conclude that 'the insertion of third world countries into the world economy, during the age of imperialism was centred on economic stagnation in poorer nations', turning them into consumers and a cheap, ill-educated workforce, and global brands into the dream of a better life, such as Nike trainers for a young boy.

The dependency theory, unlike the evolutionary theory, recognises the political and economic ties among countries that would have different consequences for each of these countries and that countries are not self-contained units. The studies of the dependency theory took an integrative approach in an attempt to be holistic and interdisciplinary instead of the divided efforts seen in the evolutionary theory and its interpretations of modernism among economists, political scientists and sociologists (Frank 1969; Amin 1974). This holistic approach enabled the dependency theory to apply historically specific analysis to national development and to recognise the material bases of organised social life (manifested in global brands), and the spread of the capitalist system in the global market. In contrast, the evolutionary theory took an idealistic approach to social change designing an artificial stages model (Parsons 1967).

The economic dependency of peripheral countries on core economies and the influence of multinational corporations (MNCs) became evident in Evans' (1979) work. The level of dependence of a country's economy on other countries' production and markets increases as it ends up providing primary products and cheap labour services for core economies with little added value and limited revenues (the peripheral countries) (Taylor 1992). The MNCs with their global brands obtain most of the surplus value through the control of investments in manufacturing, extracting and the channels of both exportation and the overseas markets. Unstable global economic conditions and the resulting shrinkage of demand in core countries usually hit peripheral countries harder as their economy and employment heavily rely on economic conditions in rich countries.

Free-market economists such as Peter Bauer and Martin Wolf criticised some of the economic policies they assign to the dependency theory, such as subsidising specific national industries to reduce imports, which may in the long term reduce the incentive to compete on quality; and maximising efficiency and innovations, which will not be sustainable. Continuing to support such industries can also reduce public funding to socio-cultural development projects, welfare and development programmes. The detractors cite the Indian economy's improvement as it moved from the state-controlled market to open trade as a contradicting example to the practice of dependency theory. Protectionism is reappearing in today's market in the trade war between the US and China during the Trump administration in the US, and the exit of the UK from the European market after a referendum in 2016. The open-market leaders are mixing and matching policies as the political interests dictate or going full circle leaving the vulnerable, dependent economies of the developing and underdeveloped economies dependent on the global market, free trade and outsourcing.

The dependency theorists' alternative unilinear growth models have aimed to address the unequal relationships between countries due partly to historical colonialism and imperialism (Shah 2019). Empirical evidence, however, is limited on both sides, modernism and the dependency theory, particularly when it comes to a comprehensive national development consideration in the long term. The dependency theories can be abstract and tend, like modernism, to homogenise countries in two categories: developed and underdeveloped. They consider ties with MNCs and global brands as detrimental, although these ties can be important means to transfer technology. They also believe in the need to develop industrial capital and capabilities to produce value when developing the economy rather than depending on consumption and exported knowledge.

The spirit of modernisation theory today is embedded in *neo-modernisation* theorists such as Jeffry Sachs (2005). Like Rostow, Sachs perceives development as gradual progress towards economic and social well-being. However, he argues that there are a billion people below the poverty line – as defined by the World Bank – in the world, who are unable to climb the development ladder because they lack the capital which the Western developed economies enjoy, in terms of health and nutrition, wealth and knowledge. Sachs suggests that since they are trapped in a cycle of deprivation, these people require targeted aid injections from the West to develop. He even calculated the required fund that amounts to 0.7 per cent of gross national product of the 30 or so most developed countries over a few decades. MNCs' ambition for wealth is suggested to be adding to the marginalisation of the world's poorest populations (Heslam 2004) through cheap labour, sweatshops, child labour and encouraging credit-buying behaviour. In an effort to show a sense of social responsibility towards those consumers in poverty, MNCs engage in dispersed projects to offer charity to those contributing to their abundance, such as Procter and Gamble's (P&G) Children's Safe Drinking Water Program offering P&G Purifier of Water packets of powder in 90 countries across the Americas, Africa and Asia (www.csdw.org).

As the dependency theorists argued for a radical reversal of the modernisation approach, underdevelopment is no longer a prehistoric, endogenous natural state of the 'third world', or a result of a historical process of unequal integration into the capitalist world market. Dependency theorists analyse the asymmetrical relations of 'peripheral' economies with 'central' industrialised economies as stemming from the colonial period and especially the course of the nineteenth and twentieth centuries, leading to a phase-accentuated monopoly and transnational capital. The new paradigm had epistemological and political implications opening the economic debates of capitalism to interdisciplinary and (neo-)Marxist horizons, Ruvituso (2020) explains. The dependency approach included in centre-periphery structural analysis stimulated debates regarding the interrelation of external and internal factors of dependency; the ruling classes and the marginality phenomenon; and the internal colonialism and the historical modes of production, that explain the unilateral patterns of brand consumption. Global brands continue to manifest the modernisation approach as they inspire changes in the social fabric and identity of their consumers competing with religious values, such as purity and modesty. Many developing economy consumers continue to look up to global brands and their MNCs dreaming of a modern lifestyle where they can flourish; while the struggle to identify an economic development approach that benefits the nation and other dependent economies continues.

'Western brands are associated with heritage, creativity, originality, and quality,' says Wang Sharay, a senior marketing director working in Beijing (in Liang 2018). Linking to this, it is relevant to note that global iconic brands, in many cases, offer emerging market consumers a new way of life such as the American fast-food legendary brands McDonald's, KFC and Burger King, or a point of view. For example, United Colours of Benetton and Cheerios taking a stand on racial issues, REI opting outside the Black Friday discounts phenomenon by closing their stores that day, Mozilla championing web freedom and user choice, and P&G challenging culturally embedded sexism by encouraging people to rethink the phrase 'like a girl'. These brands also learn from their experiences with other cultures. McDonald's experience in the Indian market and their unwelcome beef burger in a culture where cows are holy creatures taught McDonald's brand management to adopt local tastes and respect local beliefs. In China and Bangladesh, McDonald's is flourishing due to their adaptations; at the same time, they are changing the way these nations eat and their healthy diets. Best Buy, Tesco, eBay, Google, Amazon, Gap, Marks & Spencer (Graham 2019) and Dunkin' Donuts are all Western brands that have either struggled or failed to succeed in the Chinese market. China is a country that many global brands are yet to understand. China is modernising, but is it following a Western modernisation approach or has it developed a different approach to avoid overdependence on advanced Western economies?

MODESTY AND CONSUMPTION IN RELIGIOUS READINGS

Religiosity: A Conceptual Overview

Religiosity is a multidimensional and complex concept. Its definition may vary across religions. Religiosity is used to measure the religious commitment and devoutness of individuals. According to McDaniel and Burnett (1990: 101),

religiosity is 'a belief in God accompanied by a commitment to follow principles believed to be set by God'. Geser (2009), citing other scholars such as
King (1967), offers a more comprehensive definition suggesting that religiosity
is a complex, multidimensional construct that encompasses cognitive values
and beliefs, affective feelings of spirituality and commitment and behaviours
such as prayer and church attendance. Religiosity refers to the extent to which
a person is devoted, committed and adheres to religious values and beliefs; as
a continuous rather than a distinct variable (Beit-Hallahmi and Argyle 1997).
It is not a unidimensional concept (King and Hunt 1972; Abou-Youssef et al.
2015), but rather a multidimensional and complex construct that relates to
several elements of religion which in turn affect how people live their lives
in a number of ways. These elements include beliefs, values and attitudes,
knowledge, experience and practices that affect our daily activities (O'Connell
1975; Abou-Youssef et al. 2015).

People's devoutness to their religion tends to be used to classify their religiosity, taking into consideration the entangled human–religion relationship
and the centrality of religion in human history (Khan et al. 2005). However,
as a complex construct with several variables and a number of impact points,
religiosity is not easy to measure. Several scales have been developed over the
years, the majority of which measured Christian religiosity. The scales that
measure religiosity are mostly either measuring practices and beliefs such as
Taai's scale (1985) or intrinsic and extrinsic motivated religious orientation as
per Albehairi and Demerdash's scale (1988). While practices and beliefs are
self-explanatory, extrinsic and intrinsic motivated religious orientation can be
more complicated. Extrinsic religiosity is suggested not to involve spirituality
or beliefs (Vitell et al. 2005). Still, it is concerned with how social networks
perceive someone's religion, where practices are a means to an end, as they
are meant to conform to the accepted practices and way of life and enhance
the person's sense of belonging, acceptance and social status (Abou-Youssef
et al. 2015).

In some cases, one may argue that extrinsic religiosity may also be a way
to distinguish the self from its surroundings and keep a sense of identity such
as wearing a religious symbol in a foreign country or in a workplace where
the person is a minority. Intrinsic religiosity, on the other hand, is motivated
by internalised beliefs where people tend to develop a way of life matching
those beliefs (Khan et al. 2015). It is spiritual, and the practices, whether in
daily life or religious rituals, are an end goal rather than a means to an end.
Khan et al. (2015) infer that intrinsic religiosity has more impact on behaviour
than extrinsic religiosity. The scales measuring religiosity can differ in detail
from one study to another and from one religion to another. Measuring Islamic
religiosity in research, which is relatively new in comparison with Christian
religiosity measures, for example, shows that an effective reflection of the

Islamic conceptualisation of religiosity according to the understanding of Muslims requires relatively different measurement scales (Krauss et al. 2005).

Religion and Consumer Behaviour

Consumer decisions are influenced by many factors, some of which could be categorised as personal and socio-cultural (Gbadamosi 2016). Religion is a component of culture that influences people's lives and consumption decisions (McCullough and Willoughby 2009), particularly important decisions such as marriage or engagement in extramarital affairs.

Rich religious narratives help us to understand people, organisations, societies and the involvement of material objects, including what the marketplace provides (Muniz and Schau 2005). Organisational decisions can also be affected by religiosity, such as the level of engagement in financial risk (Hilary and Hui 2009). For example, Islamic banks have proved to take fewer risks than conventional banks. As a result, the spillover from Western markets, e.g. the US to the rest of the world during the 2008 financial crisis, has less impact on Islamic banks (Tabash and Dhankar 2014; Zehri et al. 2012; Hasan and Dridi 2010).

Engelland (2014) states that religion is considered a predecessor to culture where individuals with different religious beliefs based on their religion exhibit differing levels of Hofstede's (2003) cultural dimensions, whether speaking of individualism, power distance, uncertainty avoidance or masculinity. For example, Jost et al. (2003) and Schwartz and Huismans (1995) suggest that religiosity is positively associated with the desire to preserve tradition and to protect against uncertainty and is negatively associated with openness to new experiences. Risk aversion is considered an attribute associated with religiosity, whether it is manifested in fastening seat belts or increasing financial savings as ways to reduce risk (Khan et al. 2013). Meanwhile, not fastening seat belts has been a major factor in devastating car accidents in Saudi Arabia (Mansuri et al. 2015) which is considered a conservative Islamic community. The extent to which these dimensions are embedded in individuals' beliefs and attitudes may differ due to differences not only in religion but also in personal characteristics, other cultural factors and background and the surroundings at the time. These dimensions, in turn, have been proven to influence behaviours, whether in terms of ethical behaviour (Schrader 2007) or consumption behaviour (Abou-Youssef et al. 2015). It is recommended, therefore, not to expect a unified understanding of religion as well as its impact on individuals' behaviours. Jafari and Sandıkcı (2015) emphasised the need to understand identity dynamics while examining the complex relationships between the religion of Islam and consumption.

El-Bassiouny (2014) suggests that committed believers in Islam would want all business and marketing practices to adhere to their religious values and beliefs. This understanding indicates that a committed Muslim's life is inspired by religious values, including their engagement with markets and marketing practices (Jafari and Sandıkcı 2015). The increased global mobility among tourists, businesses, migrants and refugees with an identity to reserve and integration to achieve in the new market is a difficult balance to achieve. The balance between the two would determine their cultural reflexivity (Beck 2011) and attempts to influence the internal and external policies of the new destination (Akhter 2007). Such a balance can lead to engagement in the local culture and in time may develop into a modified identity, especially across generations. An example is the differences between the engagement of the majority of British-born and educated Pakistani Muslim descendants and their parents in British life. The cultural engagement of Muslims, for example, includes their consumption of products and services that fulfil their needs from Apple's smart mobile phones (iPhone) to KFC's halal chicken in areas where Muslim density is high in a multicultural city like London. However, in developing economies and modernised cities like Dubai, Western expatriate culture is prevailing as mixed-gender schools, universities, working and socialising places are the majority and bars that serve alcohol are spreading. Western culture of the global brands and the way of life it offers to these expatriates are modifying the developing country's city culture and challenging its religious values which, for example, prohibit alcohol drinking and revealing clothes, such as bikinis.

GLOBAL BRAND CONSUMPTIONS AND MODESTY IN DEVELOPING ECONOMIES

Islamic consumption practice theory is based on two concepts: (1) income defines spending ability (Quran, Al-Talaq: 7) which reduces the tendency to borrow money; and (2) economic consumption, which involves: (a) preventing the consumption of harmful products and services; (b) preventing extravagant luxury and waste (Quran, Al-Esra': 16 and 26–7; and Al-Waqeah: 41–5; and (c) encouraging reasonable and wise spending (Quran, Al-Furqan: 67; Al-Esra': 29; Al-A'araf: 32; Al-Talaq: 7). These economic and consumption concepts are embedded in the meaning of modesty in Islam. Quran does not mention 'modesty' directly. The Quran refers to its broader meaning in the Arabic language (*Zouhd*), which promotes spirituality over materialistic possessions, calls for self-discipline to pursue knowledge and work to high standards reaching 'Ehsan', as well as encourages investing incomes over spending and saving. The concept behind these encouraging behaviours is that money and wealth are a gift from God entrusted to us to utilise and invest in a way that spread its benefits. Modesty in Islam is not just about behaviours, but also attitudes and characteristics.

Similarly, modesty in *Christianity*, in its broad sense, represents a mode of moral conduct that is related to humility (Statman 1992). A person who behaves modestly refrains from extroverted behaviour that is supposed to speak of him or herself. The expansive view of modesty in Christianity as it is in Islam is about attitude and behaviour, e.g. 'to walk modestly with your God' (Micah 6: 8), which is understood as humbleness and self-discipline in their search for wisdom. In *Buddhism*, modesty is about proper conduct, that is guarding the three 'doors' to the self – body, speech and mind – so unwholesome actions are not committed through any of them (Bommarito 2018).

Modesty is also fundamental in *Judaism*. There is common thinking that it applies primarily to women, and it is a desirable quality in men, but actually it is for all (Arthur 1999). In the West, Muslims' dress code has been described as modest. This is not a term used in the Quran or known to be used in the Prophet's teachings (*Hadeeth*). It is a view based on sexual modesty; whereas modesty in its wider meaning is a requirement for both men and women in Islam. The Bible, as well, contains only two expressions related to modesty, neither of which is expressly connected with sexual modesty (Arthur 1999; Morin 2013).

Being modestly dressed is not what modesty is about in these religions. The way modest clothing is trending in the marketplace, on social media and in mass media, dressing modestly is becoming more of a lifestyle and fashion statement, which is reflected in segmenting and targeting fashion consumers in the high street and even by a few of the haute couture. The hijab, for example, became one of the product lines at Nike as well as Dolce Gabbana (www .dolcegabbana.com cited in www.theatlantic.com/entertainment/archive/2016/ 01/dolce-gabbana-high-fashion/423171/) and widely marketed in developing countries with Muslim majorities such as the countries in the Arabian Gulf. Haute Hijab is a specialist brand that offers different styles of hijab. One of their styles is called *The Modern* in a product line titled *Better Days Ahead*, which suggests a change in how the hijab is worn, which in turn can influence why it is worn (www.hautehijab.com).

In two photos by Binniam Eskender and Iman Melo of hijabs designed by Iman Aldebe in Fairobserver (www.fairobserver.com/region/europe/the-rise -of-islamic-chic-and-hijab-haute-couture-31097/), the hijab is presented in a way that is far from modest. For example, one of the photos shows naked shoulders with artistic tattoos and a headscarf that covers the hair more like a hat and leaves the neck and shoulders exposed. These artistic promoting photos transform the headscarf into a fashion and sensual statement of modern life. Religion in what is described as modern society is moving from collectivist shared religious values and practices to individualistic intrinsic beliefs.

Expectations of daily collective manifestations and symbols of religion are discouraged. Progress in modern society elicits this change at various levels of assertiveness, including the consumption of brands and global brands in particular. The fashion industry and media are focused on creating a multi-ethnic and supra-national consumer demographic defined by modest religious identity and cultures (Lewis 2019). However, modest clothing that is worn by Muslims and non-Muslims alike is merging in modern fashion trends, as shown in the marketing communication examples above, whether by the look of the model or the artistic design of the presented lifestyle.

Another example of the modern economy is the rise of online dating, which is penetrating religious communities such as Muslims. It promises them equal opportunities to find love and future spouses online through a few filtering questions based on religiosity in the personality questionnaire subscribers complete when joining sites such as eHarmony. Other specialised online sites designed for Muslims looking for a potential spouse are encouraging self-promotion, pride and sharing personal traits and private feelings with hundreds of thousands of strangers online. These characteristics contradict the broader meaning of modesty in Islam which appreciates privacy, humility and bashfulness, and which appreciates all without imposing onto their private life and feelings (Rochadiat et al. 2018). An example of this is discussed below from Hawaya from Egypt, a developing economy of Muslim majority. Rochadiat et al.'s (2018) qualitative research of online dating and Muslim women in the US exposed various tensions surfacing between religious values and current practices online (Abdel-Fadil 2015). These findings contradict the stigma associated with online dating reported in quantitative research that suggested the normative use of online dating among Muslim immigrants due to practicality and flexibility driven by pragmatic religious and cultural norms (Bunt 2009; Lo and Aziz 2009; Hammer 2015). Research has not yet examined this phenomenon closely, particularly in developing countries, and the examples below suggest a need for further research to understand the dynamic between religious values, social identity and online brand communications and consumption including dating.

Dating is a modern phenomenon which may not be complying with the values of religious Muslims where love and marriage are entwined and experienced in social contexts with community blessing. The modern economy brand agents are weakening the connections of traditional communities and dislocating many in favour of new online and professional connections. Modern lifestyles which are developed around careers and lengthy working hours reduce traditional communities' connections and offer different priorities in life. This new lifestyle made meeting potential spouses harder for committed Christians and Muslims, particularly as places of worship are unable to compete for their time. Consumers are developing self-concepts that value individualism and have an ideal self represented in the global heroes of modern society such as Bill Gates (co-founder of Microsoft), Steve Jobs (late chief executive officer (CEO) of Apple), Mark Zuckerberg (CEO of Facebook), Jeff Bezos (CEO of Amazon), Lynne Doughtie (CEO of KPMG) and Cathy Engelbert (CEO of Deloitte), or modern celebrities. Whether they are business-oriented or cultural or environmental activists the modern generations in the so-called developing economies are forming new types of connections that enable them to achieve a modern lifestyle where online dating is a norm and marriage as a religious commitment is less popular. Cultures, values and beliefs differ around the world. Thus, the idea of 'one size fits all' that global brand trends promote while penetrating new markets for growth is distracting and can be disturbing to societies and have serious consequences.

The religion- or culture-specific dating and marriage sites or apps are an illustration of the socio-cultural battle with modernism as it reshapes the social identity in developing countries. Brands such as Harmonica, the Egyptian matchmaking app that was acquired in 2019 by Match Group, the company behind dating apps such as Tinder, Match and Meetic, is now called Hawaya (in reference to love in Arabic), Arabian Date (a global dating app for Arabs) and Muzmatch (a Mulsim-specific marriage site) are major players in this field, aiming to solve a problem that emerged with the modernised economy to further modernise society.

The Covid-19 pandemic led to a dramatic increase in online shopping in 2020, as it forced millions of shoppers to stay at home to stop the spread of the virus. Consumers had to turn to the internet to procure everyday items such as groceries (fruit, vegetables, milk and cheese) or toilet paper and they were more focused on the availability of an item than on a particular brand. As a result, retail platforms enjoyed a 6 per cent global traffic increase between January and March 2020 as retail sites generated 14.34 billion visits in March alone, up from 12.81 billion worldwide visits in January (Statistica.com, March 2020). The lockdown that followed from March 2020 led consumers to attempt to buy more and more of their daily essential products online. This necessity, coupled with more time spent at home, led to unusual buying behaviours, some of which market research recognised earlier. E-commerce statistics from 2017, for example, show that 43 per cent of online shoppers have reported making purchases while in bed, and 20 per cent from the bathroom or while in the car (Osman 2020). So, would a limited time discount from a favourable brand communicated in a text at night with a link to the brand's online store prompt psychological buying? Are there brand-buying behaviours that lead to overspending?

Think with Google research (2014) suggests that 48 per cent of online shoppers worldwide overspent or bought something unplanned while shopping online. Eighty-five per cent of customers start a purchase on one device and finish it on another, at another time. The timing of the purchase is important as some of the behaviours that increase spending online are combining shopping with alcohol consumption. Ten per cent of customers reported that they made a purchase while drunk. Gender is a significant variable here as 14 per cent of male buyers reported buying drunk in comparison with 6 per cent of female buyers (Osman 2020).

Spending online is growing around the world, as internet access increases. The World Bank reports that the percentage of individuals using the internet in Saudi Arabia, for example, was 93.3 per cent in 2018, an increase from 64.7 per cent in 2014 (Market Line 2020). Using mobile devices for online shopping became a growing trend, which made online purchases more accessible and convenient in developing economies. Saudi Arabia had a smartphone penetration of 46.0 per cent (Newzoo 2018). The increased availability of mobile internet and m-commerce platforms is enabling the rise of online retail value in developing countries. Amazon, the global online retail brand, expanded into many developing countries, including the Middle East, benefiting from this accessibility. By 2017, 58 per cent of online shopping in the Middle East was from international vendors (Go-Gulf 2017) such as Amazon. Forty-two per cent of jewellery and watch purchases, 48 per cent of health and beauty purchases and 44 per cent of electronics and computers bought in the Middle East moved online (Go-Gulf 2017).

The Saudi Arabian online retail sector has experienced double-digit growth. The industry generated total revenues of $1.8 billion in 2018, with an annual growth rate of 25 per cent between 2014 and 2018. In comparison, the Emirati and Israeli online retail sectors grew by 13.8 and 17.9 per cent, respectively, over the same period, to reach respective values of $1.7 billion and $2.0 billion in 2018 (Market Line 2020). Online retailers are benefiting from the wide reach of internet access and the convenience of mobile devices to enhance their mobile optimised websites and shopping applications as they simplify and speed up the process. Hence, consumers have fewer opportunities to reconsider a buying decision. One-click purchase features and personalised home pages and filters are examples of features that simplify the buying process and make it more enjoyable. The one-click purchase also makes it easier for a consumer to buy something by mistake.

In 2018 the electrical and electronics retail segment was the sector's most lucrative in Saudi, with total revenues of $688.2 million, equivalent to 39.2 per cent of the sector's overall value, and 24.2 per cent of the apparel sector ($424.5 million) was also sold online (Market Line 2020). The ease of buying online and the increased access and convenience accompanied with spending more time at home alone, such as the elderly and children, suggest a rich soil for continuous growth in online shopping trends where overspending can be an easy mistake to make, particularly when buying with credit. The risk of overconsumption and overspending is higher among vulnerable consumers, particularly when it comes to online and mobile games. Examining the examples of the Souq, an Amazon leading online retailer in Saudi Arabia with online displays exhibiting a range of global brands sold online in the Saudi market, brings the modern lifestyle of the West to shoppers at home offering entertainment as much as convenience. Western models dominate the site, and there is no evidence of cultural customisation, for example, the site offers female shoppers over 1,000 bikinis in comparison with few dresses. The site www.amazon.sa (accessed on 14 July 2020), which used to be www.Saudi .souq.com (accessed on 2 June 2020), highlights luxury accessories. Watches, sunglasses and bags each have their own category. There is also a wide range of prices and offers, as is the case with Amazon, that can serve and penetrate a wide range of market segments, encouraging possessions and materialism (Amin 1977).

Food home delivery is another sector flourishing online around the world and in developing economies such as Saudi Arabia and the Middle East, China, India and Brazil. Food delivery market research shows that China is first in the world in 2020 with predicted revenue at US$51,514 million, while the US is second (US$26,527 million), India is third (US$10,196 million) and Brazil is fifth (US$3,300 million) after the UK (US$5,988 million). Saudi Arabia is ranked 15th with a market value of US$1,556 million (Statistica.com 2020). The average customer consumption in each of these countries depends on the market size out of the size of the population. With online food delivery consumers, 40.9 per cent are low-income customers followed by medium-income customers at 33.7 per cent (Statistica.com 2020), which is a concerning observation as most of the consumers are between 25 and 44 years of age. This is, however, an age of productivity, and convenience tends to be appreciated more by busy professionals. Still, it is not expected that those with the lowest income and a family to feed to resort to ready meals. This is not usually the most cost-effective option for low-income families and can lead to overspending in a vulnerable segment of the market. It is also a significant change in culture from home cooking to home delivery. There is a wide range of online food delivery platforms in addition to restaurant home delivery in Saudi, but the Delivery Hero dominates over 65 per cent of the market. In comparison, the second player is Dominos, with only a 10 per cent market share, and Uber Eat is 5 per cent, while the rest is shared among a number of providers (Statistica. com 2020). It is clear that the market is dominated by MNC brands and almost monopolised by Delivery Hero, the German-based MNC.

The expected worldwide growth rate of online food delivery is 9.8 per cent (Statistica.com 2020), and eMarketer predicts that worldwide business-to-consumer e-commerce sales will increase by 20.1 per cent. With such rapid and significant growth comes responsibility. The higher the buying temptation that online retailers create, the bigger is their responsibility to enable shoppers to shop wisely – within their socio-cultural parameters – and securely. A responsible approach to global brand experience online, including communication and content, shopping and consumption promises a sustainable future to all – the brands, the retailer and their global consumers. Overconsumption such as overeating or poor diet is a social responsibility that global brands and retailers need to consider. Overspending is the exception and not the norm and online retailing provides a great service to communities, as the Covid-19 pandemic has shown. They will continue to grow and develop, and it is essential to reconsider the role they play across the world as global retail brands and the platform that brings other global brands to homes around the world. Separating modern styles of consumption from perceived development in knowledge, infrastructure, higher added-value manufacturing and economy can enhance national development. Strengthening the competitiveness of national brands may require rethinking legislation to reduce market dependency and increase choice in the emergent market.

The Balancing Act of Brand–Consumer Interaction

Country-of-origin image research shows a strong preference in developing countries for international and global brands, and in particular Western brands (e.g. Kleppe et al. 2002; Saffu and Scott 2009; Al-Abdulrazak 2020). The superiority perceived in global brands stimulates a strong desire to self-identify with many of these brands. Hence, iconic global brands offering a new lifestyle become activists of culture change in developing economies. This is evident in the rapid cultural change seen in many developing countries across all continents including the Arabian Gulf, namely the United Arab Emirates and recently Saudi Arabia. The experiential consumption of the FIBA 3x3 Basketball World Tour, the Spanish Super Cup in Saudi and Formula One in Bahrain encouraged the consumption of other global and iconic brands associated with the lifestyle and dress code of such experiences, e.g. Nike, TISSOT, Wilson, Mercedes and Ferrari. In a comparative study of luxury brand consumption in Russia and Romania, whether buying luxury brands to demonstrate status and welfare (social identity) or as a treat for working hard (self-concept), as most Russian respondents stated, or to enjoy perfection, high quality and attention to detail (self-concept) as Romanian respondents reported, both countries show a global brand preference over national brands (Ochkovskaya 2015).

International and global brands – which reflect modernisation as a symbol of the developed economy – encourage some consumption behaviours that can take consumers away from modesty in its broader religious meaning. They challenge the national cultural values and beliefs such as humility, generosity, purity and mindfulness. The promoted practices of credit spending that can easily lead to overspending, a competitive drive to possess for self-identification and social identity change can stimulate pride and greed and reduce gratitude and sharing values in society. The conversation among modernism, postmodernism and dependency theorists can inform a balancing act in the interaction between global brands as agents of modernisation and consumers in developing economies. Figure 5.1 is an attempt to illustrate the interaction between a global brand and consumers in a developing economy and the balancing act that different readings and practices with economic development (dependency theory and postmodernism) can play. The imbalance of power between the brand and the developing economy is illustrated in the size of the power-of-influence arrow travelling from the brand to the emerging market consumers and vice versa. The self-identification of consumers with the global brand forms and reforms the values and cultures of these individuals and societies, as seen with modesty as a religious value in the examples discussed above. Understanding this interaction can be beneficial in balancing the influences of the interacting powers and in helping national brands compete with global brands.

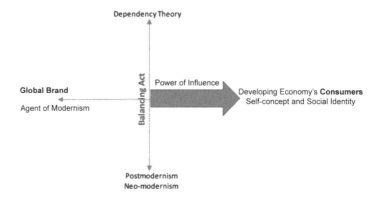

*Figure 5.1   The balancing act of a global brand and consumer
                interaction in developing economies*

CONCLUSION

Global brands, such as Facebook, Amazon, Apple, Microsoft, Samsung, Chanel, Coca Cola, Disney and McDonald's (some of the top 100 brands ranked by Inter Brand (2019) based on their financial value and dominated in the top 10 by American brands), are reshaping not just the consumption of the developing economy nations, but also their lives. As these brands change how people live and work, they become agents of change. The revolutionary root to modernisation as recommended by the evolutionary theory was enabled by the iconic global brands of social media in what was called in Western media, the 'Arab Spring' (an uprising in Middle Eastern countries in 2011, with its conflicts continuing until today in 2020). Facebook, Twitter and other global social media platforms played a significant role in the fuelling of the movement that ended up bloody and disappointing, to say the least. Many countries lost political and economic stability, bleeding their wealth and offering human sacrifices in wars that had no winners, apart from businesses that profit from wars and that can be described as ghost colonisers. Such extreme cases make the agency role of global brands based on the modernisation theory evident.

Consumers' identification with global brands contributes to their self-concept through the ideal self and the social self (Gonzalez-Jimenez 2017). Global brands' ethnocentric strategies and culture play a great part in the social identity of many of their consumers, from social categorisation and identification to belonging to specific groups and comparisons with other groups of society. Nike can represent the dream of a better life, a modern life, to a starving child somewhere because his favourite African athlete – who he watches on the only television in the village – wears Nike. The self-identification of a child with Nike, and the social identification of Saudis with McDonald's and Coca-Cola, Abu Dhabi and the Emiratis with the Louvre and Parisians with Disney form and reform the values and cultures of these individuals and societies. Religiosity as a major element of the self-concept and social identity of believers and non-believers alike (Agarwala et al. 2018) can influence and be influenced by consumers' identification with these global brands. Understanding this interaction can be beneficial in balancing the influences of the interacting powers and in helping national brands compete with global brands. Would a multidomestic approach to a global brand help balance the power of influence in the interaction with international consumers? Empirical research in brand as an agent of modernisation and the role of religiosity in consumers' identification with global brands would have its applications in understanding consumer choices and brand preferences, brand loyalty and self-concept, segmentation, targeting and positioning. Further exploration with the enquiry of global brands as agents of modernisation and the potential cultural conflict including religiosity would enhance our theoretical understanding of the brand phenomenon and the scope of its social and economic contribution as an agent of change.

The responsibility of global brands as modernisation agents that can be used for good or evil, such as online bullying and the abuse on some of our favourite social media platforms, and the goodwill consumers put in these brands not to misuse their data and to keep them secured, is gigantic and can be above these businesses' capabilities. Some shareholders can also see it as a conflict of interest between profit and social responsibility. Dominating global brands reduce the competitiveness of developing markets. They gain tremendous bargaining power due to their resources which can be intimidating to national brands and national authorities alike. The market penetration of national brands becomes harder, which leads to limited market options and reduces consumers' democratic choice to select a service or product provider. Consumers live to a global brand's promise, and the dream of being part of modern life is what may limit these consumers' choices and national brands' opportunities. Also, brands as agents of modernisation tend in many cases to conflict with consumers' identity traits and socio-cultural values as with religiosity and religious values such as modesty. These conflicts can have a dramatic impact on brand choices and consumer self-concept, social belonging and connections. Trendy hijab, online shopping, online dating and gambling are online-aided brand consumption platforms. Their accessibility on mobile devices associated with modern entertainment images under global iconic brands can prove challenging to consumers and contradict with their beliefs, or can lead to overspending which may, in turn, cause social conflict. The postmodern conundrum suggests that the world is a very complicated place and that there are a number of ways to interpret it. Therefore, no one solution is preferable to any other, so solutions are imposed by power (Peterson 2018) and, in this case, the power is in the hands of the global brands.

REFERENCES

Aaker, D.A. (1996) Measuring brand equity across products and markets, *California Management Review*, 38, 102–20.

Aaker, D.A. (2002) *Building Strong Brands*, London: Simon and Schuster.

Abdel-Fadil, M. (2015) Counseling Muslim selves on Islamic websites: Walking a tightrope between secular and religious counseling ideals? *Journal of Religion, Media and Digital Culture*, 4(1), 1–38. Available at: www.jrmdc.com/journal/issue/view/8.

Abid, M. (2004) Political modernisation: The concept, contours and dynamics, *Indian Journal of Political Science*, 65(4), 590–602.

Abou-Youssef, M.M.H., Kortam, W., Abou-Aish, E. and El-Bassiouny , N. (2015) Effects of religiosity on consumer attitudes toward Islamic banking in Egypt, *International Journal of Bank Marketing*, 33(6), 786–807.

Agarwala, R., Mishra, P. and Singh, R. (2018) Religiosity and consumer behaviour: A summarising review, *Journal of Management, Spirituality and Religion*, 16(1), 32–54.

Ajayi, A.K. (2015) *Dependency Theory and the Third World*, Ogbooro: Banselian Book Services.

Akhter, S.H. (2007) Globalisation, expectations model of economic nationalism, and consumer behaviour, *Journal of Consumer Marketing*, 24(3), 142–50.

Al-Abdulrazak, R.M. (2016) *The Branded Nation: A Comparative Analysis with Reference to Syria and the United Arab Emirates*, Thesis, Royal Holloway, University of London.

Al-Abdulrazak, R.M. (2020) SMEs market growth, in S. Nwankwo and A. Gbadamosi (eds), *Entrepreneurship Marketing: Principles and Practice,* London: Routledge.

Albehairi, A. and Demerdash, A. (1988) *Religious Orientation Scale*, 2nd ed., Cairo, Egyptian Renascence.

American Marketing Association (n.d.) *Definition of Marketing*. Available at: www .ama.org/the-definition-of-marketing-what-is-marketing/ (accessed 24 November 2019).

Amin, S. (1974) *Accumulation on a World Scale: A Critique of the Theory of Underdevelopment*, translated by Brian Pearce, 2 vols. New York: Monthly Review Press.

Amin, S. (1977) *The Law of Value and Historical Materialism*. London: Harvester.

Aronczyk, M. and Powers, D. (eds) (2010) *Blowing Up the Brand: Critical Perspectives on Promotional Culture*, Bern: Peter Lang Publishing.

Arthur, L. (ed.) (1999) *Religion, Dress and the Body*. Oxford: Berg.

Avruch, K. (1998) *Culture and Conflict Resolution*. Washington, DC: United States Institute of Peace Press.

Bagaeen, S. (2007) Brand Dubai: The instant city; or the instantly recognisable city, *International Planning Studies*, 12(2), 173–97.

Basar, S. (2006) Dubai: Self-help for those wanting to build a 21st century city, *Static*, 4. Available at: http://static.londonconsortium.com/issue04/basar_selfhelp .php (accessed 22 October 2014).

Beck, U. (2011) Cosmopolitanism as imagined communities of global risk, *American Behavioural Scientist*, 55(10), 1346–61.

Beit-Hallahmi, B. and Argyle, M. (1997) *The Psychology of Religious Behaviour, Belief and Experience*, London: Routledge.

Beverland, M. (2018) *Brand Management: Co-Creating Meaningful Brands*, London: Sage.

Bob, C. (2002) The merchants of morality, *Foreign Policy*, 129(March–April), 36–45.

Bob, C. (2005) *The Marketing of Rebellion: Insurgent, Media and International Activism*, Cambridge: Cambridge University Press.

Bommarito, N. (2018) Modesty and humility, *Stanford Encyclopedia of Philosophy* (Winter), Edward N. Zalta (ed.). Available at: https://plato.stanford.edu/archives/ win2018/entries/modesty-humility/ (accessed 25 May 2020).

Borgerson, J.L. and Schroeder, J.E. (2002) Ethical issues of global marketing: Avoiding bad faith in visual representation, *European Journal of Marketing*, 36(5/6), 570–94.

Brakus, J.J., Bernd, H.S. and Lia, Z. (2009) Brand experience: What is it? How is it measured? Does it affect loyalty? *Journal of Marketing*, 73(3), 52–68.

Brown, S. (2016) *Brands and Branding*, London: Sage.

Bunt, G.R. (2009) *iMuslims: Rewiring the House of Islam*, Chapel Hill, NC: University of North Carolina Press.

Cammack, P. (2001) Neoliberalism, the World Bank and the new politics of development. In U. Kothari and M. Minogue (eds), *Development Theory and Practice: Critical Perspectives*, London: Palgrave, 157–78.

Coleman, J. (1968) Modernisation, *International Encyclopedia of the Social Sciences*, 10. New York: Free Press.

De Chernatony, L. (1999) Brand management through narrowing the gap between brand identity and brand reputation, *Journal of Marketing Management*, 15(1/3), 157–80.

De Chernatony, L. (2009) Towards the holy grail of defining 'brand', *Marketing Theory*, 9(1), 101–5.

El-Bassiouny, N. (2014) The one-billion-plus marginalisation: Toward a scholarly understanding of Islamic consumers, *Journal of Business Research*, 67(2), 42–9.

Engelland, B.T. (2014) Religion, humanism, marketing, and the consumerism of socially responsible products, services and ideas, *Journal of Business Research*, 67(2), 1–6.

Evans, P. (1979) *Dependent Development, The Alliance of Multinational, State and Local Capital in Brazil*, Princeton, NJ: Princeton University Press.

Ferraris, M. and Segre, A.T. (1988) Postmodernism and the deconstruction of modernism, *Design Issues*, 4(1/2), 12–24.

Ferraro, V. (2008) Dependency theory: An introduction, in S. Giorgio (ed.), *The Development Economics Reader*. London: Routledge, pp. 58–64.

Firat, A.F. and Venkatesh, A. (1992) The making of postmodern consumption, in R. Belk and N. Dholakia (eds), *Consumption and Marketing: Macro Dimensions*, Boston, MA: PWS-Kent Publishing.

Frank, A.G. (1969) The sociology of development and the underdevelopment of sociology, *Catalyst*, 3, 20–73.

Gbadamosi, A. (2016) Consumer behaviour in developing nations: A conceptual overview, in A. Gbadamosi (ed.), *Handbook of Research on Consumerism and Buying Behaviour in Developing Nations*, Hershey: IGI Global, pp. 1–29.

Geser, H. (2009) Work values and Christian religiosity, *Journal of Religion and Society*, 11, 1–36.

Girma, M. (2018) Religion, politics and the dilemma of modernising Ethiopia, *HIT Teologiese Studies/Theological Studies*, 74(1), 1–9.

Go-Gulf (2017) *Middle East Shoppers Online Shopping Behaviour – Statistics and Trends*, 7 October. Available at: www.go-gulf.com (accessed 2 June 2020).

Gonzalez-Jimenez, H. (2017) The self-concept life cycle and brand perceptions: An interdisciplinary perspective. *AMS Review*, 7, 67–84.

Graham, L. (2019) China is proving a tough market for western brands – here's the common mistakes that companies keep making, *CityAM.com*. Available at: www.cityam.com/china-proving-tough-market-western-brands-heres-common/ (accessed 27 May 2020).

Hammer, J. (2015) Marriage in American Muslim communities, *Religion Compass*, 9, 35–44.

Hasan, M. and Dridi, J. (2010) The effects of the global crisis on Islamic and conventional banks: A comparative study, International Monetary Fund, Working Paper, Monetary and Capital Markets Department and Middle East and Central Asia Department, September.

Heslam, P.S. (2004) *Globalisation and the Good*, Grand Rapids, MI: William B. Eerdmans Publishing.

Hilary, G. and Hui, K.W. (2009) Does religion matter in corporate decision making in America? *Journal of Financial Economic*, 93(3), 455–73.

Hofstede, G. (2003) *Culture's Consequences: Comparing Values, Behaviours, Institutions and Organisations across Nations*, 2nd ed., Thousand Oaks, CA: Sage.

Hollensen, S. (ed.) (2017) *Global Marketing*, 7th ed., Harlow: Pearson Education.

Holt, D.B. (2003) What becomes an icon most? *Harvard Business Review*, 81(3), 43–9.

Holt, D.B. (2004) *How Brands Become Icons: The Principles of Cultural Branding*, Boston, MA: Harvard Business School Press.

Holt, D.B. (2006) Toward a sociology of branding, *Journal of Consumer Culture*, 6, 299–302.

Ind, N. (1997) *The Corporate Brand*, New York: New York University Press.

Inter Brand (2019) Best Global Brands 2019 Rankings. Available at: www.interbrand .com/best-brands/best-global-brands/2019/ranking/ (accessed 6 June 2020).

Jafari, A. and Sandıkcı, Ö. (2015) Islamic consumers, markets, and marketing: A critique of El-Bassiouny's (2014) The one-billion-plus marginalisation, *Journal of Business Research*, 68(12), 2676–82.

Jost, J.T., Glaser, J., Kruglanski, A.W. and Sulloway, F.J. (2003) Political conservatism as motivated social cognition, *Psychological Bulletin*, 129(3), 339–75.

Keller, K.L., Apéria, T. and Georgson, M. (2012) *Strategic Brand Management: A European Perspective*, 2nd ed., Harlow: Pearson Education.

Khan, R., Misra, K. and Singh, V. (2013) Ideology and brand consumption, *Psychological Science*, 24(3), 326–33.

Khan, Z.H., Watson, P.J. and Habib, F. (2005) Muslim attitudes toward religion, religious orientation and empathy among Pakistanis, *Mental Health, Religion and Culture*, 8, 49–61.

Khan, Z.H., Watson, P.J., Naqvi, A.Z., Jahan, K. and Chen, Z.J. (2015) Muslim experiential religiousness in Pakistan: Meaning in life, general well-being and gender differences, *Mental Health, Religion and Culture*, 18(6), 482–91.

Kim, S.H. (2002) Rapid modernisation and the future of Korean Christianity, *Religion*, 32, 27–37.

King, M. (1967) Measuring the religious variable: Nine proposed dimensions, *Journal for the Scientific Study of Religion*, 6(Fall), 173–90.

King, M. and Hunt, R. (1972) Measuring the religious variable: Replication, *Journal of the Scientific Study of Religion*, 11, 240–51.

Klein, N. (1999) *No Logo*, London: Fourth Estate/Harper Collins.

Kleppe, I.A. Iversen, N.M. and Stensaker, I.G. (2002) Country images in marketing strategies: Conceptual issues and an empirical Asian illustration, *Brand Management*, 10(1), 61–74.

Krauss, S., Hamzah, A., Juhari, R. and Abd Hamid, J. (2005) The Muslim religiosity personality inventory (MRPI): Towards understanding differences in the Islamic religiosity among the Malaysian youth, *Pertanika Journal of Social Sciences and Humanities*, 13(2), 173–86.

Levy, M.J., Jr. (1953) Contrasting factors in the modernisation of China and Japan. *Economic Development and Cultural Change*, 2(3), 161–97.

Levy, M.J., Jr. (1966) *Modernisation and the Structure of Societies*, Princeton, NJ: Princeton University Press.

Lewis, R. (2019) Modest body politics: The commercial and ideological intersect of fat, Black, and Muslim in the modest fashion market and media, *Fashion Theory*, 23(2), 243–73.

Liang, L.-H. (2018) *What Innate Advantages Do Western Brands Have in China – Part I*, Nanjing Marketing Group, 8 August. Available at: www.nanjingmarketinggroup .com/blog/innate-advantages-western-brands-have-in-china-part-1 (accessed 22 March 2019).

Lo, M. and Aziz, T. (2009) Muslim marriage goes online: The use of Internet matchmaking by American Muslims, *Journal of Religion and Popular Culture*, 21(3), 1–20.

Mansuri, F.A., Al-Zalabani, A.H., Zalat, M.M. and Qabshawi, R.I. (2015) Road safety and road traffic accidents in Saudi Arabia, *Saudi Medical Journal*. Available at: http://www.ncbi.nlm.nih.gov/pmc/articles/PMC4404474/ (accessed 10 December 2015).

Market Line (2020) *Industry Profile, Online Retail in Saudi Arabia*. Available at: www.Marketline.com, February.

Mathras, D., Cohen, A.B., Mandel, N. and Mick, D.G. (2015) The effects of religion on consumer behaviour: A conceptual framework and research agenda, *Journal of Consumer Psychology*. Available at: http://dx.doi.org/10.1016/j.jcps.2015.08.001

McCullough, M.E. and Willoughby, B.L.B. (2009) Religion, self-regulation, self-control: Associations, explanations, and implications, *Psychological Bulletin*, 135(1), 69–93.

McDaniel, S.W. and Burnett, J.J. (1990) Consumer religiosity and retail store evaluative criteria, *Journal of the Academy of Marketing Science*, 18, 101–12.

Menhas, R., Umer, S., Akhtar, S. and Shabbir, G. (2015) Impact of modernisation on religious institution: A case study of Khyber Pakhtun Khwa, Pakistan, *European Review of Applied Sociology*, 8(10), 23–8.

Morin, K.M. (2013) Men's modesty, religion, and the state: Spaces of collision. *Men and Masculinities*, 16(3), 307–28.

Muniz, A.M. and Schau, H.J. (2005) Religiosity in the abandoned Apple Newton brand community, *Journal of Consumer Research*, 31(March).

Newzoo (2018) Global mobile market report 2018. Available at: www.Newzoo.com (accessed 1 June 2020).

O'Connell, B.J. (1975) Dimensions of religiosity among Catholics, *Review of Religious Research*, 16(3), 198–207.

Ochkovskaya, M. (2015) Perception and consumption of global luxury brands in Russia and Romania: Comparative cross-cultural aspects, *Management Dynamics in the Knowledge Economy*, 3(2), 279–99.

Osman, M. (2020) Ecommerce statistics for 2020 – chatbots, voice, omni-channel marketing, *Kinsta.com*, 20 May. Available at: www.Kinsta.com/blog/ecommerce-statistics (accessed 5 June 2020).

Parsons, T. (1967) *Sociological Theory and Modern Society*, New York: Free Press.

Parsons, T. and Shils, E.A. (eds) (1951) *Toward a General Theory of Action*, Cambridge, MA: Harvard University Press.

Peterson, J.B. (2018) The psychology of identity (talk), The Dutch Lion (De Nederlandse Leeuw), Rijswijk, 19 January. Available at: www.youtube.com/watch?v=HFIk5RIJfAg (accessed 1 June 2020).

Reid, J. (2013) Immaterialism, Working paper, King's College London, May, 1–25. Available at: https://kclpure.kcl.ac.uk/portal/files/10052380/ImmaterialismJReid.pdf (accessed 26 December 2019).

Rochadiat, A.M.P., Tong, S.T. and Novak, J.M. (2018) Online dating and courtship among Muslim American Women: Negotiating technology, religious identity and culture, *New Media and Society*, 20(4), 1618–39.

Rosenbaum-Elliott, R., Percy, L. and Pervan, S. (2015) *Strategic Brand Management*, 3rd ed., Oxford: Oxford University Press.

Rostow, W.W. (1964) *View from the Seventh Floor*, New York: Harper and Row.

Ruvituso, C.I. (2020) From the south to the north: The circulation of Latin American dependency theories in the Federal Republic of Germany, *Current Sociology*, 68(1), 22–40.

Sachs, J. (2005) *The End of Poverty: Economic Possibilities for Our Time*, New York: Penguin Press.

Saffu, K. and Scott D. (2009) Developing country perceptions of high- and low-involvement products manufactured in other countries, *International Journal of Emerging Markets*, 4(2), 185–99.

Schlosser, E. (2002) *Fast Food Nation*, New York: HarperCollins.

Schrader, U. (2007) The moral responsibility of consumers as citizens, *International Journal Innovation and Sustainable Development*, 2(1), 79–96.

Schroeder, J. and Morling, M.S. (eds) (2006) *Brand Culture*, New York: Routledge.

Schwartz, S.H. and Huismans, S. (1995) Value priorities and religiosity in four western religions, *Social Psychology Quarterly*, 58, 88–107.

Shah, S. (2019) Critics of dependency theory, social science theories. Available at: www.sociologydiscussion.com/capitalism/critics-of-dependency-theory-social -science-theories/672 (accessed 31 December 2019).

Sherry, J. (1989) Postmodern alternatives: The interpretive turn in consumer research, in H. Kassarjian and T. Robertson (eds), *Handbook of Consumer Research*, Englewood Cliffs, NJ: Prentice-Hall.

Simões, C., Dibb, S. and Fisk, R.P. (2005) Managing corporate identity: An internal perspective, *Journal of the Academy of Marketing Science*, 33(2), 153–68.

Spencer-Oatey, H. (2008) *Culturally Speaking: Culture, Communication and Politeness Theory*, 2nd ed. London: Continuum.

Spencer-Oatey, H. (2012) What is culture? A compilation of quotations. GlobalPAD Core Concepts. Available at: GlobalPAD, Open House. Available at: www.warwick .ac.uk/globalpadintercultural (accessed 27 December 2019).

Statman, D. (1992) Modesty, pride and realistic self-assessment. *Philosophical Quarterly*, 42(169), 420–38.

Taai, N.M. (1985) *Religious Behaviour Scale*, Kuwait: Arrobyaan Publishing.

Tabash, M.I. and Dhankar, R.S. (2014) The flow of Islamic finance and economic growth: An empirical evidence of Middle East, *Finance and Accounting*, 2(1), 11–19.

Taylor, P.J. (1992) Understanding global inequalities: A world-systems approach, *Geography*, 77(1), 10–12.

Think with Google research (2014) available at: https://www.thinkwithgoogle.com (last accessed 10 December 2019).

Venkatesh, A. (1992) Postmodernism, consumer culture and the society of the spectacle, in John F. Sherry, Jr. and Brian Sternthal (eds), *Advances in Consumer Research*, Vol. 19, Provo, UT: Association for Consumer Research, pp. 199–202.

Vitell, S.J., Paolillo, J.G. and Singh, J.J. (2005) Religiosity and consumer ethics, *Journal of Business Ethics*, 57(2), 175–81.

Wallerstein, I. (1967) *The Modern World-System: Capitalist Agriculture and the Emergence of the European World Economy in the Sixteenth Century*, New York: Academic Press.

Wohlforth, W.C. (1995) Realism and the end of Cold War, *International Security*, 19(3), 91–129.

Zehri, C., Abdelbaki, A. and Bouabdellah, N. (2012) Effects of the current financial crisis on Islamic banks compared to conventional banks, *Banks and Bank Systems*, 7(1), 83–93.

6. Ethics, religion and consumer behaviour in developing nations

Ayodele Christopher Oniku

INTRODUCTION

The influence of religion on ethical belief of consumers cannot be disputed, especially when it comes to socio-economic activities of mankind. To a greater extent, religion or faith plays a pivotal role to determine the likely ethical orientation of average consumers in a market in terms of purchase decisions and patterns. Studies have shown the different areas that consumers are concerned about or exhibit their level of ethical beliefs and religion orientations, for instance, the likelihood of returning excess change, the chance of engaging in fraudulent activities during shopping, the likelihood of being fraudulent during exchange processes with buyers, overinvoicing, choice of fashion, issues of religion economics, etc. (Vitell & Muncy, 2005; Leahy, 1986; Gokariksel & Secor, 2009, 2010a; Iyer, 2016). Previous studies have shown that religious tenets and doctrines may shape consumers' inclinations and therefore make them behave appropriately, in line with religious tenets and doctrines (Knox, 1902; Gras, 1944; Fort, 1997). Savulescu (1998) stresses that ethics are about reason while religion is about faith, and other studies have found out that the level of faith that influences ethical behaviour is a function of the teachings of the holy books, traditions inherent in certain faiths and the advice, commands or instructions of religious figureheads or leaders (Lynch, 1990; Rashid & Ibrahim, 2008). By and large, the effects of these are on the propensity of consumers to be ethical or unethical when it comes to commercial dealings and relationships.

The chapter will clearly examine the effects of the duo of ethics and religion on consumer behaviours in that the religious orientations and interaction with consumption behaviours of consumers will be examined to understand how the inter-relationship of religion and ethics affects both consumers' buying decisions and patterns in the market. Importantly, consumers' buying behaviours and decisions will be examined in the prism of marketing strategy and decisions like advertising, and purchase decisions in the areas of clothing, eating, relationships, marketing communication effects and adornment. The under-standing of the discourse will help marketing organisations and government institutions that focus on consumer rights, protection and product standard to understand how the interaction and interplay of religion and ethical consider-ation is dominating buying decisions and behaviours in contemporary market.

The understanding and manifestation of ethics as a business issue and decision, especially in marketing which dominantly serves, protects and inter-acts with buyers' decisions in the marketplace, are strategic in contemporary organisations. Ethics pertinently focuses on morally acceptable behaviour on the part of individuals. In other words, it is the judgemental decision on what is wrong and not wrong in behaviours based on individuals' background of religious beliefs and tenets. So, as it is applicable to individuals, likewise it is applicable to corporate organisations in their relationship with clients. Importantly, the study focuses on the ethics and ethical judgement of con-sumers relatedly to the consumption behaviours, decisions and patterns across certain goods and services.

ETHICS AND RELIGION IN DEVELOPING MARKETS

The peculiarity of developing markets is that religion plays tactical and pivotal roles in determining the socio-economic lifestyle of many people (Nwosu, 2013; Hamdani et al., 2004), and this subsequently informs producers' and organisations' business decisions (Singhapakdi et al., 2000). The influence of religion subsequently affects ethical considerations on how to approach markets in terms of product offering, market communication mediums and contents and other strategic business and marketing decisions. It is not an uncommon development for individuals to grow up under an influence of a particular religion in many communities in the developing economies. Thus, consumers and producers as individuals have a tone of religion influencing their respective buying decisions, and this further directly or indirectly affects their disposition to issues of ethical decisions and practices.

In many developing countries, prior to Islamic economics and Christian economics (Iannaccone, 1986, in Hamdani et al., 2004) which have dominated contemporary socio-economic behaviours, traditional or local beliefs and reli-gions existed that laid the foundations of ethics that influenced the economics of business in many societies. For instance, African Traditional Religion (ATR) existed and had ethics and ethical values on the way business was conducted and equally mediated the relationship between producers (sellers) and consumers (buyers). According to Pew Research Centre (2010) 57 per cent of Africans are Christians, 29 per cent Muslim and 13 per cent practise ATR (Patterson, 2014). Equally, Indonesia has the largest population of Muslims, and according to Pew Research Centre (2008) more than nine in every ten

Indonesians belong to a religion or faith and that religion influences their economic, social and political life. Index Mundi (2019) reveals Indonesian index demographic profiles, with a 262.8 million population in 2018, has a religion distribution of 87.2 per cent Muslim; 7 per cent Protestant; 2.9 per cent Roman Catholic; 1.7 per cent Hindu; and 1.3 per cent others. The 2019 India Demographics Profile revealed that Hindus constitute 79.5 per cent; Muslims constitute 14.2 per cent; Christians constitute 2.3 per cent; Sikhs 1.7 per cent; and Buddhists and other religions constitute 2 per cent (2019). In the same line, Onaiyekan (2011) alludes that the demography of religion in Nigeria is in the three main religious practices in the country – ATR, Islam and Christianity. One significant fact about religion that cuts through the developing economies is that religious tenets and doctrines greatly influence the social, political and economic lives of people, and this further extends to business definitions and operations (Lu & Lu, 2010; Khan, 2014; Parboteeah et al., 2008). Generally, in marketing practice the influence and dictates of religion cannot be underestimated due to its influence on consumers' buying decisions in terms of consumption patterns that manifest in terms of frequency, volume and occasion. Obviously, the dictates of religious tenets and doctrines as stipulated by the holy books or religion manuals have really dominated consumer psychology vis-à-vis buying behaviours. For instance, the case of religion-approved consumption patterns or behaviours unfolds what a religion forbids eating, what amounts to sacrilegious market practice or acceptable practices in terms of time, purpose and motives behind consumption behaviours.

Religion is more than gatherings of the faithful to perform rites; it is expected that believers should imbibe the tenets and doctrines to shape daily conducts in society, and this influences certain observations like dress, morality, adornment and relationships. Equally, in commercial relationships and business conduct, the effects of religion cut across issues like types of business relationship and conduct, the management of money and usury, the disposition to sensitive issues like tips and gifts and giving and receiving bribes (Rashid & Ibrahim, 2008). Thus, it isn't uncommon to see certain businesses or commercial relationships forbidden in certain societies because of popular religion therein or the tenets and doctrines preached. Further to this is the issue of ethics which expressly creates boundaries and checks to conduct socio-economic activities like business. People who act contrarily to the rules of religion are believed to be committing sins, turpitudes or acts of iniquity. For instance, the Bible stipulation of the Ten Commandments provides a reference point to the expected lifestyle and behaviours of Christians, not only in the religious circle but equally in relationships in business and other socio-economic conduct. Likewise, other religions have such laws and commands, for instance the *Hadith* and *Shunna* in the Quran for Muslims, the laws of *Manu* for Hindu and the *Sutras* for the Buddhist that guide the faithful in their daily conduct.

By and large, religious laws like Shar'ia and the Ten Commandments have by omission or commission become bases to define what constitutes acceptable ethics in many social systems (Parboteeah et al., 2008).

Another dimension to the relationship between religion and ethics is projected in the studies of Hamdani et al. (2004) which stress the roles of divine economics and the influence on the disposition of people towards religion. The need to uphold the sacredness of life-after, the sharing of income with others, helping those in need, philanthropic gestures and other injunctions in the holy books is sacrosanct to many believers' views of religion vis-à-vis economic behaviours. In fact, Hamdani et al. (2004) stress the indisputable roles of divine economics as a pivotal tool in Islamic socio-economic behaviours.

Fundamentally, the discourse on ethics and religion is founded on the interaction and combination of deontological and teleological thoughts and evaluation. According to Savulescu (1998), religion is about faith while ethics is about reason, yet the interaction of both variables has been found imperative in contemporary business decisions and management. Importantly, the focus of deontological evaluation is on the specific actions or behaviours of an individual, while teleological evaluation focuses on the consequences of actions or behaviours of an individual as well (Schneider et al., 2011). In other words, the effect of religion on human decisions and behaviours is a function of the impacts of teachings and doctrines of faith involved. There is a connection between the texts of the holy books, religious traditions and the figureheads and the behaviours of followers or believers in that the culmination of religions' impacts determine behaviours and understanding of consequences of actions (Savulescu, 1998). For instance, the teachings and inherent traditions attached to each faith determine consumers' disposition to issues that affect buying decisions, patterns and understanding and interpretation of marketing communication. Equally, the roles of figureheads in what is preached as rights and wrongs to a large extent affect consumers' market behaviours and simultaneously influence responses to marketing communication and offerings in market.

CONSUMERS, ETHICS AND RELIGION AND DEVELOPING ECONOMIES

In marketing, it is expected that the effective interaction of religion and business strategy generates customer satisfaction which ultimately leads to customer retention and repeat purchase, and further becomes a benchmark for organisations to maintain and improve market share and turnover. It can be deduced that unethical practices or business decisions on the part of the producers, sellers or salesmen can have adverse effects on businesses and vice versa. In other words, organisations that produce products not needed by consumers based on religious beliefs and doctrines might not be successful in business. Or business that is not known for altruism and equally notorious in issues that violate societal values or run contrary to religious doctrines and teachings may suffer adverse effects on the bottom line. Likewise, a business that has good and effective social responsibility, especially in religious circles (e.g. sponsorship of religious events like holy pilgrimage, Father Christmas, etc. or other rites classified as religious economics, be it Islamic or Christian economics) may enjoy enduring patronage as a result of religious gestures (Hamdani et al., 2004). A candid example of this was in November 2002 when the Miss World pageant was cancelled in Nigeria because it was slated to come up in the Muslim-dominated city of Kaduna and this led to religious-motivated riots that claimed over 200 lives. The event was later hosted in Alexandra Palace, London, United Kingdom on 7 December 2002 (*The Guardian*, 2002). On 14 April 2006 there was a Muslim riot in Indonesia over the Indonesian edition of *Playboy* magazine despite the fact that the woman on the front page was clothed (*The Guardian*, 2007). Also, there have been cases of riots and anti-business movements against alcohol sales in many societies based on the fact that such commercial operations run contrary to religious teachings and doctrines. The underpinning factor is that business ideas or models contravene religious teachings, beliefs and tenets. Aptly, consumers tend to exhibit a high level of sensitivity to patronage, consumption and the adoption of products or services when religious factors or elements are involved.

The work of Savulescu (1998) itemises factors and business developments where their execution or business owners' disposition along with the societal value determine their ethical views or position, e.g. selling hazardous items, misleading instructions, padding expense accounts, insider information, falsifying reports, favouring relatives, etc. Importantly, societal values system, culture and the teachings and tenets of religions define whether the occurrence of any of these constitutes ethical practice or otherwise (Vitell, 2010). Furthermore, studies have thrown more light on what may constitute unethical practice of business from religions' angle especially in the execution of marketing communications in terms of the use of religious symbols (Taylor et al., 2010) and sexually appealing objects (Putrevu & Swimberghe; 2013) and the findings show that religious symbols might not violate ethical consideration of consumers. Studies conclude that sexually appealing objects and the use of religious symbols are strategic to improve sales among those who moderately uphold such religious beliefs and but they might lead to lower purchase intention among those who uphold stronger religious beliefs (Putrevu & Swimberghe, 2013; Taylor et al., 2010). Likewise, consumers with high intrinsic religious orientation or high-religiosity consumers might disapprove sexual appeals and be favourable to non-sexual appeal communication, and their ethical intentions and judgements cannot be disconnected from biblical injunctions or religious beliefs (Kim et al., 2009). Singhapakdi et al. (2013) further stress that organisation decisions on the execution of policy with religious undertones is a function of managers' religiosity whereby their intrinsic religiosity tends to be guided by their religion's tenets and teachings in their ethical judgements and intentions while managers with high extrinsic religiosity tend to be less so in ethical judgements and intentions.

The consumer side of ethics is fundamentally underpinned by the level of religiosity which in turn influences purchase decisions, buying patterns and responsiveness to marketing communications and other marketing strategies. Studies have shown that consumers' ethical decisions and judgements or beliefs are largely determined by religion but the manifestation in the type of religion and level of religiosity may vary due to their disposition to religion (Vitell et al., 2005, 2006; Roth et al., 2012; Chowdhury & Fernando, 2013; Kim et al., 2009).

RELIGION: INTRINSIC AND EXTRINSIC FACTORS

One of the cardinal studies that unravel religious orientations of individuals in a society is the Religious Orientation Scale of Allport (1950) and Allport and Ross (1967). Basically, the study premises religiousness or religiosity on two dimensions of intrinsic orientation and extrinsic orientation. Succinctly, 'intrinsically-oriented person considers religion as an ultimate end in itself; it is a master motive in life' (Neyrinck et al., 2010). In other words, intrinsicness represents high religious piousness and a total submission to the teachings and tenets of religion as the guide for all human activities and endeavours, and this definitely and ultimately affects market behaviours of consumers in their disposition to unethical practices. Irrespective of the position as a buyer, an intrinsic-oriented person upholds the values of ethics and religious values or doctrines and these are internalised. Such people exercise personal abhorrence towards bribery, kickbacks, product adulterations, cheating, exaggeration, lies and other forms of unethical business practices that are frowned on by their religions.

Extrinsic orientation implies that religion is approached in a 'utilitarian or instrumental fashion' (Neyrinck et al., 2010). Extrinsic-oriented people see religion as a means to an end in that religion is an instrument to achieve goals in life without much resolution or an enduring believe in the tenets, doctrines or teachings. The operation of extrinsic orientation is to use religion for selfish ends and in order to seek solace as it is not integrated into the deeper life of the person concerned. In business, the manifestation of extrinsic orientation is the incidence of unethical practices (both buyers and sellers) and the essence is to boost performance on the expense of the other party or the larger society.

On a larger consideration, many studies on the relationship between extrinsic and intrinsic and consumers' behaviours show that extrinsic orientation leads to consumers' unethical beliefs and intentions which equally lead to questionable consumer behaviours in business, while intrinsic orientation rarely leads to unethical or questionable consumer behaviours or intentions (Vitell et al., 2005, 2006; Genia, 1993; Schneider et al., 2011). Equally, the extrinsic and intrinsic orientation effects in marketing communication show that consumers are affected by the level of indecency and inappropriateness projected in sexual appeal advertising, thus the level of religiosity determines consumers' perceptions and attitudes (Putrevu & Swimberghe, 2013; Taylor et al., 2010). Equally, the dimensions of extrinsicness and intrinsicness may determine the operation and interpretation of marketing communication strategies in the market.

While it may seem as though many studies have focused on the examination and investigation of the extrinsic and intrinsic scale from a Christianity angle (Gras, 1944; Jacobson, 1998; Vitell et al., 2009; Kim et al., 2009; Taylor et al., 2010; Chowdhury & Fernando, 2013), other recent studies have focused on the integration and implication of the intrinsic and extrinsic scale on Islam. The effects of the scale on Islam share the same implications and effects on consumer ethical beliefs, judgements and intentions (Khan, 2014; Schneider et al., 2011; Rashid & Ibrahim, 2008). However, the work of Rashid and Ibrahim shows a slight difference in the interpretation of religiosity levels across different cultures because of the influence of the cultural factor on Islam. The general application and understanding of intrinsic and extrinsic factors is nonetheless relevant and strategic in understanding the behaviours and orientations of believers of other religions in that believers of ATR, Buddhists, Hinduists, Jews, Sikhists, etc. may hold an extrinsic or intrinsic position. It is not uncommon in different parts of Africa to see traditionalists who are wholly believers of their faiths and this they manifest in clothing, diet, relationships, medication, etc. to express the intrinsicness factor. On the other hand, there are believers who are partially involved in the faith in that they express outward characteristics of traditionalists but there is a limit to this in their daily living and buying behaviours. It is expected that a Buddhist should be a vegetarian, and there are believers who may shun certain dictates of the religion to express the extrinsic factor. The works of Miller and Dixon-Roman (2011) and van der Geutgen et al. (2013) show that the effects of modernity, peer pressure, hip-hop culture and the redefinition of morality are affecting youths' religious orientations. In other words, the effects of changes in society may impact adherence of many believers to tenets, doctrines and commands, which in turn affect market behaviours in terms of buying decisions and patterns.

Importantly, larger studies on the relationship between religion, ethics and buying behaviours have tilted more towards major religions like Christianity,

Islam and Buddhism with fewer works devoted to other religions; however, this study will delve on major religions in the developing economies to show the interaction of religion and consumer buying behaviours and decisions. Kim et al. (2009) stress that what constitutes ethical behaviours and judgements on the part of consumers has its root in the tenets and teachings of the Bible in the case of Christian environments, specifically the injunctions of the Ten Commandments. In Islam, the basis of consumers' market behaviour is enshrined in the Quran with emphasis on *Hadith* and *Shunna*; Judaism practice has its doctrines enshrined in the Torah; Buddhists the Tripitaka or Pali Canon; and in Hinduism it is the Vedas.

Christianity and Islam are the world's most popular religions and worshippers cut across the developing economy. Buddhism is popular and practised in Cambodia, Thailand, Myanmar, Sri Lanka, Laos and Japan. Hinduism is practised in India, Nepal, Bangladesh, Indonesia, Pakistan, Sri Lanka and Malaysia. The popularity of Judaism is high in developed countries; however, there is a large presence in South Africa in the developing economy. ATR cuts across the African continent and comes in different names and forms based on the beliefs of the community, natives and ancestors, e.g. *Ifa* worship among the Yoruba in Nigeria, Brazil, Barbados, Peru and some other parts of South American and West African communities; *Akuj* and *Were* among the Kenyans; *Nzambi* among the Congolese; *Cagn* among the Central African communities; *Jok* among the Zaireans and Ugandans; *Kuomboka* among the Zambians; and *Mujaji* and *Nomhoyi* among the South Africans.

FIELD STUDY: METHODS

In order to understand the influence of religion on ethical behaviours of consumers, a survey exercise was carried out in Nigeria to explore the influence of religion and ethics on consumers' buying behaviours and decisions. The study adopts qualitative methods based on the peculiarity of the research objective. Thus, managers of selected businesses were interviewed based on their interactions and experiences with customers and their buying decisions and behaviours in the face of religion, religious orientations and ethical decisions, and the selected businesses covered banking/finance, pharmaceutical, beauty/cosmetic, fashion, public services, etc. The managers selected for the interviews have MBAs or equivalent professional qualifications in sales, marketing, management, etc. with over ten years' experience. However, the scope of the study did not involve small or medium-sized enterprises because of the size and volume of operations which limit the scope of managers and interaction with customers. The qualifications of managers aided the stratification process of the samples into industries, and in total 28 managers were interviewed for the study. Also, due to factors such as availability, tight business schedules of many managers and time demands for the interviews, only nine managers were successfully directly interviewed while the remaining 19 managers preferred to submit responses in an open-ended questionnaire. The design of the questionnaire enhanced the opportunity to give an account of their experiences without limiting their narrative.

The interview approach adopted lent credence to a discovery-oriented approach which gave room to accommodating wider horizons and larger audience (Taylor et al., 2010; Wells, 1993), and the open-ended questionnaire approach was able to achieve this as well. As a result, emphasis was focused on discovery with dedicated attention to managers' activities and responses. Thus, a set of questions was addressing or stressing the same enquiry in order to receive deeper and comprehensive information or discovery from interviewees that could generate robust findings. Equally, connections were established that helped to relate responses to earlier and previous works on the variables. The approach further lends support to the interpretive analysis in the study (Taylor et al., 2010). The essence of the interpretive approach is to bring social reality into the study and this was achieved by encouraging managers/interviewees to give their account based on their experiences in work, especially in their relationships with subordinates, customers, suppliers and colleagues in their day-to-day activities. The findings of the study were then narrated under different subheadings to reflect the different issues in the study.

FINDINGS AND DISCUSSION

Ethics and Religion: Consumers' Case

From the interviews, it was asserted that what informed consumers' ethical behaviours are borne out of religion's tenets, teachings and faith declarations that solidly embed moral behaviours and beliefs. Largely, what amounts to consumers' core values and buying behaviours irrespective of religion orientation are offshoots of the Bible's teachings like the Ten Commandments; the *Hadith* and *Sunnah* in the Quran and the moral codes of ATR and *Pali* canon of Hinduism. Importantly, consumers with extrinsic orientation are described as buyers with high inherent values or behaviours to subvert religion's beliefs and tenets to accommodate personal enjoyment and desire. Such consumers, in spite of physical appearance, identity by religious names and adornment intentionally consume products that run contrary to religion teachings, e.g. alcoholic brands or demands for 'settlements' or bribes to get work done. On the other hand is the case of consumers with intrinsic orientation who show high propensity to uphold moral values, religious values and tenets that influence their ethical behaviour in the market. An example of targeted marketing to this group is Islamic insurance policies that are being embraced by many insurance firms that have a larger percentage of Muslim customers, many of whom are converting policies to be based on *Takaful* principles.

The prevalence of unethical practice vis-à-vis religious tenets and beliefs among consumers is a function of core values, morality decisions, modernity and peer influence. In other words, unethical practice (i.e. subversion of moral codes and religious doctrines) prevalence among consumers manifests in terms of consumption patterns that may not be in consonant with the practised religious requirements, or there could be a situation where consumers hide their religious identity to avoid any embarrassment that may be generated as a result of perceived 'negative' buying decisions, e.g. consumers asking for a blank invoice to be completed by himself or the consumption of pork by a Muslim client in the company of Christian friends. These situations clearly reveal what instil intrinsic and extrinsic orientations among consumers. The fact is that organisations recognise these behaviours in the market and integrate them into strategies to improve turnover and market share. A consumer aptly commented: 'in the face of modernity and social acceptability requirements many youths and other category of consumers will jettison religion doctrines and tenets and be swayed by peers influence and modernism'.

It is revealed, based on experience, that piousness and outward appearance are not a benchmark and yardstick to determine customers' religiosity. It is only on rare occasions that customers' appearance and piousness reflect or determine religiosity or religious orientation, and become a pointer to form decisions about their market behaviours. Resultantly, extrinsic and intrinsic orientations are revealed in continuous relationships of organisations with customers which later inform customer profiling and strategic relationships with clients. While some customers tend to maintain permanent positions in their religious orientations (extrinsic or intrinsic), others tend to be 'switchers' in that economic pressure, cultural influence (change in social values) and peer pressure can turn an intrinsic-oriented client into an extrinsic-oriented one. For instance, a manager in the beauty industry disclosed that change in societal values and peer pressure can turn an intrinsic-oriented customer to extrinsic-oriented and persuade them to buy skin-lightening cream, despite the fact that many religions frown on it as a sign of waywardness, rebelliousness and immoral practice. Also, it was found that peer pressure and the effect of 'keeping up with the Joneses' make many youths feel that they need to eat spiced barbecue meat sourced from pork which Islam, Judaism and Hinduism forbid for their worshippers.

Interpretations of religious teaching and injunctions in the holy books to suit personal purpose are one way to identify customers with extrinsic orientation, e.g. use of phrases like 'God understands' or citations from the Bible in the books of Matthew 22:21, Mark 12:17 and Luke 20:25: 'Render therefore unto Caesar the things which are Caesar's; and unto God the things which are God's' at the point of anti-faith consumption behaviour to subvert biblical teachings and tenets in order to satisfy personal desire is a common occurrence among extrinsic-oriented Christians. Invariably, manifesting extrinsic orientation is a deliberate ethical and religious behaviour among consumers who indulge in or cultivate the forbidden act. It is further found, on the contrary, that organisations' brand integrity, professionalism and superior service/product quality could turn a supposed extrinsic-oriented customer into an intrinsic-oriented one in his/her dealing with such an organisation. In other words, an organisation that distinguishes itself based on professionalism, superior services and excellent customer relationships that are uncommon in an industry may affect the religious orientation of customers in dealing with such firms. Thus, customers with extrinsic religious orientation will be ready to trade off short gains attached to unethical dealings for superior services with organisations reputed for ethical organisational culture and core values. A customer testified that 'In spite of my religion background as a Muslim, I patronise a fashion designer that is a Rosicrucian based on his expertise and professionalism that I couldn't find among Muslim tailors in spite of objection among friends and relatives'.

Also, intrinsic orientation is popular and upheld by many customers based on different reasons. For instance, many customers are intrinsic-oriented purely on religion and faith. The values, teachings and doctrines of religion make them uphold intrinsic orientation, especially the resolute teaching about 'life thereafter'. There is a set of customers whose intrinsic orientation has political activism connotations as they confess that they belong to social/political groups that advocate that 'things must be done right'. Their stance on ethical values, fairness and justice goes beyond religious values but is mixed with the political ethos of building a just and corruption-free society. Experiences with organisations further reveal that such intrinsic-oriented customers can be more aggressive by seeking legal action or other formal means to ensure that ethics are followed and practised. Another set of intrinsic-oriented customers are those whose religiosity manifests to fight moral decadence in society. They mix religious values with societal uprightness to express their market behaviours. In all these sets of consumers the internalising of religious values is expressed on different notes to achieve the same goals of life-thereafter and a fair and just society.

Religion and Ethics: The Case of 'Switchers'

The peculiarity of consumers in developing markets reveals one important fact that in the struggle to exercise religious orientation and to keep with modernism, peer pressure, personal desire and culture changes many consumers switch from being intrinsic to extrinsic, which ultimately affects ethical judgement. From the survey exercise, religious orientation switching is a situation where a consumer known for a particular religion orientation is found to behave differently at the point of buying and consumption decisions, and this behaviour is temporary as the occasion demands. Due to this development many consumers do not have a fixed religious orientation in the market but switch across product decisions depending on their desire and goals.

Consumers consciously, and at times unconsciously, switch between being extrinsic and intrinsic in their religious orientation as a result of the need to make purchase decisions, and the switching may constitute ethical and unethical behaviours. From the study, it was found that there are a few factors that underpin religious orientation switching which invariably affect the behavioural decisions of consumers.

Firstly, socialisation across religions manifests in different forms depending on the tenets and teachings that inform the ethical behaviours in each religion. Generally, however, there are certain acts and behaviours that cut across every society and the disposition of each religion to these acts and behaviours determines their acceptance. For instance, alcohol consumption, cigarette smoking, casinos, clubbing, etc. are behaviours that many religions may tolerate as an act of socialisation while other religions will frown on it as forbidden or a sinful act. On the part of consumers, some indulge in acts as part of socialisation while their religion may forbid it. Also, some consumers may hold or exhibit intrinsic orientation in all their mannerisms but occasionally socialisation makes them extrinsic in certain areas of consumption behaviour. A consumer in the survey attested that 'my religion forbids any entertainment that involves cinema but my long stay in UK has made me to cultivate cinema outing as a way of relaxation and socialisation with friends and co-workers'. Also, a Hindu businessman declared 'my business sojourn across African nations introduces me to cold beer and dry meat barbecue as a form of socialisation with clients'. Thus, in spite of religious teachings and doctrines, consumers occasionally consume forbidden items to get along socially.

Secondly, peer pressure is prominent in the reasons given by many consumers as a determinant of occasional change in religious orientation. Peer pressure manifests in terms of the influence of friends and associates on buying behaviours and decisions. Association brings people to new discoveries, new lifestyles and changes in consumption behaviour. The issue of peer pressure is largely experienced among youths and in the areas of fashion, food, entertainment, finance, etc. For instance, the influence of friends makes certain consumers make decisions on issues around alcohol consumption, engagement in certain entertainment like clubbing and music, the consumption of certain foods that their religion may forbid. The act of pork consumption among Hindus, Muslims and Jews is forbidden and sacrilegious, while to Christians and traditionalists it is acceptable and encouraged. Equally, while alcoholic drinks are forbidden in Islam, *Vedas* in Hinduism merely discourages it as sinful behaviour; Buddhism also condemns the act as sinful. But to Catholics, beer and other alcoholic drinks are not forbidden while the Evangelical and Pentecostal denominations in Christianity forbid the acts as a hindrance and antithetical to the 'in-dwelling of the Holy Spirit'. In all these, peer pressure and keeping up with the Joneses might force many consumers to occasionally indulge in the consumption irrespective of the teachings and commands of their religion.

The need to make short gains in the course of buying decisions causes many consumers to switch behaviours from being intrinsic-oriented to extrinsic-oriented in consumption decisions. Short gains may be inherent in behavioural tendency and the manifestation determines ethical judgement of consumers vis-à-vis religious beliefs and doctrines. In order to make quick gains many consumers may resort to engaging in giving bribes, over/underinvoicing and tax evasion, while nearly all religions admonish the act of being a good citizen and shunning negative financial dealing or activities. In the study, based on many organisations' experience, piousness and consumers' religiosity may not determine ethical behaviour when it comes to giving and receiving bribes. A consumer confirmed 'I had to give a bribe to fast-track my application in government office for approval of land acquisition and surveying plan paper'. The implication of short gains and financial subversion is that religious consumers with intrinsic orientation may intermittently or occasionally give or receive bribes and may contradict the religious ethical proclivity expected.

Change in culture is evident in the response of many consumers as a major factor that may cause intermittent and occasional switching in religious orientation. The essence is that change in culture necessitates conformity that consumers have to embrace but many religious tenets and doctrines struggle to accept it as a new order in buying decisions and behaviours. Culture change affects consumption and buying behaviour decisions in the areas of fashion, entertainment, financial products like insurance, investment options, etc. The position of many religious organisations on the influence of culture is regarded as infiltration by many religious authorities and is regarded as sacrilege or sinful depending on the teaching and canons. A consumer affirmed that her church still frowns at her dressing style which she enjoys for comfort and fashion: 'wearing a pair of trousers in spite of the fact that it is feminine-designed is a struggle for the church to accept as a conventional female dress for service'. Many Pentecostal affiliations of Christianity believe that trousers are meant for men and not for women. Thus, consumers' religious orientation is tested when they appear contrary and unethical based on the religious tenets and doctrines. A traditionalist also confirmed using an imported modern and expensive whisky, gin or any form of spirit for worship that is not accepted by traditionalists, rather than the local brew and schnapps brands.

Such buying behaviour is frowned on because it is perceived as modernity that is unethical, and worshippers are regarded as being extrinsic-oriented.

ETHICS, CONSUMER BEHAVIOUR AND RELIGION: FURTHER REFLECTIONS

In addition to the findings from the empirical study reported above, there are other themes worth discussing to address the interaction of ethics, religion and their manifestation in consumers' consumption behaviours, decisions and patterns.

Advertising, Marketing Communication and Religion

It is imperative to state that the issue of marketing communication is strategic in marketing decisions across industries irrespective of the products or brands involved. However, the limits set by religious proclivity and the manifestation of tenets and doctrines have meant the practice of advertising and other forms of marketing communication is evaluated on the basis of infringement of religion beliefs and religiosity in the economy. With the growth of neo-liberalism in Islamic nations like Turkey, Jordan and other parts of the Middle East, the criticisms levelled against the prominence of marketing communication in business management and especially the fashion industry are dividing secularism and Islam and also tradition and modernism. According to Gokariksel and Secor (2009), the adoption of catwalks and exhibitions in the veiling sector is being evaluated as anti-Islam and a mismatch of Middle Eastern culture and religion. The nascent economic liberalism that fuels the fashion industry calls for the use of fashion shows and catwalks to drive awareness, show their wares and in that way sell particular fashion styles or brands. The modes of marketing communication have gained a negative press with veiling which is an identity of piousness and religiosity among Muslim women in the Middle East. Hence, to many Islamic scholars and ardent worshippers, catwalks and fashion parades are seen in the prism of the sexualisation of women and the commodification of Muslim women, using Islamic identity – veiling – as a tool of sex appeal in the course of marketing communication (Gokariksel & Secor, 2009, 2010b; Gokariksel & McLarney, 2010). Equally, the creation of boutique days as a marketing communication tool to raise awareness about the latest fashion, styles and trends in the veiling sector is condemned on the basis of its contradiction with Islamic-ness and ethical guides of Islam in business (Gokariksel & Secor, 2009). While the conventional method of marketing communication is embraced and adopted to improve business performance, the position of religion and ethical judgements of many Muslims has bred polarisation among consumers in that certain consumers believe in the potential of marketing communication strategies to spur their buying decisions and other consumers believe that marketing communication is a corruption to Islamic tenets as enshrined in *Hadith* and *Shunna*, and in Islamic economics. The development may be further interpreted as the case of intrinsic-oriented Muslims whose behaviour is labelled *Halal* and extrinsic-oriented Muslim consumers in the fashion industry whose behaviour is denoted as *Haram*.

The position of Pontifical Council on the use of advertising in business, which is regarded as 'cultural harms of advertisements' for Catholics (Foley, 1998, p. 314), is a pointer to the position of Christianity on marketing communication strategies in business management and consumers' education and awareness. Ringold (1998) stresses that consumers should use advertising rather than advertising using consumers; the statement is founded on the grounds that the prevalence of advertisements based on consumers' consumption; decisions leading to misleading and offensive advertising, information manipulation and the triggering of sexual instincts are the negative and unethical effects of advertisements. The contents of advertisements are described as 'lapses unto superficiality, tawdriness and moral squalor' (Ringold, 1998, p. 333). By and large, advertising effects will make capitalism and modernity redefine religion (Lewis, 2010). The ethical position of religious institutions and bodies may adversely affect buying decisions of many consumers and their disposition to trust and have confidence in marketing communication content and message. Subsequently, it will deny or rob businesses of pecuniary gains from the fraction of the market that are regarded as intrinsic-oriented believers due to the reflection on their buying behaviours and decisions.

Religion, Food and Consumers' Ethical Decisions

One of the potential areas that religion has influenced consumers' buying behaviours and decisions is the area of food based on the fact that diet remains a sacred area that religions use to instil spiritual behaviours and mannerisms. The dos and don'ts of religions in food determine diet, vegetables, meat consumption, and the dictates of religions further determine the timing, frequency and combination of food consumption, and believers adhere to the rules as part of displaying religious orientation.

According to *The Economist* of 22 November 1997 (Doole & Lowe, 2000), McDonald's had to learn from the failure of KFC in India, a nation with over 80 per cent Hindus and 40 per cent devoted vegetarians at that time. KFC had failed to understand the peculiarities of the culinary specification of the Hindu-dominated market of India to adapt their fast foods to the needs of Indian consumers. In 1996, when McDonald's opened their first restaurant in a franchising agreement with Amit Jatia, a staunch vegetarian, the success of the business was as a result of offering an appropriate menu that factored in the religious diet of Hinduism. The departure from the regular McDonald's menu in the North American and European markets opened the door for vegetarian menus like the Tikki Burger, Chicken Maharaja, McSpicy Paneer, McMasala and Mclmli, and the ingredients and preparations were in total compliance with Hindu specifications. One of the strategic turning points of the franchise was the need to allay the fear of Hindu/vegetarian consumers that the vegetarian menus were cooked in a separate area of the kitchen using separate utensils. This is based on the *Vera* of Hinduism which requires that separate cooking utensils are used for vegetarian cooking to avoid contamination. While the ethical judgement of McDonald's in India informed the decision to adapt menus to Hindu dietary laws in order to gain quick acceptance, consumers' ethical decisions are based on religious doctrines, rules and teachings that guarantee acceptable worship, dedication, faithfulness and righteousness that give desired peace and tranquillity. The result of the ethical behaviours on both sides saw the opening of over 350 McDonald's outlets in the first 14 years of operation by 2001 (www.mcdonaldsindia.com).

Halal is the popular name for foods recommended for Muslims on the basis that they are prepared in conformity to Islamic prescription in *Sunnah*. According to Tayob (2016), halal is the Islamic dietary law based on the Quran and the prophetic traditions of *Sunnah*, and the prohibitions cover 'meat of swine, dead meat and meat that has been sacrificed in the name of other deities' (p. 72). On a broader note, the application of halal extends to processed foods like cheese based on their source and content; it also involves shared utensils and cutlery and the mixing of ingredients in the kitchen. Invariably, the necessity of halal in Islamic communities informs how and where Muslims eat in public and the reason that in many advanced and religion-sensitive societies it is imperative to display halal slogans either on the restaurants or food items in supermarkets in order to meet the needs of and satisfy Muslim customers.

In South Africa, WIMPY carries halal labels on menus and outlets to show the organisation is Islam-consciousness in their service and this in turn commands the patronage of certain Muslims in their choice of restaurant (Tayob, 2016). The ethical judgement of the company in the preparation and separation of utensils is fundamental to the acceptance of their products among the faithful in order to pursue and uphold their religion orientation.

Religion, Ethics and Fashion among Muslim Women

The connection between fashion and religiosity is as old as religion based on the fact that religions in all forms distinguish themselves by adornment, fashion style and the specification of colours or design and tailoring. From the priest in a Catholic parish; the layman in an Anglican parish; the imam in a mosque; the chief priest/priestess in shrines; pujari in the Hindu temple to the monk or abbot in the Buddhist temple, their choice of adornment and fashion reveals who they are. Importantly, adornment and fashion are given a general connotation and interpretation in religion circles – reverence, holiness, sanctity, godliness, purity and sacredness. However, there may be differences among the different faiths, even intra-faith in terms of application, usage and styling. For instance, in Christianity the use of jewellery varies among denominations; while orthodox churches permit moderate usage certain denominations among the Pentecostal and Protestants totally forbid it. Equally, while Islam permits adornment, jewellery, finished accessories and heavy perfume (Kastner, 2018; Gokariksel & Secor, 2010a), Christianity sets limits and a time for total prohibition. The position of each denomination on jewellery sets the benchmark for acceptance, membership and ethical values of religiosity which ultimately determine the evaluation and definition of piousness, purity, righteousness and iniquitous acts or behaviours.

The interpretation of adornment and fashion among Muslim women is not given the same qualification as is found in other religions, especially in men's fashion. The commodification of women is a popular word today among conservative Islamists in that instead of presenting fashion to represent women's piousness, religiosity and devoutness they are 'selling Islam' (Gokariksel & Secor, 2010a, p. 119). *Tesettur* is the Islamic term for women's adornment that covers heads and bodies and helps them to avoid contact with unrelated men (Gokariksel & Secor, 2010a). There is a wider condemnation in certain quarters of Islam on the new definition and usage of *Tesettur* as a result of the influence of modernism and capitalism. The display, image and branding have tainted the true meaning of *Tesettur* in Islam; resultantly *Tesettur* is no longer Islamic but is classed as fashion. Jones (2010), in her study on Indonesian Muslim women, concludes that the boundaries between image and substance and between virtue and value are blurring. This shows that the ethical view of believers determines religiosity among members.

Traditionally, *abaya* is associated with Islam to express the dignity, reputation, morals, decency and chastity in womanhood and it is the traditional female dress throughout the Arab Gulf States (Al-Quasimi, 2010). However, the prevalence of modernity in certain quarters of the region coupled with the effect of emerging capitalist entrepreneurs that propel their business with applications of contemporary business and marketing strategies have defeated the original purpose of *abaya* as veiling that brings equality among women irrespective of class. According to Al-Quasimi (2010), the new 'Abaya-as-fashion' comes with competition among women and extravagance; modern designs with no Islamic veiling, and a deviation from the traditional black colour to different colours adorned with floral attachments. The traditional piety associated with censure consciousness in *abaya* is eliminated. Moors (2003) claims further that *abaya* is now designed with Western fashion consciousness which has infiltrated Islamic fashion and adornment for women, and violates Islam's veiling and scarfing tradition for women. Today, *abaya* is designed with tightly cut fittings, dropping shoulders and 'covering what is ugly and shows what is beautiful' (Moors, 2003, p. 45). The polarisation among women is a choice between conservative Islam and modernity which manifests in the choice of fashion between *hijab Islami* (for the conservative) and *Islamic hijab* (that shows the face and hands for the modernists) (Moors, 2003). By and large, Al-Quasimi (2010) concludes that based on *Hadith* the rise of *Kafirat* (clothing of infidel women/men) has infiltrated Islamic fashion.

The rise in the infiltration of Islamic fashion is further expressed in *sanse* which has become part of Islamic fashion among women in francophone African countries, especially among Senegalese women. *Sanse* is described as the act of beautifying oneself through clothing (Kastner, 2018), and the source of this is the integration of, and influence of, French couture on women's clothing design in the region, an idea that has its source in the impact of colonial rule. *Sanse* basically requires that the body shape is essential and crucial to reflect in designing and cutting women's clothing in order to distinguish between married and unmarried women. Married women are expected to be more rounded with shapes and curves than single ladies, and the contours must be shown in the clothing (Kastner, 2018). The incursion of colonialism in the name of Westernisation has changed the religious consciousness associated with fashion in the system.

Critically, the embrace or infiltration of foreign culture into the social life of other people may have effects on religiosity. Equally, the adoption of modern neo-liberalism and capitalist practice in business (Gokariksel & McLarney, 2010; Moors, 2003; Gokariksel & Secor, 2009, 2010a) might as a matter of necessity change the disposition of people to religion because of exposure to foreign practice that may be seen as relevance to business profitability but antithetical to religious values, ethics and doctrines.

Religion, Ethics and Online Dating

The advent of modern technology is not limited to business, economics, medical fields and science and the inclusion of social life has gained prominence in recent times, including online dating. The use of match making is as old as man and many holy books like the Bible, Quran and ancient practice among traditionalists testify to the potential of family members establishing relationships and marriage among children and kinsmen in society. The challenge of online dating among many people in developing economies is the disposition of religion to engagement in the act. The popularity of online dating to seek relationships with the opposite sex or the potential of finding a spouse is prevalent among youths but the adaptation in many developing countries is rooted in religious tenets and doctrines. According to Fair et al. (2009), the adoption among Ghanaian youths is based far more on lifestyles, new identities and economic reasons than religion or religiosity. The development may not be disconnected from the fact that the culture borne out of ATR and other religions still upholds the old-age tradition of parents' match making and inter-family relationships. The work of Adesina and Ayodele (2004) stresses that more Christians are involved because of the strong connection between Christianity and Westernisation, so it is easier for Christians to adapt to and adopt online dating; also Western education is an influence in that Muslims who engage in online dating are usually those who have had a Western education and are people who refuse to be swayed by religious dogma. The assertions herein reveal that religiosity may need to be downplayed to be fully engaged in online dating which may be interpreted as there still being room for religious orientation influence to determine engagement in online dating. To corroborate this, studies in many developed societies reveal that many Christian participants hide their religious identities because there is an inherent perception of Christian denominations like Evangelicals, Pentecostals and Protestants based on their doctrines on issues like pre-marital sex, abortion, homosexuality and chastity which may hinder finding companions and interested persons (Bobkowski & Kalyanaraman, 2010; Bobkowski & Pearce, 2011).

Religion, Ethics and Financial Services

The growth of Islamic banking with operations based on *Shar'ia* principles of Islamic law as an interest-free banking system allows social development. The underpinning principle is that the elements of *halal* and *haram* should guide financial and banking services, thereby *riba* is guided against. Its acceptability and growth across the globe put its value at more than $1 trillion in 2010 (Schottmann, 2014) and this is possible because of the modalities that many people found strategic to business and personal needs in many developing economies. The rise of Islamic banking has been found in countries like Saudi Arabia, Sudan, Iran, South Africa, Nigeria, Malaysia, Pakistan and Egypt (Qasaymeh, 2011; Schottmann, 2014; Siddique & Iqbal, 2016). Importantly, the spread of Islamic banking is not limited to Muslim countries because of the profit and loss system that distinguishes it from conventional banking systems (Siddqui, 2012).

The principle of *Shar'ia* guides the *Takaful* which is the insurance system that operates on the principle of Islamic banking. The operations of *Takaful* focus on the coverage of conventional insurance policies but its operation is underpinned by *Shar'ia* law in that social prosperity is fundamental as it is enshrined in the Quran and *Sunnah*. According to Anand (2014) the word

Takaful means 'joint guarantee whereby a group of participants agree among themselves to support on another jointly for the losses arising from specified risks' (p. 6). Participants agree to contribute a sum of money known as *Tabarru* or a commitment into a common fund that will be mutually used to assist members against stated risk or damage. Conservative Islamists believe and propagate *takaful* as suitable insurance products among Muslims because there are *fatwas* (religious decrees) in many sects and countries against conventional policies. Unlike conventional insurance products, *takaful* is devoid of excessive instalments associated with the former but instead relies on a donation, or voluntary and mutual contribution in a special fund to be used as compensation against any peril, loss or damage (Bekkin, 2007). A participant is entitled to income from another part of his instalment based on the *Shar'ia* principle of profit and loss sharing.

The ethical factor that makes *Shar'ia* or Islamic financial systems more acceptable among Muslim clients is the administration of the profit and loss-sharing system and the social prosperity that underpin the operations. Among the five central pillars of Islam is *Zakat* which represents charity work among the faithful (arms to the needy). Social prosperity is central to the religion and this principle underpins the modality and operation of the Islamic financial system or Islamic economics. As a result the acceptance of the Islamic financial system is growing beyond the shores of Islamic countries to non-Muslim nations (Qasaymeh, 2011; Siddiqui, 2012). Unlike the conventional financial system that gives rise to a growing bourgeoisie in global economics and an unequal distribution of wealth, Islamic economics promotes economic emancipation.

The relationship of other religions with economics is clearly denoted as economics of religion (Iyer, 2016) and the bottom line is that every religion derives its economic practice and disposition to money management and pursuit from its respective holy book. According to Iyer (2016), the growth of secularism and pluralism has greatly influenced economic development and this is further witnessed in the growth of education and urbanisation which has led to a decrease in religiosity. Invariably, it can be juxtaposed that economic development in a society or the effects of education and urbanisation on individuals may affect religious orientation – both intrinsicness and extrinsicness.

Ethics, Religion and the Consumers: The Balance

It is imperative to understand the relationships and to create a balance in the operations of the variables and impacts in the marketplace, especially on the buying decisions and behaviours of consumers which provide the basis for business decisions and strategies. While religion is fundamentally a crucial part of man and livelihood, its significance in man's daily living is its relationship with economic activities which strategically affect buying behaviours (Iyer, 2016). How religion defines consumers' buying decisions and behaviours is hinged on the tenets, doctrines and teachings of each religion which invariably become the base for consumers' ethical behaviours and judgements among people, including the producers of goods and services. Thus, the decisions of consumers across all religions are not largely personal but a dictate of faith and religion to achieve conformity with other members, and to remain acceptable. Importantly, culture and religion derive their common ground from societies' interpretations of religious tenets and doctrines which influence the cultural behaviour of consumers in the marketplace.

Where the prevailing culture in society leans towards material acquisition, wealth display and ostentatious consumption, it is influenced by the teachings and commands of religious tenets and this will to a great extent determine the disposition of worshippers' behaviours towards riches and wealth. Hence, the level of acquisition or obedience to religious tenets will further determine the religious orientation of consumers/worshippers. All the holy books and ATR doctrines believe that wealth acquisition and religiosity have inverse relationships, and studies further confirm that the acquisition of more wealth may have reverse effects on individual devotion and spirituality and the organisational pursuit of ethical practice (Keir, 2016; Leahy, 1986; Fort, 1997). For instance, in a society where inordinate wealth and material acquisition is celebrated and is used to determine the level of societal influence, social status and respect, there is a high probability that people tend to be extrinsic oriented because the quest to be rich and relevant in society will dominate the market behaviours of buyers, and may cloud ethical intention and judgement. In other words, consumers' tendency to be unethical in the consumption of fashion, food and services like banking is a function of the extent to which the religion influences culture in a society. By and large, in a society where the urge for inordinate wealth acquisition and unnecessary material pursuit is discouraged and religiosity is celebrated, the religious orientation will have a direct impact on ethical intention and the behaviours of people/consumers in the marketplace.

Importantly, the quality of religious values, teachings and tenets may go a long way to determine consumers' buying behaviour and decisions, especially in a society like developing markets where religion plays a strategic role in individuals' market and social behaviours and lifestyle. It was understood during the survey that the incidence of wrong and watered-down religious teachings in many religious sects and denominations is influencing the unethical practices and values system. There is a symbiotic relationship between religion and ethical values in society, and the content of religious teachings may influence the religious orientation imbibed and exhibited.

Essentially, the level of Westernisation or Westernised orientation in a society, or the extent that a socio-economic system has embraced neo-liberalism, may determine the direction or practice of religious orientation among people or consumers. Neo-liberalism that manifests in capitalist economic practice and the resultant effects on socio-economic lifestyles directly affects religion and religiosity because the ethical foundation of neo-liberalism runs contrary to the piousness, devoutness and conservative practices of the intrinsic orientation associated with religions like Islam, Christianity, Buddhism and Hinduism (Jones, 2010; Al-Quasimi, 2010; Iyer, 2016; Gokariksel & McLarney, 2010). The differences in societies' display, consumption or usage of fashion, religious economics and other socio-economic activities are influenced by the extent of acceptance or influence of neo-liberalism on religion. The tendency for neo-liberalism to influence religiosity and religious orientation of people is high when the socio-economic foundation is built on Western capitalism and liberalism.

CONCLUSION

Irrevocably, the relationship between religion and ethics remains a synergy that influences and determines many developments in society. The influence of religion on ethics is a superior function in that the former influences the tempo, ethos and operationalisation of the latter, and is the reason that the religious orientation of consumers may affect their stance on evaluation and understanding of ethics. Consumers' market behaviours depend on the influence of culture (prevailing societal values that support either intrinsic or extrinsic orientation) and neo-liberalist culture (influenced by Westernisation and capitalist practices) that will drive their behaviours in the market. By and large, the symbiotic relationships and connections between religion and business ethics are inseparable (Knox, 1902; Gras, 1944; Keir, 2016) and recognition of every society's peculiarities will make business policies and decisions enjoy continuity and a profitable performance.

REFERENCES

Adesina, W. & Ayodele, O. (2004). Shaping the Internet for Match-Making/Dating: A Challenge for the Contemporary Nigerian Family Institution, *African Sociological Review*, 8(2), pp. 103–14.
Al-Quasimi, N. (2010). Immodest Modesty: Accommodating Dissent and the 'Abaya-as-Fashion' in the Arab Gulf States, *Journal of Middle East Women's Studies*, 6(1), pp. 46–74.
Allport, G.W. (1950). *The Individual and His Religion: A Psychological Interpretation*, New York: Macmillan.
Allport, G.W. & Ross, J.M. (1967). Personal Religious Orientation and Prejudice. *Journal of Personality and Social Psychology*, 5, pp. 432–43.
Anand, M. (2014). Islamic Insurance in Malaysia: Insights for the Indian Insurance Industry, *Singapore Journal of Legal Studies*, pp. 1–23.

Bekkin, R.I. (2007). Islamic Insurance: National Features and Legal Regulations, *Arab Law Quarterly*, 21(2), pp. 109–34.

Bobkowski, P.S. & Kalyanaraman, S. (2010). Effects of Online Christian Self-Disclosure on Impression Formation, *Journal for the Scientific Study of Religion*, 49(3), pp. 456–76.

Bobkowski, P.S. & Pearce, L.D. (2011). Baring their Souls in Online Profiles or Not? Religious Self-Disclosure in Social Media, *Journal for the Scientific Study of Religion*, 50(4), pp. 744–62.

Chowdhury, R.M.M.I. & Fernando, M. (2013). The Role of Spiritual Well-being and Materialism in Determining Consumers' Ethical Beliefs: An Empirical Study with Australian Consumers, *Journal of Business Ethics*, 113(1), pp. 61–79.

Doole, I. & Lowe, R. (2000). *International Marketing Strategy: Analysis, Development and Implementation*, 2nd Edition, London: Thompson Business Press.

Fair, J.E., Tully, M., Ekdale, B. & Asante, R.K.B. (2009). Crafting Lifestyles in Urban Africa: Young Ghanaians in the World of Online Friendship, *Africa Today*, 55(4), pp. 28–49.

Foley, J.P. (1998). Ethics in Advertising: A Look at the Report by the Pontifical Council for Social Communications, *Journal of Public Policy and Marketing*, 17(2), pp. 313–15.

Fort, T.L. (1997). Religion and Business Ethics: The Lessons from Political Morality. *Journal of Business Ethics*, 16(3), pp. 263–73.

Genia, V. (1993). A Psychometric Evaluation of the Allport-Ross I/E Scale in a Religiously Heterogeneous Sample. *Journal for the Scientific Study of Religion*, 32(3), pp. 284–90.

Gokariksel, B. & McLarney, E. (2010). Muslim Women, Consumer Capitalism, and the Islamic Culture Industry, *Journal of Middle East Women's Studies*, 6(3), pp. 1–18.

Gokariksel, B. & Secor, A.J. (2009). New Transnational Geographies of Islamism, Capitalism and Subjectivity: The Veiling Fashion Industry in Turkey, *Area*, 41(1), pp. 6–18.

Gokariksel, B. & Secor, A.J. (2010a). Between Fashion and Tesettur: Marketing and Consuming Women's Islamic Dress, *Journal of Middle East Women's Studies*, 6(3), pp. 118–48.

Gokariksel, B. & Secor, A.J. (2010b). Islamic-ness in the Life of a Commodity: Veiling Fashion in Turkey, *Transactions of the Institute of British Geographers*, 35(3), pp. 313–33.

Gras, N.S.B. (1944). Religion and Business. *Bulletin of the Business Historical Society*, 18(2), pp. 27–32.

Hamdani, S.N.H., Ahmad, E., Khalid, M. & Tahir, S. (2004). Study of Philanthropic Behaviour in Divine Economics Framework, *Paper of Proceedings Part II Twentieth Annual General Meeting and Conference of the Pakistan Society of Development Economists*, Winter, pp. 875–94, Pakistan Institute of Development Economics, Islamabad.

IndexMundi (2019). www.indexmundi.com

Iyer, S. (2016). The New Economics of Religion, *Journal of Economic Literature*, 54(2), pp. 395–441.

Jacobson, C.K. (1998). Religiosity and Prejudice: An Update and Denominational Analysis. *Review of Religious Research*, 39(3), pp. 264–72.

Jones, C. (2010). Images of Desire: Creating Virtue and Value in an Indonesia, Islamic Lifestyle Magazine, *Journal of Middle East Women's Studies*, 6(3), pp. 91–117.

Kastner, K. (2018). Making Fashion, Forming Bodies and Persons in Urban Senegal, *Africa Development*, 43(1), pp. 5–20.

Keir, J. (2016). From Religion to Business Hans Kung's Final Bridge-Building Challenge. *The Journal of Corporate Citizenship*, 62(Special Issue), pp. 131–42.

Khan, J.M. (2014). Construction of Muslim Religiosity Scale, *Islamic Studies*, 53(1/2), pp. 67–81.

Kim, D., Fisher, D. & McCalman, D. (2009). Modernism, Christianity and Business Ethics: A Worldview Perspective, *Journal of Business Ethics*, 90(1), pp. 115–21.

Knox, G.W. (1902). Religion and Ethics. *International Journal of Ethics*, 12(3), pp. 301–16.

Leahy, J.T. (1986). Embodied Ethics: Some Common Concerns of Religion and Business. *Journal of Business Ethics,* 5(6), pp. 465–72.

Lewis, R. (2010). Marketing Muslim Lifestyle: A New Media Genre, *Journal of Middle East Women's Studies*, 6(3), pp. 58–90.

Lu, L. & Lu, C. (2010). Moral Philosophy, Materialism, and Consumer Ethics: An Exploratory Study in Indonesia, *Journal of Business Ethics*, 94, pp. 193–210.

Lynch, J. (1990). Marketing and the Religious Right: An Application of the Parallel Political Market Place Conceptualisation. *Journal of Public Policy and Marketing*, 9, pp. 154–66.

Miller, M.R. & Dixon-Roman, E.J. (2011). Habits of the Heart: Youth Religious Participation as Progress, Peril, or Change? *Annals of the American Academy of Political and Social Science*, 637, pp. 78–98.

Moors, A. (2003). Islam and Fashion on the Streets of San'a, Yemen, *Fashion and Hypes*, 16(2), pp. 41–56.

Neyrinck, B., Lens, W., Vansteenkiste, M. & Soenens, B. (2010). Updating Allport's and Batson's Framework of Religious Orientations: A Re-evaluation from the Perspective of Self-Determination Theory and Wulff's Social Cognitive Model. *Journal for the Scientific Study of Religion*, 49(3), pp. 425–38.

Nwosu, P. (2013). *Introducing the Study of Comparative Religion: Perspective in the Study of Religions*, Lagos: K. Success.

Onaiyekan, J. (2011). Dividends of Religion in Nigeria, Public Lecture at University of Ilorin, 12 May.

Parboteeah, K.P., Hoegl, M. & Cullen, J.B. (2008). Ethics and Religion: An Empirical Test of a Multidimensional Model, *Journal of Business Ethics*, pp. 387–98.

Patterson, A.S. (2014). Religion and the Rise of Africa. *Brown Journal of World Affairs*, 21(Fall/Winter), pp. 181–96.

Pew Research Centre (2008). Religious and Public Life: US Religious Landscape Survey: Religious Beliefs and Practices. www.pewforum.org

Pew Research Centre (2010). Religion and Public Life: Tolerance and Tension: Islam and Christianity in Sub-Saharan Africa. www.perforum.org

Putrevu, S. & Swimberghe, K. (2013). The Influence of Religiosity on Consumer Ethical Judgement and Response towards Sexual Appeals, *Journal of Business Ethics*, 115(2), pp. 351–65.

Qasaymeh, K. (2011). Islamic Banking in South Africa: Between the Accumulation of Wealth and the Promotion of Social Prosperity, *Comparative and International Law Journal of Southern Africa*, 44(2), pp. 275–92.

Rashid, M.Z. & Ibrahim, S. (2008). The Effects of Culture and Religiosity on Business Ethics: A Cross-Cultural Comparison, *Journal of Business Ethics*, 82(4), pp. 907–17.

Ringold, D.J. (1998). Comment of the Pontifical Council for Social Communications' Ethics in Advertising, *Journal of Public Policy and Marketing*, 17(2), pp. 332–5.

Roth, D.L., Mwase, I., Holt, C.L., Clark, E.M., Lukwago, S.N. & Kreuter, M.W. (2012). Religious Involvement Measurement Model in a National Sample of African Americans, *Journal of Religion and Health*, 51(2), pp. 567–78.

Savulescu, J. (1998). Two Worlds Apart: Religion and Ethics, *Journal of Medical Ethics*, 24(6), pp. 382–4.

Schneider, H., Krieger, J. & Bayraktar, A. (2011). The Impact of Intrinsic Religiosity on Consumers' Ethical Beliefs: Does It Depend on the Type of Religion? A Comparison of Christian and Moslem Consumers in Germany and Turkey, *Journal of Business Ethics*, 102(2), pp. 319–32.

Schottmann, S.A. (2014). From Duty to Choice: Marketing Islamic Banking in Malaysia, *South East Asia Research*, 22(1), pp. 57–72.

Siddique, M.Z. & Iqbal, M. (2016). Theory-Practice Convergence of Islamic Banking in Pakistan: An Empirical Analysis, *Islamic Studies*, 55(1–2), pp. 33–56.

Siddiqui, S.H. (2012). Anatomy and Critique of Islamic Banking, *Pakistan Horizon*, 65(3), pp. 35–58.

Singhapakdi, A., Salyachivin, S., Virakul, B. & Veerayangkur, V. (2000). Some Important Factors Underlying Ethical Decision Making of Managers in Thailand. *Journal of Business Ethics*, 27(3), pp. 271–84.

Singhapakdi, A., Vitell, S.J., Lee, D., Nisius, A.M. & Yu, G.B. (2013). The Influence of Love of Money and Religiosity on Ethical Decision-Making in Marketing. *Journal of Business Ethics*, 114(1), pp. 183–91.

Taylor, V.A., Halstead, D. & Haynes, P.J. (2010). Consumer Responses to Christian Religious Symbols in Advertising, *Journal of Advertising*, 39(2), pp. 79–92.

Tayob, S. (2016). 'O You who Believe, Eat of the *Tayyibat* (Pure and Wholesome Food) That We Have Provided You': Producing Risk, Expertise and Certified Halal Consumption in South Africa, *Journal of Religion in Africa*, 46(1), pp. 67–91.

The Guardian (2002). Miss World Will Go Ahead Despite Riots. 25 November. www.theguardian.com/uk/2002/nov/25/gender.world

The Guardian (2007). Indonesian Playboy Editor Cleared of Indecency. 5 April. www.theguardian.com/media/2007/apr/05/pressandpublishing.indonesia

van der Geutgen, J., Van Meijel, B., den Uyl, M.H.G. & de Vries, N. (2013). Virginity, Sex, Money and Desire: Premarital Sexual Behviour of Youths in Bolgatanga Municipality, Ghana, *African Journal of Reproductive Health*, 17(4), pp. 93–106.

Vitell, S.J. (2010). The Role of Religiosity in Business and Consumer Ethics: A Review of the Literature. *Journal of Business Ethics*, 90, pp. 155 67.

Vitell, S.J. & Muncy, J. (2005). The Muncy-Vitell Consumer Ethics Scale: A Modification and Application. *Journal of Business Ethics*, 62(3), pp. 267–75.

Vitell, S.J., Paolillo, J.G.P. & Singh, J.J. (2005). Religiosity and Consumer Ethics, *Journal of Business Ethics*, 57(2), pp. 175–81.

Vitell, S.J., Paolillo, J.G.P. & Singh, J.J. (2006). The Role of Money and Religiosity in Determining Consumers' Ethical Beliefs, *Journal of Business Ethics*, 64(2), pp. 117–24.

Vitell, S.J., Bing, M.N., Davison, H.K., Ammeter, A.P., Garner, B.L. & Novicivec, M.M. (2009). Religiosity and Moral Identity: The Mediating Role of Self-Control. *Journal of Business Ethics*, 88(4), pp. 601–13.

Wells, W.D. (1993). Discovery-Oriented Consumer Research. *Journal of Consumer Research*, 19(4), pp. 459–504.

7. Consumption, religion and digital marketing in developing countries

Ayantunji Gbadamosi

INTRODUCTION

Who would have thought that the sudden change the world experienced in consumption patterns during the Covid-19 pandemic would turn out as it did? Nations of the world introduced lockdown measures to prevent physical interactions between people as a means of curbing the spread of the virus. Restaurants and pubs were asked to close, fashion retailers and banks were given a similar order for the same reason of saving lives. Similar measures were applied to schools and other education institutions as well as conference events to be held around the period of the outbreak. The simple message is that a 'new normal' life has emerged that permeates virtually all walks of life including consumption. Emphatically, one remarkable issue that accompanied this dynamic of consumer behaviour in an unprecedented form is the significant increase in the use of digital measures to aid consumption activities. Online shopping for needed products which could not be bought through the usual physical presence in the stores, students' educational activities that suddenly moved online to redeem the educational system, and the proliferation of online conferences around the time are some of the examples of how the world responded to the global pandemic that altered our way of living. The use of social media to check on the welfare of loved ones and access global news is another clear example that cannot be ignored. By and large, digital marketing came in handy for daily living. This major phase of life and several other changes in the business world experienced prior to that bring the discourse of this phenomenon to the fore.

In consistency with the overarching focus of this book, this chapter explores how digital marketing interacts with religion to influence consumption in developing nations. The content of the chapter is arranged as follows. Following this introduction is an overview of digital marketing, providing a robust foundation for the content of the chapter. This is followed by online customer behaviour that presents the dynamics of what consumers buy, why they buy them, and how they engage in the purchases vis-à-vis the use of digital technologies. The section also examines the relevance and application of some theories around the nexus of consumer behaviour and technology. The notion of an online marketing environment is also discussed and comes after the online consumer behaviour segment. Similarly, segmentation, targeting, and positioning is also examined with specific reference to digital marketing and religion. This is followed by a discussion on the use of social media in relation to consumption activities with specific relevance to religion and developing countries.

AN OVERVIEW OF DIGITAL MARKETING

It is now widely accepted that our consumption patterns have been significantly revolutionised in many ramifications (Gbadamosi, 2019). At every phase of the consumer decision-making process, digital technologies are considered important. Although it may vary in scale, it is interesting to note that this development straddles developed and developing countries. It is stated that digital channels facilitate people's purchase decisions in that they can search, evaluate the information obtained, make recommendations, influence decisions of others, and offer feedback to consumers (GE Capital, 2013). A good number of studies has emphasised that the proliferation of social technologies has significantly contributed to the shift in how people collaborate, communicate, share information, and consume (Hsu et al., 2007; Aral et al., 2013; Susarla et al., 2013; Benson et al., 2015). One observation which is also logically shared by many is that the internet has spawned completely new categories of products and services that could be produced, promoted, and distributed with networked computers, and it is important to study how these market offerings are moved from various points on the value chain to the ultimate consumer (Key, 2017). Increasing evidence shows that religious products such as food, clothing, and other religious artefacts are not excluded, especially as these are moved from one country or context to another.

  Meanwhile, it is important for us to have a brief and operational definition of digital marketing that could help our understanding of the discourse in this chapter. Smith (2012: 86) defines digital marketing as 'the practice of promoting products and services using digital distribution channels via computers, mobile phones, smart phones, or other digital devices'. While this definition seems useful to a great extent, especially in highlighting some of the tools used in this new phenomenon, its focus is more on the marketing communications aspect of the construct. A rather succinct definition but with a wider scope is given by Chaffey and Ellis-Chadwick (2016: 11) which defines the term as 'achieving marketing objectives through applying digital technologies and media'. Historically, this change in the form of connection of people to the digital world could be linked to the first production of the personal computer in 1981, and interest in this phenomenon continues to grow astronomically and even increases in significance thereafter such that the marketing channels in the twenty-first century are notably virtual worldwide (Karatum, 2017). So, the internet has changed consumption considerably in the past decades among consumers of different characteristics including those of different religious beliefs.

Increasing evidence now continues to show that consumers of today, especially those in the category of Generation X, are now more pragmatic, socially connected, and could be considered to multitask in the digital marketing environment (Schiffman et al., 2008). Interestingly, this consumer group is present in various religious groups, and in both developed and developing countries. Grant et al. (2013) put it very simply to indicate that the internet has actually become a fully fledged distribution channel, hence marketers will have to deal with the reality of complexity associated with behaviour linked to this especially in the area of online information exchanges. An example could be seen in the form of consumers that are based in countries where certain religious-oriented products are not readily available. They could order and receive them to satisfy their needs. This is an example of a case in which the divide between the developing countries and developed countries is less visible. So, a consumer in the United States could order a specific abaya (a type of Muslim's women dress) from Dubai or Malaysia to her doorstep, so could a customer in the United Kingdom receive his kumkuma (a powder often used for religious and social events in Hinduism) from India. Ultimately, the gap between consumers and producers is being bridged through various technological opportunities.

One may wonder why this is the case. These are closely connected to the several benefits associated with the use of digital technologies to consumers over the more conventional approach to consumption. Some of these benefits as listed in the literature include convenience, broader selection of market offerings, product diversity, more access to competitive pricing, richer and participative information, efficiency, and cost reduction (Bayo-Moriones & Lera-López, 2007; Tiago et al., 2014). For example, it is noted that online reviews provided by customers are beneficial in that they are a trusted source of information for consumers which could be a sign for marketers to explore this in depth towards identifying what motivates those who write the reviews (Smith, 2011). Reviews are often provided concerning virtually all religion-related products ranging from financial services products to food and fashion items.

As a link to this, it is shown that Millennials have a preference for certain digital advertising over others implying that there are specific digital marketing strategies that would be amenable to reaching them, like websites with brightly coloured graphics (Smith, 2012). If we look at it from the perspective of the marketers, there is a claim that digital media enhances direct dialogue with the consumer (Tiago et al., 2014). This is a crucial development in the world of marketing generally, and in marketing communications in particular. So, there could be dialogue between consumers in Malaysia, Ghana, and Mexico and marketers in other parts of the world, say Canada, Germany, or Japan. One of the ways by which this is facilitated is the low cost. It is argued that the cost efficiency of digital communications compared to the traditional media is considerable. This digital marketing, also known as e-commerce, is not only being used frequently by marketers to reach their target audience, but also attracts billions of dollar investments from various organisations (Smith, 2011). At the global level, the number of active internet users has been noted as 4.54 billion (Statista, 2020). ICT Facts and Figures provides some useful statistics that could be of use to our discourse of digital marketing in this chapter. Firstly, it is indicated that 70 percent of the world youth are online in one form or another. To be specific, it is noted that in developed countries, 94 percent of young people whose ages range from 15 to 24 use the internet whereas the number in developing countries is put at 67 percent. The percentage is even lower (30 percent) in least developing countries (International Telecommunications Union, 2017). The same information source (ICT Facts and Figures, 2017) shows that the proportion of homes with internet access in developed countries is double that of developing countries. Generally, interest in the use of the internet and the associated activities including consumption is on the increase but these records show that developing countries are still relatively behind in the rate of adoption of this phenomenon for transactions.

There are various ways and tools often used to bring digital marketing execution to fruition and these have different ways of influencing consumers in terms of how they make their consumption decisions. One of these classifications is the use of in-bound and out-bound systems. As explained by Patrutiu-Baltes (2016), in-bound marketing gives room for open and smart communications towards purchasers that pay attention to the organisation's market offerings and create personal relationships with them in the form of promoting content that is adapted to their needs. This approach to reaching consumers encourages interactions online. Ultimately, the key focus here is that the consumer is active in searching for a solution or interaction with brands and is attracted to stimuli through social media marketing and content search (Chaffey and Ellis-Chadwick, 2016). On the other hand, the out-bound is about how the firm communicates personalised messages to customers through its website or email formats. Unlike the in-bound marketing that involves the consumer searching for the brand or products, the out-bound is initiated by the digital marketer towards generating action from the target customers (Maheshwari et al., 2019). The twenty-first-century marketers and consumers of products are amenable to various types of these approaches which explain why firms tend to emphasise the integrated marketing communications in their strategies. The relevance of each of these tends to vary with the nature of the products, religious sensitivities, and consumers' religiosity.

ONLINE CONSUMER BEHAVIOUR

Just as we discuss the issue of consumer behaviour in its wider context, the discourse also has significant implications associated with how people make their consumption decisions using digital technologies. Products offered on the internet lack some salient features such as opportunities to taste, smell, and tangibility, which explains why it is important to mitigate these through the provision of information to consumers in various forms with the option to zoom in and out to make the products more visible for evaluation (Talpau, 2014). Perhaps a good way to start is to look into the issue of who are these digital consumers, how can they be categorised, and how are they influenced? What is the place of religion in their consumption?

An interesting contribution by Hanlon (2019) provides a good starting point. In this publication, distinction is made between digital natives and digital immigrants. Explaining this further, Hanlon (2019) shows that the terms are discussed in relation to a generational cohort of people to depict digital natives as those who were born in the digital era and are therefore more versed in the use of digital technologies. Hence, they were born into a time characterised by the predominance of gadgets such as tablets and smart phones and are accustomed to the use of social media such as YouTube, Facebook, Twitter, and Instagram to mention but a few. So, whether one practises Judaism, Hinduism, or Buddhism is not really the issue, the focus is on the dispensation of birth of that consumer falling within the period characterised by the surge of digital technological tools. On the other hand, as the notion of immigrants is often discussed in relation to people who are born in a different country but migrate to a host country, digital immigrants are considered as those whose births do not fall within this period. Hence, the divide between these groups is expected to show in terms of their understanding of the use of these technological gadgets. This is an interesting illustration of customer behaviour in relation to this phenomenon as teased out from the literature. Nonetheless, this typology has been criticised by many on the ground that the terminologies cannot neatly provide exact explication of how consumers use these tools in that the line between the two could be very blurred. For instance, some digital native individuals might not be as keen on technology as depicted, whereas some people considered to be digital immigrants may have a keen interest in technology and great understanding of how they work. A closely related erroneous point that could be made is to claim that consumers from developing countries such as Burundi,

Lesotho, and Belize do not use internet technologies. There are small groups of consumers within these contexts that are more technology savvy than others that are in developed countries where the technological usage rate is very high.

Apart from the generational divide embedded in the typology of digital natives and digital immigrants, online customer behaviour could also be explained through the information obtained by consumers online and how they use it. Chen (2010) provides two types of information that consumers seek online in order to evaluate their choice of market offerings. In this explanation, the first could be noted as all in-born features of the product or service such as the purpose, price, and functionality, whereas the second information type is about the social characteristics of the products in the form of data relating to the review of the products from other consumers who have used and experienced the products in the past. While the former type of information revolves around the static features of the products, the latter is social in nature (Chen, 2010; Mou & Shin, 2018). Both classifications are amenable to religious illustration and explication. For example, a specific product could be consumed for the purpose of religion. In this, we can see the examples of purchases for religious ceremonies and holy pilgrimages. Also, Islamic banking services fit the functionality illustration of this type of data usage by consumers. When consumers are interested in social interactions and reviews, the examples could be in the form of adherents of the religion specifically joining social media groups of their religion where information could be given about the appropriateness of the specific market offerings relating to their religion. From another perspective, the digital divide has been noted from the point of inequality (Lissitsa & Cohen, 2018). Hence, on the one hand, as noted in the literature (Dimaggio & Hargittai, 2001; Hargittai, 2003), there are those consumers with connectivity who have the full opportunities associated with it and there are others who are without, while the other classification relates to differentiating them on various types of users.

As noted by Valvi et al. (2013), some of the online customer behaviour discussions are guided by these theories which will be examined in relation to religion and the context of developing countries.

- Technology acceptance model (Davis et al., 1989)
- Theory of reasoned action (Fishbein & Ajzen, 1975)
- Theory of planned behaviour (Ajzen, 1991)
- The innovation diffusion theory (Rogers, 1962).

Consumers' Acceptance of New Technology

One of the key theories that could help us to understand how consumption in developing nations is linked to religion within the digital context is the technology acceptance model (TAM), developed by Davis et al. (1989). To have a deep understanding of this model and its link to this discourse, it will be useful to reflect back several years to the time when computers were new and just being introduced and there was scepticism around their use by people in relation to difficulties associated with using them. The key message behind the model was to see a way of explaining the link of perceived benefits of adopting new technology and the experience of users of the technology. As noted by Hanlon (2019), the origin of this model is linked to the seminal work of Fishbein and Ajzen (1975) entitled the theory of reasoned action. Overall, the TAM indicates that people accept using technology based on their perception of how useful or beneficial it will be to help them get their job done, but this model suggests that this will be weighed alongside 'perceived ease of use'. Hence, if the new technology is too difficult for them to understand and use such that the difficulty outweighs the benefit, then acceptance will be affected. Overall, the key factors taken into consideration in this model are:

- external variables
- perceived usefulness
- perceived ease of use
- attitude towards using the technology
- behavioural intention to use the technology
- actual system usage.

Although the application of this model started with the use of computers, it is now widely used to explain acceptance of other technological tools such as apps and mobile phones. Similarly, we can extend the understanding to explain how followers of a religion embrace the use of technology. Accordingly, apart from the personal factors which include religiosity that may influence the decision of how to embrace technology, external factors which include perspectives of others towards the adoption will also be key to this explanation. Wahyuni (2016) conducted a study on the influence of the TAM model on students' behaviour to the Sharia financial system (Sikesya), used for learning about this financial product, in Indonesia. It shows that users' perceived ease of use is not influenced by experience but the perceived usefulness of the system influences the attitudes and behaviour of these users positively. Also, social influence is found to influence behavioural intention. Similarly, in another study conducted in Iran, Kashi and Zheng (2013) found that perceived usefulness significantly impacts the behavioural intentions of job applicants for e-recruitment systems whereas this is not the case for perceived ease of use. Although there is a high likelihood of differences in reactions to digital technologies based on various factors, by and large, the usefulness of digital technologies in terms of how they facilitate transactions is expected to prompt further use in developing countries even in various religious contexts. Meanwhile, there is great potential for further empirical studies on how this model applies in several religious-related contexts and consumption in developing countries.

The Innovation Diffusion Theory

Another useful theoretical explication around consumption that can be applied to digital marketing and religion in developing nations is the theory of diffusion of innovation (Rogers, 1962). In its general terms, the theory provides explanation around how consumers adopt new innovation in the marketplace. In this theory, it is believed that there are variations around how quickly an innovation spreads among consumers in the marketplace. In this, different categories of consumers are identified as follows:

- innovators
- early adopters
- early majority
- late majority
- laggards.

These different consumer categories display different consumer behavioural patterns for the new products beginning with the most enthusiastic group (innovators) to the laggards who are not particularly keen to adopt the new invention until others have tried it and ensured that the risk involved in buying the product is minimal. In the analysis of the society, such as in developing countries, the relevance of different religious groups like Christians, Buddhists, and Muslims is pivotal to new product adoption (Rehman & Shabbir, 2010).

Interestingly, given the nature of the topic involved, we can draw experiences and examples from different contexts to an extent, to initiate the discussion in relation to developing countries. For instance, Lissitsa and Cohen (2018) in a study that revolves around online shopping note a different level of religiosity among the Jewish population to be secular, religious, traditional, and ultra-orthodox. In this typology, the secular Jews are interested in religious ceremonies and rituals due to their cultural resonance whereas they would still like to be seen as secular. Hence they are torn between these two influences (Lissitsa & Cohen, 2018). The traditionalists are different in that they tend to be closer to the religious than the secular group, supportive of Jewish religiosity, but do not observe most of the associated commandments (Peres & Ben-Rafael, 2006; Yuchtman-Ya'ar & Peres, 2000; Lissitsa & Cohen, 2018). As shown in the study, the majority of those considered religious are well integrated into Israeli society in terms of participation in military service, participation in a residential pattern, and participation in the labour force. According to Lissitsa and Cohen (2018), citing a body of literature (Friedman, 1991; El-Or & Watzman, 1994; Cohen & Susser, 2000), the ultra-orthodox segment accept rabbinic authority as unquestionable, and are characterised by their rigid interpretation of Jewish religious law, strong adherence to Torah study, and, to them, the use of the internet can be a threat to religious conservation. According to Lissitsa and Cohen (2018), this latter segment (ultra-orthodox) could be likened to the laggards category in Rogers' (1962) diffusion of innovation theory.

As in the conventional understanding of adopting new products, consumers consider a number of key factors which include perceived relative advantage, perceived usefulness, trust, attitude, compatibility, and perceived ease of use. The study of Agag and El-Masry (2016b) that revolves around understanding consumer intention to participate in the online travel community specifically emphasises these listed factors. So, while there may be resistance on the part of the consumers to digital technologies due to their deep level of religiosity, the relevance of these factors that underpin the adoption of new technology cannot be underestimated. For instance, the relative advantage of using the new technology could understandably tilt the interest of religious consumers who may be overly conscious of adopting new technology to consider it positively. For instance, the relative advantage of technology came to the rescue significantly all over the world during the global pandemic of Covid-19 such that various religious groups now turn to digital technology to maintain their religious practices. One of the dominant examples is the Easter celebration by Christians that was unavoidably done online across the world as various governments of the world instructed their citizens to observe social distancing and avoid going to houses of worship to prevent the spread of the virus among worshippers. This adoption of technology to stream religious services online through the use of communication packages such as Skype, Zoom, Microsoft Team, and WhatsApp took place both in the developed and developing countries.

As reported by the United Nations, while 57 per cent of member states have indicated details about Covid-19 on their national portals, as at 25 March 2020, this number had surged to 86 per cent, totalling 167 countries by 8 April 2020 (UN, 2020). This is a significant use of digital technology for guidance on lockdowns, social distancing measures, and other related issues. Meanwhile, there are specific observations relating to developing countries. In a recent online panel discussion which revolved around digital health in developing countries with perspectives from Sri Lanka, Benin, and Pakistan, mobile technology services were noted as useful for people in understanding their Covid-19 symptoms. Within this context, the health-tech start-ups reported a several fold increase in the usage of their technologies as a result of the pandemic (GSMA, 2020). Many commentators described it as a 'new normal' that will continue to influence practices even in developing countries for many years to come.

DIGITAL MARKETING ENVIRONMENT AND THE NEXUS OF CONSUMPTION AND RELIGION IN DEVELOPING COUNTRIES

Just as we discuss the conventional marketing environment as a crucial topic to the discussion of consumer behaviour, so is the discourse of the digital marketing environment. Consumers and businesses interact within this environment constantly and the changes within it determine how successful or otherwise a business will be. However, the focus in this chapter is more around consumption. Hence, attention will be directed to how consumers and their religious

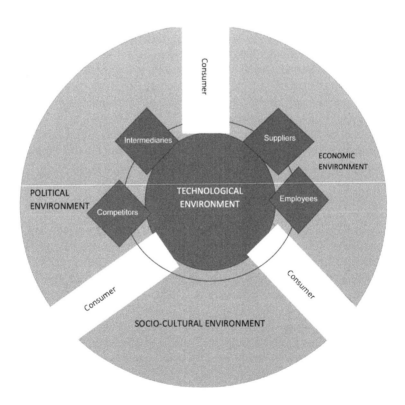

Figure 7.1   Digital marketing environment

beliefs operate within the macro- and micro-environmental factors which are depicted in Figure 7.1.

MACRO-ENVIRONMENTAL FACTORS

Economic Environment

Consumers' decisions are influenced by a number of economic issues such as interest rates, exchange rates, gross domestic product (GDP), gross national product, inflation, and unemployment that depict the overall health of the economy. Generally, the economic strength and purchasing power of developing nations are notably different from those of developed countries. Furthermore, specific consumer groups have more access to resources than others which could be linked to proficiency and access to digital resources for consumption transactions. As an example, statistics available indicate some of the economic data of Bangladesh as a developing country. The percentage increase of the projected GDP for the year 2020 is put at 7.4 per cent while the percentage for the projected change in consumer prices is indicated as 5.5 per cent. For the Philippines, another country among the developing countries, the projected GDP growth for 2020 is estimated to be 6.2 per cent while the change in consumer prices for the same year is recorded as 2.3 per cent. These are simply examples of what determines the economic strength of nations in developing countries and will ultimately be linked to the rate of development to expect in relation to the use of digital technologies in the countries. Similarly, this would most likely be linked to the proportion of those exploring digital technologies for their religious-related consumption activities.

Political Environment

A number of political issues are linked to consumption as associated with the digital technologies. This tends to moderate the business environment to ensure that all stakeholders operate for the fairness of all. However, in some cases that are quite broad in scope, the involvement of politics is more noticeable than others. For example, Lewis (2015) raises the issue of the use of the hijab by Muslim women in the West and noted that it has been overpoliticised which prevents people from having the knowledge of how it works as a fashion item. The more liberal the political system of countries towards these things, the more likely they will be used by people. The internet penetration in a specific developing country is understandably dependent on the political system of the country. The political will of the government to direct attention to development around technology is crucial to whether significant progress will be made in that direction or not. One of the key challenges noted about some developing countries is government instability which implies that government regulation on developmental projects around technology may be affected. It is important for governments in developing countries to encourage technology innovation. This is emphasised by Wetmore (2017), that beyond looking into adapting to technology, giving priority to technology innovation is a core issue that developing countries need to bypass for effective digital systems to function. Besides, it is also emphasised that ensuring equitable distribution of technology between the citizens is important (Wetmore, 2017). Hence, the political system could focus on these to ensure further improvement in how consumption systems are facilitated which will ultimately be linked to religion.

Socio-Cultural Environment

This layer of the marketing environment revolves around the dynamics of people's way of life. The issues around culture and social interaction remain a valuable topic with interesting dynamics in marketing over the years (Gbadamosi, 2015a, 2015b, 2019). One of the highly cited and widely used cultural studies is that of Hofstede (1981), whose national culture typology classified nations on the basis of power distance, individualism, uncertainty avoidance, and masculinity. This varies from one society to another, and even within developing countries. Given the key relevance of this, changes in the socio-cultural environment are being monitored and analysed by marketers. For example, with reference to Xiao and Benbasat (2011), Agag and El-Masry (2016a) highlight the proliferation of internet fraud that accompanies the increasing growth of e-commerce. Drawing from the data from the National Fraud information centre, there was a loss of $781,841,611 for the year 2013 alone and this was notably higher than the records for the preceding years (www.fraud.org). The notion of ethics which is about the moral principles guiding consumers in their various consumption transactions and deciding on questionable cases (Agag & El-Masry, 2016a) can moderate the extent to which some embrace internet transactions. In relating this to religion, Choi et al.'s (2013) study shows that the consumer switching behaviour of the Protestants and those of Catholics, Buddhists, and non-religious consumers are not significantly different, which brings these authors to conclude that their teaching, values, and beliefs do not specifically align with their consumption switching behaviour.

Technological Environment

The significant change in the technological dimension of the marketing environment has launched new product development opportunities for businesses. More importantly, consumers' ways of life have been altered in a myriad of ways. Chang (2011) notes that Web 2.0 sites are becoming more effective in that they make it possible to have user-generated content. This reflects in a number of examples such as Instagram and YouTube platforms where consumers are able to upload and share videos of goods and services. The increasing use of this digital opportunity has been attributed not only to the associated convenience but also in terms of its resilience as a medium of education, entertainment, and communication (Lissitsa & Cohen, 2018). This explains why it has been positioned at the centre of the marketing environment in Figure 7.1, as compared to the usual illustration we often have in the conventional discussion of macro-environmental factors. Of course, this is meant to illustrate and emphasise its all-encompassing role among marketing environmental factors. In the context of the focus of this chapter, consumers of the same religious affiliation could offer advice to one another in terms of the availability of certain products and details of how they work within the tenets of their religious beliefs. This is also closely linked to how ideas of new products and services develop from various digital communities based on available expert opinions and resources that exist within those systems (Rehman & Shabbir, 2010).

MICRO-ENVIRONMENTAL FACTORS

While micro-environmental factors consist of the consumers themselves, channel members, suppliers, and the competitors of the firms offering goods and services desired by the consumer, their operations are also interlocked by some form of digital marketing activity in various ways. As the tastes of contemporary consumers in developing nations are becoming increasingly patterned in favour of technology-oriented or technology-facilitated consumption, these key stakeholders are left with almost no option but to move in a similar direction with their roles in the consumption system. For instance, the channel members mediating between the producers and the ultimate consumers will be looking into digital facilities to make order processing easier and accompanied by an expeditious delivery system. This will aid their roles of delivering time, place, and possession utilities. In the same vein, suppliers of inputs will have to contribute to the flow with appropriate use of technology otherwise the system will suffer.

A considerable level of evidence shows an increasing level of competition in the marketing environment among marketers offering goods and services to various consumers, including those in the developing countries. This, in a way, reinvigorates the position of the consumer as the king in the marketing system in that they have many options on how to fulfil their consumption desire. Accordingly, customers increasing demand for value in their transactions including the benefits of digital marketing cannot be ignored by a business as any firm unwilling to operate to conform to consumers' pattern of needs will be operating at their own peril. A clear example is the experience during the Covid-19 pandemic period when consumers were left with almost no option but internet transactions. Businesses that were not ready for that mode of interaction were affected in varying ways such as loss of revenue and even loss of the business. As technology occupies a central part of consumers' consumption system, so does religion to a great extent. Accordingly, the activities of channel members and suppliers are expected to take the religious characteristics of the target market into consideration. As a typical Muslim would expect suppliers of their products to ensure that such foods are halal compliant, so would adherents of Zoroastrianism, Sikhism, or Unitarianism expect channel members they are relating with to respect their religious beliefs. The move away from standardisation of marketing strategies to adaptation strategies by multinationals such as McDonald's and Subway in developing countries exemplified this contention further.

MARKET SEGMENTATION, TARGETING, AND POSITION IN ONLINE CONSUMPTION

Marketing is basically about identifying needs and wants and providing relevant market offerings to satisfy those at a profit to the organisation. Meanwhile, by nature, the market being served, including the digital market, is heterogeneous. This explains why it is indicated that the key rationale for the study of consumer behaviour revolves around understanding consumer markets better so as to be able to segment and target them effectively (Robson et al., 2013; Gbadamosi, 2009). This is especially so when considering basic differentiating factors like religious beliefs, the degree of interest in internet usage for transactions, and the society of the consumers. Blackwell (2016) notes that media companies have shifted attention from focusing on broad demographic divisions of consumers to a more nuanced focus on segmentation; with consideration for their lifestyle categorisation and psychological and cultural influences on their purchases. Hence, one can be interested in how consumers in developing countries use religion and digital marketing to aid their day-to-day consumption activities. For example, the study of Choi et al. (2013) indicates that there is merit in considering religiosity in market segmentation by businesses.

Before delving deeply into religion, religiosity, and digital marketing, one useful study around segmenting consumers in developing countries by Al-Khatib et al. (2005) pinpoints that extant knowledge around international segmentation on developing countries (such as Amine & Cavusgil, 1986; Hofstede, 1991; Malhotra et al. 1998) adopts macro-environmental factors such as political system ideologies, income levels, language, culture, and geographical location. As a form of improvement on this, it has been suggested that this effort has limitations and the use of micro factors such as personality, moral development situational factors, and lifestyle could provide richer insight into this phenomenon (Souiden, 2002; Al-Khatib et al., 2005). Accordingly, Al-Khatib et al.'s (2005) study yields three consumer segments in the developing countries that constitute the context of this study. These are:

- principled purchasers
- suspicious shoppers
- corrupt consumers.

While the principled purchasers are less opportunistic, more trusting of others, and perceive questionable actions in a negative way, the suspicious consumers in this context are less trusting of others, somewhat opportunistic but tend to be cautious in dealing with others, and place a high emphasis on ethical behaviour. The segment labelled 'corrupt' were not ethically oriented, they were Machiavellianistic, and took advantage of others. Logically, and to a great extent, these characteristics about consumers in the developing countries could be applied to their behavioural pattern in relation to the dynamics of their involvement in digital transactions.

Focusing on adolescents as consumers is also an interesting endeavour in itself. It has been shown that this consumer group is very close to the internet as it has access to various tools and gadgets that facilitate this in various places such as public libraries, school, family, and friends (Hill et al., 2013). The literature suggests that young consumers that belong to privileged socio-cultural systems are the most adept at internet usage (Lissitsa & Cohen, 2018). However, it is also important to note that adolescents' online consumption transactions have associated limitations especially in terms of their dependence on their parents for approval of transactions as they do not independently own credit cards (Hill et al., 2013). In terms of online segmentation in a specific context, Lissitsa and Cohen (2018) identify four consumer segments within contemporary Israeli society: ultra-orthodox, religious, traditional, and secular. These segments have interesting and varying behavioural patterns towards the use of the internet. Meanwhile, in relation to adolescents specifically, Hill et al. (2013) identify three segments which are:

- internet conquerors
- virtual pragmatists
- recreational shoppers.

As shown in this study, the internet conquerors are the group with the highest online accessibility, spend the greatest amount of time on the internet, and are the oldest of the three groups. This study also shows that this segment has the highest online self-efficacy, and most of them have the opportunity to make purchases with the permission of their parents (Hill et al., 2013). Unlike the internet conquerors, the virtual pragmatists are the youngest of the three segments, characterised by the lowest levels of online social motivations, lower consumer self-efficacy, and lower online accessibility. According to Hill et al. (2003), this consumer segment is least likely to make online purchases with the permission of their parents. Meanwhile, the recreational shoppers are in-between internet conquerors and virtual pragmatics. In view of its keen and enduring interest in internet shopping and for buying 'cool' things online, this segment is notably the highest in ranking in terms of shopping with the permission of their parents. This is quite revealing as a study and has great value in terms of the enrichment of knowledge on the use of digital technology for shopping. Nonetheless, while it is logical to argue the application of digital technologies to religion-related consumption, a deeper understanding of the dynamics in terms of segmentation of adherents on the basis of their religiosity, especially in developing countries, will benefit from further empirical studies.

Meanwhile, it is interesting that a wider scope of application of internet usage for consumption practices continues to emerge. For instance, the prevailing online dating transactions like Match.com and eHarmony are now being extended to cover various consumer groups including religious and race segments (Blackwell, 2016). Also, the shopping motives of consumers are useful in segmenting them such as having those shopping for utilitarian motives and those buying for hedonic experiences (Childers et al., 2001; Hill et al., 2013). In this schema, when consumers are driven by utilitarian motives for online transactions, they are keenly interested in rational cues linking to the market offerings towards making a rational decision that will give them an optimal outcome. On the other hand, consumers driven by hedonic motives would be interested in entertainment, fun, and emotional worth of the transaction experience (Sherry, 1990; Arnold & Reynolds, 2003). In a further explanation offered by Pandey and Chawla (2018), consumers buying experiential market offerings such as clothing may perceive that the quality and fit vary and could see the online option being riskier as they do not have the opportunity to touch or feel the product prior to purchase. In their study, which revolves around the evolving segments of online buyers in India, an emerging market, Pandey and Chawla (2018) identify three consumer segments:

- disengaged averse online shoppers
- adept online shopping optimists
- interactive convenience shoppers.

Those who are disengaged averse online shoppers have a low loyalty level and go for which of the channels meets their needs at the time, show apathy for online clothes shopping, and are drawn to online shopping by the availability of deals and offers and the availability of a higher range of different sizes of clothing. Meanwhile, the consumer segment known as adept online optimists enjoys online shopping and finds it logically useful, convenient, and trustworthy. Nonetheless, they may be switching and migrating to new websites as they have a superior level of technological prowess. The third segment, the interactive convenient shoppers, is not adept at using technology, and has a high level of e-distrust but does not mind spending a high amount on clothing compared to the other segments, despite their low-income status. Each of these segments offers distinct and interesting online dynamics that could extend understanding but considering the impact of this will be even more enlightening.

SOCIAL MEDIA CONSUMERS AND RELIGIOSITY IN DEVELOPING NATIONS

Evidently, the discussion of digital marketing and consumption within a religious context would be incomplete without reference to social media activities of consumers. Tracing the trend of events around the dynamics of this phenomenon, social media was originally a set of leisure tools through which people, friends, and family members could connect with one another by sharing information and networking, but it has now grown into a big part of most business organisations (Aral et al., 2013; Benson et al., 2015). Banks, educational institutions, grocery merchants, estate agents, and several other businesses are now on one social media platform or another to relate to their existing and potential customers. They realised that customers in various contexts and religious groups are social consumers. This development is understandable as it opens up opportunities for an increase in revenue for these businesses (Agarwal et al., 2008; Malthouse et al., 2013). To strip this down for clarity purpose, social media could be seen from two key interrelated areas which are the communication and content-sharing part and the part of social interaction through networking (Wasserman & Faust, 1994; Benson et al., 2015). Kaplan and Haenlein (2010) classify social media into six groups: content communities, collective projects, social networking sites, blogs and micro-blogging, multiplayer online role-playing games, and virtual social worlds. Each of these social media types has several examples that we relate with fairly regularly. For instance, YouTube is a type of content community, Wikipedia falls within collective projects, while LinkedIn and Facebook are types of social networking sites (Kaplan & Haenlein, 2010; Benson et al., 2015).

Consumers are different in terms of which of these social media platforms are amenable to depicting their consumption patterns. In the same vein, there will also be some interesting dynamics around how they are interlinked to religion and religiosity in the developing countries.

One of the challenges associated with the use of these social technologies is security breaches. Several cases reported in the press make some consumers have concerns about how social media organisations operate and the security of their data. One of the well-reported cases is that of Cambridge Analytica and Facebook in which security breach about the personal data of users was raised. Besides this, fraudsters, scammers, and other unscrupulous individuals are making incursions into the arena, stealing personal data of users associated with business organisations. In a study on the role of security notices and online consumer behaviour with reference to social networking users, Benson et al. (2015) explored the relationship between various factors. There are several types of social networking sites, purchase intentions, user victimisation, propensity towards risk, purchase experiences, and attention devoted to notice of security given by social media users. Their findings show that there is a strong link between consumers' purchase intentions and paying attention to notices and features of security on social networks. However, their study did not find a link between user victimisation, purchase experience, and the perception of security notices/features.

A TYPOLOGY OF DIGITAL CONSUMERS IN RELIGIOUS CONTEXT: REFLECTIONS FOR FURTHER STUDIES

This chapter explores a number of key issues on the relevance of digital technologies to religion in developing countries and it has opened an avenue for future studies. The interesting themes discussed in the chapter show some thought-provoking contentions and it will be beneficial in various ways if further studies could examine them empirically. Based on reflections on the issues discussed in this chapter, a four-segment typology on the explication of the religion–consumption nexus in relation to the use of digital technologies in developing countries is proposed as shown in Figure 7.2, in which the issue of segmentation targeting and positioning in relation to consumption around digital technologies is proposed.

As shown in Figure 7.2, when targeting consumers in relation to religion and digital marketing strategies in developing countries, it is logical to hold that undifferentiated marketing may not be as effective as expected. This is because consumers vary in terms of their religiosity and knowledge of the dynamics of digital technologies in relation to the purchase of goods and services. A typology of four consumer segments simply identified as the 4Cs (conservative, circumstantial, centric, and contemporary) in terms of their digital activities and engagement is hereby proposed in this chapter. The conservative consumers are not too keen about the use of digital technologies and would prefer all conceivable alternatives to this mode of satisfying their consumption needs. As

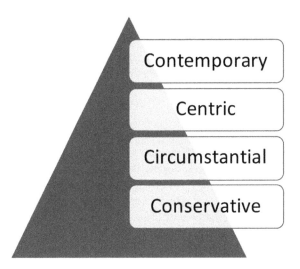

Figure 7.2   4Cs typology of digital consumers in a religious context

indicated earlier in this chapter, it may be misleading to rigidly conceptualise consumers in this category in terms of their age. Hence, the key identifier is the lifestyle in terms of aversion to digital technology. The circumstantial digital consumers are expected to share many characteristics of the conservatives. Nonetheless, when they encounter opportunities to use digital marketing for the purchase of goods and services, then their interest becomes kindled. However, they are not actively searching for opportunities to use these digital technologies except when circumstances bring them their way. The centrics are so identified in this typology due to their positioning in the schema. They are occasionally interested and use the digital mode of transaction even to address their religious needs. However, their sporadic engagement in digital marketing makes them lower in the hierarchy of digital usage than the contemporary consumers who are very adept in the use of various digital technology tools, using them to fulfil their secular and religious needs. The contemporaries are expected to be on several social media platforms and explore the benefits of these in various ways. Most of the contemporary consumers would also use this means to advance messages about their religious affiliations and explore it to fulfil their social needs. As shown in the arrow in Figure 7.2, there is potential for each of these segments to move up the latter towards reaching the 'contemporary consumer stage'.

While the 4cs typology is provided as an explication of the digital marketing segmentation approach for targeting consumers with specific relevance to religion, exploring it further in empirical studies could be academically rewarding. Hence, it has huge potential to lead to strategic direction for marketers when exploring the use of technology and religion in developing nations. Accordingly, it is expected that the basic segmentation norms of ensuring that the market segment is measurable, actionable, accessible, differentiable, and substantial will be maintained to achieve efficiency and effectiveness.

CONCLUSION

The practice of using technology to solve problems associated with consumption has come to stay. The proliferation of digital marketing permeates every facet of the human consumption system, from the purchase of low-involvement products such as fast-moving consumer goods to luxury products like fashion items. Nonetheless, the rate at which people embrace digital marketing varies in relation to many factors. One of these is the level of their religiosity. This could be viewed to be on a continuum ranging from the point where someone has no link to any religious belief to the other end where one is ardently associated with specific religious values. So, having a thorough understanding of online customer behaviour vis-à-vis their religiosity will extend the current understanding in consumer behaviour. Closely related issues under this are the existing models that explain the dynamics of consumer behaviour in relation to their use of digital technologies. Among these are the TAM, theory of reasoned action, theory of planned behaviour, and the innovation diffusion theory. In one form or another, the notion of religion and religiosity could be linked to how these theories explain the digital ramifications of consumption. In doing so, the notion of segmentation, targeting, and positioning becomes core to the discourse in that there are variations in what constitutes needs among various consumer groups. For example, the interest of Atheists, Muslims, Buddhists, and Christians, to mention but a few, for exploring the internet may well be different. Meanwhile, a further probe within each of these religions could also introduce further degrees of diversity and interest. For instance, the age difference between consumers in specific religious groups differentiates the rate and purpose of the use of internet facilities. Similarly, while some are more conservative in a particular religious belief, others are more open to the dynamics of these innovations. Hence, the 4cs typology of segmenting consumers for digital marketing strategic targeting is proposed (see Figure 7.2).

No consumer exists in a vacuum. Apart from religion, a myriad of other factors are at play. This introduces the relevance of the digital marketing environment. This consists of actors and forces whose roles and impact influence consumers' decisions. Conventionally, these are conceptualised as macro and micro forces. While the macro forces have a broad impact on businesses, the micro are closer to specific organisations. Within the terrain of this discourse, it could be logically argued that all of these factors are in turn influenced by changes and trends in the world of technology. Hence, the technological environment is considered core to these environmental forces. One of the emerging issues in the world of technology is the increasing engagement rate in social media activities. Although the original scheme of operations in social media platforms is merely around facilitating social interactions among members, its use has now been widely explored for consumption activities as well as facilitating business operations. The popularity of this medium is evident in the soaring number of people connected to one social media platform or another such as Facebook, Instagram, and Twitter. Meanwhile, this trend is challenging the commonly stated perspective that there is a dearth of digital activities in the developing nations. The explosive trend of technological advancement is evident albeit in varying scales when compared to developed nations. Hence, the impact of religion and technology on consumer behaviour is now more prominently evident in the contemporary developing nations.

REFERENCES

Agag, G. M., & El-Masry, A. A. (2016a). Cultural and religiosity drivers and satisfaction outcomes of consumer perceived deception in online shopping. *Internet Research*, *26*(4), 942–62.

Agag, G. M., & El-Masry, A. A. (2016b). Understanding consumer intention to participate in online travel community and effects on consumer intention to purchase travel online and WOM: An integration of innovation diffusion theory and TAM with trust. *Computers in Human Behavior*, *60*, 97–111.

Agarwal, R., Gupta, A. K., & Kraut, R. (2008). Editorial overview: The interplay between digital and social networks. *Information Systems Research*, *19*(3), 243–52.

Ajzen, I. (1991). The theory of planned behavior. *Organizational Behavior and Human Decision Processes*, *50*(2), 179–211.

Al-Khatib, J. A., Stanton, A. D. A., & Rawwas, M. Y. (2005). Ethical segmentation of consumers in developing countries: A comparative analysis. *International Marketing Review*, *22*, 225–46.

Amine, L. S., & Cavusgil, S. T. (1986). Marketing environment in the Middle East and North Africa: The forces behind market homogenization. *Advances in International Marketing*, *1*, 115–41.

Aral, S., Dellarocas, C., & Godes, D. (2013). Introduction to the special issue: Social media and business transformation: A framework for research. *Information Systems Research*, *24*(1), 3–13.

Arnold, M. J., & Reynolds, K. E. (2003). Hedonic shopping motivations. *Journal of Retailing*, *79*(2), 77–95.

Bayo-Moriones, A., & Lera-López, F. (2007). A firm-level analysis of determinants of ICT adoption in Spain. *Technovation*, *27*(6–7), 352–66.

Benson, V., Saridakis, G., Tennakoon, H., & Ezingeard, J. N. (2015). The role of security notices and online consumer behaviour: An empirical study of social networking users. *International Journal of Human-Computer Studies*, *80*, 36–44.

Blackwell, D. (2016). 40 is the new 65? Older adults and niche targeting strategies in the online dating industry. *Social Sciences*, *5*(4), 62.

Chaffey, D., & Ellis-Chadwick, F. (2016). *Digital Marketing: Strategy, Implementation, and Practice*. Harlow: Pearson Education.

Chang, J. (2011). Conceptualising the value of web content in marketing research. *Marketing Intelligence and Planning*, *29*(7), 687–96.

Chen, L. (2010). Understanding buyers' social information needs during purchase decision process. *Proceeding of 12th International Conference on Electronic Commerce*, 5–12. http://dx.doi.org/10.1145/2389376.2389380

Childers, T. L., Carr, C. L., Peck, J., & Carson, S. (2001). Hedonic and utilitarian motivations for online retail shopping behavior. *Journal of Retailing*, *77*(4), 511–35.

Choi, Y., Paulraj, A., & Shin, J. (2013). Religion or religiosity: Which is the culprit for consumer switching behavior? *Journal of International Consumer Marketing*, *25*(4), 262–80.

Cohen, A., & Susser, B. (2000). *Israel and the Politics of Jewish Identity: The Secular-Religious Impasse*. Jerusalem: JHU Press.

Davis, F. D., Bagozzi, R. P., & Warshaw, P. R. (1989). User acceptance of computer technology: A comparison of two theoretical models. *Management Science*, *35*(8), 982–1003.

Dimaggio, P., & Hargittai, E. (2001). From the 'digital divide' to 'digital inequality': Studying internet use as penetration increases. Working paper 15. www.princeton .edu/~artspol/workpap/WP15%20-% 20DiMaggio%2BHargittai.pdf

El-Or, T., & Watzman, H. (1994). *Educated and Ignorant: Ultraorthodox Jewish Women and Their World*. Boulder, CO: Lynne Rienner.

Fishbein, M., & Ajzen, I. (1975). *Belief, Attitude, Intention, and Behavior: An Introduction to Theory and Research*. Reading, MA: Addison-Wesley.

Friedman, M. (1991). *Haredi Society: Sources, Trends and Processes*. Jerusalem: Jerusalem Institute for Israel Studies.

Gbadamosi, A. (2009). Cognitive dissonance. *International Journal of Retail and Distribution Management*, *37*(12), 1077–95.

Gbadamosi, A. (2015a). Brand personification and symbolic consumption among ethnic minority teenage consumers: An empirical study. *Journal of Brand Management*, *22*(9), 737–54.

Gbadamosi, A. (2015b). Exploring the growing link of ethnic entrepreneurship, markets, and Pentecostalism in London (UK). *Society and Business Review*, *10*(2), 150–66.

Gbadamosi, A. (2019). Postmodernism, ethnicity, and celebrity culture in women's symbolic consumption. *International Journal of Market Research*, 1470785319868363.

GE Capital (2013). 81% research online before making big purchases. https://chainstoreage.com/news/study-81-research-online-making-big-purchases#:~:text=%20Study%3A%2081%25%20research%20online%20before%20making%20big,website%20%28in%20order%20of%20importance%29%3A%20warranty... %20More%20 (Accessed 19 September 2020).

Grant, R., Clarke, R. J., & Kyriazis, E. (2013). Modelling real-time online information needs: A new research approach for complex consumer behaviour. *Journal of Marketing Management*, *29*(7–8), 950–72.

GSMA (2020). Innovating during crisis: COVID-19 and digital health in developing countries. *Mobile for Development*. www.gsma.com/mobilefordevelopment/ resources/innovating-during-crisis-covid-19-and-digital-health-in-developing -countries/ (Accessed 7 July 2020).

Hanlon, A. (2019). *Digital Marketing: Strategic Planning and Integration*. London: Sage.

Hargittai, E. (2003). Informed web surfing: The social context of user sophistication. In P. Howard & S. Jones (eds), *Society Online* (pp. 257–74). Thousand Oaks, CA: Sage.

Hill, W., E. Beatty, S., & Walsh, G. (2013). A segmentation of adolescent online users and shoppers. *Journal of Services Marketing*, *27*(5), 347–60.

Hofstede, G. (1981). *Culture's Consequences: International Differences in Work-Related Values*. Beverly Hills, CA: Sage.

Hofstede, G. (1991). *Cultures and Organisations: Software of the MIND*. New York: McGraw-Hill.

Hsu, M. H., Ju, T. L., Yen, C. H., & Chang, C. M. (2007). Knowledge sharing behavior in virtual communities: The relationship between trust, self-efficacy, and outcome expectations. *International Journal of Human-Computer Studies*, *65*(2), 153–69.

ICT Facts and Figures (2017). www.itu.int/en/ITU-D/Statistics/Documents/facts/ICTFactsFigures2017.pdf (Accessed 19 September 2020).

International Telecommunications Union (2017). www.itu.int/en/ITU-D/Statistics/Documents/facts/ICTFactsFigures2017.pdf (Accessed 19 September 2020).

Kaplan, A. M., & Haenlein, M. (2010). Users of the world, unite! The challenges and opportunities of social media. *Business Horizons*, *53*(1), 59–68.

Karatum, S. (2017). The place of digital marketing on Turkish small businesses. *Journal of International Trade, Logistics and Law*, *3*(2), 36.

Kashi, K., & Zheng, C. (2013). Extending technology acceptance model to the e-recruitment context in Iran. *International Journal of Selection and Assessment*, *21*(1), 121–9.

Key, T. M. (2017). Domains of digital marketing channels in the sharing economy. *Journal of Marketing Channels*, *24*(1–2), 27–38.

Lewis, R. (2015). *Muslim Fashion: Contemporary Style Cultures*. Durham, NC: Duke University Press.

Lissitsa, S., & Cohen, O. R. (2018). The decade of online shopping in the Jewish Ultra-Orthodox community. *Journal of Media and Religion*, *17*(2), 74–89.

Maheshwari, V., Dobson, P., & Lawrence, A. (2019). Digital and social media marketing. In A. Gbadamosi (ed.), *Contemporary Issues in Marketing: Principles and Practice* (pp. 221–54). London: Sage.

Malhotra, N. K., Agarwal, J., & Baalbaki, I. (1998). Heterogeneity of regional trading blocs and global marketing strategies. *International Marketing Review*, *15*(6), 476–506.

Malthouse, E. C., Haenlein, M., Skiera, B., Wege, E., & Zhang, M. (2013). Managing customer relationships in the social media era: Introducing the social CRM house. *Journal of Interactive Marketing*, *27*(4), 270–80.

Mou, J., & Shin, D. (2018). Effects of social popularity and time scarcity on online consumer behaviour regarding smart healthcare products: An eye-tracking approach. *Computers in Human Behavior*, *78*, 74–89.

Pandey, S., & Chawla, D. (2018). Evolving segments of online clothing buyers: An emerging market study. *Journal of Advances in Management Research*, *15*(4), 536–57.

Patrutiu-Baltes, L. (2016). Inbound marketing: The most important digital marketing strategy. *Bulletin of the Transilvania University of Brasov Economic Sciences, Series V*, *9*(2), 61.

Peres, Y., & Ben-Rafael, E. (2006). *Cleavages in Israeli Society*. Tel-Aviv: Am-Oved Publishers.

Rehman, A. U., & Shahbaz Shabbir, M. (2010). The relationship between religiosity and new product adoption. *Journal of Islamic Marketing*, *1*(1), 63–9.

Robson, K., Pitt, L., & Wallstrom, A. (2013). Creative market segmentation: Understanding the bugs in consumer behavior. *Journal of Public Affairs*, *13*(2), 218–23.

Rogers, E. M. (1962). *Diffusion of Innovations*. Glencoe, IL: Free Press.

Schiffman, L. G., Hansen, H., & Kanuk, L. L. (2008). *Consumer Behaviour: A European Outlook*. Harlow: Pearson Education.

Sherry, J. F., Jr. (1990). A sociocultural analysis of a midwestern flea market. *Journal of Consumer Research*, 17(1), 13–30.

Smith, K. T. (2011). Digital marketing strategies that Millennials find appealing, motivating, or just annoying. *Journal of Strategic Marketing*, *19*(6), 489–99.

Smith, T. K. (2012). Longitudinal study of digital marketing strategies targeting Millennials. *Journal of Consumer Marketing*, *29*(2), 86–92.

Souiden, N. (2002). Segmenting the Arab markets on the basis of marketing stimuli. *International Marketing Review*, *19*(6), 611–36.

Statista (2020). Global digital population as of January 2020. www.statista.com/statistics/617136/digital-population-worldwide/ (Accessed 12 February 2020).

Susarla, A., Oh, J. H., & Tan, Y. (2013). Social networks and the diffusion of user generated content: Evidence from YouTube. *Information Systems Research*, *23*(1), 23–41.

Talpau, A. (2014). The marketing mix in the online environment. *Bulletin of the Transilvania University of Brasov Economic Sciences, Series V*, *7*(2), 53.

Tiago, M. T. P. M. B., & Veríssimo, J. M. C. (2014). Digital marketing and social media: Why bother? *Business Horizons*, *57*(6), 703–8.

UN (2020). Digital technologies critical in facing COVID-19 pandemic, United Nations, New York, 15 April. www.un.org/development/desa/en/news/policy/digital-technologies-critical-in-facing-covid-19-pandemic.html (Accessed 7 July 2020).

Valvi, A. C., Frangos, C. C., & Frangos, C. C. (2013). Online and mobile customer behaviour: A critical evaluation of grounded theory studies. *Behaviour and Information Technology*, *32*(7), 655–67.

Wahyuni, T. (2016). The influence of technology acceptance model (TAM) on the users' behavior of Sikesya application in IAIN Surakarta. *Shirkah: Journal of Economics and Business*, *1*(1), 47–72.

Wasserman, S., & Faust, K. (1994). *Social Network Analysis: Methods and Applications*, Vol. 8. Cambridge: Cambridge University Press.

Wetmore, D. (2017). How technology is helping economies in developing countries. Borgen Project. https://borgenproject.org/how-technology-is-helping-economies/ (Accessed 7 July 2020).

Xiao, B., & Benbasat, I. (2011). Product-related deception in e-commerce: A theoretical perspective. *MIS Quarterly*, *35*(1), 169–95.

Yuchtman-Ya'ar, E., & Peres, Y. (2000). *Between Consent and Dissent: Democracy and Peace in the Israeli Mind*. New York: Rowman and Littlefield.

8. Religion and consumer behaviour in developing nations: A look into the future

Chahid Fourali and Ayantunji Gbadamosi

INTRODUCTION

Up to recently, religion, in its widest sense, may have been the proverbial 'elephant in the room' in marketing research, due to a lack of consideration of its influence on the general behaviour of people, including the purchase of products, services and even ideas. Although marketing has many uses it can particularly help shed light on how religion influences consumer behaviour. Religion is relevant to consumer behaviour on at least two levels:

1. As a separate field of study in the form of marketing of religious ideas. Indeed, religion is big business that is supported by huge media enterprises that reach to the highest levels of society. In some cases, this influence is officially recognised (although not necessarily accepted by members of each religion) such as in the case of the Vatican, Iran or Israel, even though many members may distance themselves from the official position. In other cases the influence is indirect through 'democratic representation' that attracts many hopeful politicians to abide by the wishes of the most powerful groups so they may stand a chance to be voted in.
2. As a pervasive presence, at least tacitly, where all consumer behaviour is at some level influenced by 'religion'.

The sheer size of the members of followers from each religion is a reminder of this important factor in our societies. Most people currently associate themselves with one of any number of religions. According to Wikipedia's list of religious populations, the latest estimates suggest that there are 2.3 billion Christians, 1.9 billion Muslims, 1.2 billion Hindus and 506 million Buddhists as well as a myriad of other religions including Judaism, Sikhism, and the variety of denominations that may be found in various parts of Asia and Africa. Religion is also a fluid field of study that shows that some religions are multiplying their memberships more than others and also that there are ongoing attempts at 'inventing new religions' (Cusack, 2010). Overall 6 billion out of the 7 billion world population consider themselves religious to some degree (PEW Research Centre, 2012).

However, given that religion can mean different things to different people perhaps we ought to start by defining what is meant by religion before proceeding with this chapter. According to Paloutzian (2017), religion can be defined at various levels, with personal, cultural, functional or 'substantial' aspects. Accordingly, a definition would reflect any of these dimensions depending on the positioning of the definition. Hence, it may be best to think of religion from the interplay of these dimensions as a definition could combine any of these four perspectives. Fourali (2018) identified four religious dimensions organised in terms of whether the religious perspective is personal or social (see Figure 8.1). It is also important to differentiate the 'religious' dimension from the 'spiritual' one. The former is about organised religions. This would refer to denominations, institutional practice, self-righteousness, sense of community and belonging while the second is about the search for meaning, personal growth and existential issues (Oman, 2013). The religious debate also shows that religion can refer to any system of belief (including secular ones) that may reflect the above dimensions, particularly in the light of recent proliferation of many secular, quasi-religious groups. This phenomenon has benefited from a recent *National Geographic* article called 'The World's Newest Major Religion: No Religion' (Bullard, 2016).

There is an increased recognition in marketing and business studies in general about the effect of religion on consumer behaviour (Johnson et al., 2017). This influence is reflected in the creation of journals and other significant publications that specialise in the religious perspective as shown in the *Journal of Islamic Marketing* or even the *Concise Encyclopedia of Church and Religious Organization Marketing*. Such initiatives only took place as a result of the realisation of the value of religious beliefs in the behaviours of customers. Here are two examples of this influence based on Islam: Nike setting up Nike Hijab and HSBC setting up Sharia-compliant products. Arguably, a marketer needs to develop a closer understanding of this influence if they are to service adequately current or future customers.

This is a conceptual chapter which sets out to critically review and integrate the themes covered throughout this book but also develop its own arguments about the urgency for marketers to advance their understanding and tools that help them identify religious needs in order to serve them profitably. In this process, the chapter reviews the link between ethics and business vis-à-vis the religious factor in the context of broader consumer behaviours, and crit-

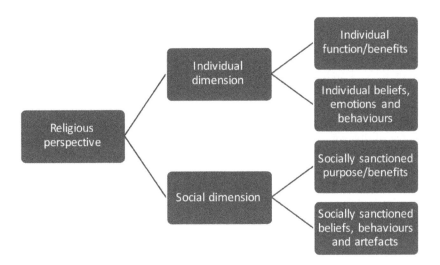

Source: Fourali (2018).

Figure 8.1   Religious dimensions

ically determines the way forward. Specifically, the chapter undertakes the following:

1. Critically review the themes developed throughout the chapters of this book.
2. Explore some key religious perspectives to business and common dimensions derived through moral values.
3. Critically review the key factors influencing consumer behaviour derived from several models of consumer behaviour and link them to the religious perspective.
4. Finally, review the themes for the future of consumer behavioural research work.

This chapter will take a broader perspective to address these objectives in that the developed arguments apply throughout 'developing' or 'developed' nations. Nevertheless, the specific focus of this book to make distinct contribution to the literature by highlighting the discourse vis-à-vis developing nations remains uncompromised, and is robustly addressed.

In the next section the themes covered in the book are reviewed towards deriving some 'golden threads'.

A REVIEW OF THE KEY THEMES FROM THE BOOK

Just as we have historical records for consumer behaviour as indicated in a number of seminal papers (Stigler, 1954; Sheth, 1985; Baumgartner, 2010), there is great value in appreciating the future associated with the discourse. While it may be easy to understand the mechanical parts that form the system of a car, the bits and pieces that underpin the electrical circuit of a home and processing units that make up a personal computer system, understanding human behaviour is more challenging especially in relation to the considerable degree of diversity that characterises that phenomenon. In a recent publication, Schiffman and Wisenblit (2019) define it as the behaviour exhibited by consumers while searching for products and services as well as that displayed while buying, using, evaluating and disposing of them. The tantalisingly complex part of the discourse is that this phenomenon is in a state of flux that changes with environmental forces. Hence, there are significant implications for consumer behaviour for changes experienced in the economy as well as the stability (or otherwise) of political systems. Similarly, consumers react to trends and changes in the socio-cultural environment while the experiences associated with Covid-19 in various ways demonstrate that the technological environment could influence not only the current behaviour of consumers but its future pattern. Accordingly, there are emerging issues around consumer behaviour with implications for how the topic is discussed and understood both in the academic milieu and practical setting.

There is consensus to a great extent that consumers are influenced by a myriad of factors which could be simply categorised as psychological and sociological in nature. Some would describe the former as internal and personal to the consumer while the latter relates to how consumers intermingle and are influenced by other people and groups in various ways. Closely related to the latter is the culture of the people that prescribes and patterns the way of life of people of a particular setting, just like an individual's personality explains his or her behaviour. Meanwhile, one of the key elements in the paraphernalia of a culture is religion. Even when one is not affiliated to any religious values or beliefs such as in the case of Atheists (see Table 1.1), this mindset in itself of being in the 'out-group' of the various religious groups could influence the consumption pattern of those holding this stance. So, the diversity of religious beliefs in various ways tends to be indicative of consumption patterns of adherents. Meanwhile, one of the commonly held perspectives is that the consumption patterns in developing nations are a radical departure from those relating to developed nations. However, this stance has been criticised on the ground that it is oblivious to the dynamics of the contemporary developing nations that crave and actualise the fantasy of the consumption world in ways that mirror the consumer behaviour of the developed nations (Gbadamosi, 2016). Given this consumption pattern, coupled with the contention that most consumers in developing nations are significantly religious, it would be a grave act of mis-judgement for marketers to ignore the impact of religion in the planning and execution of future marketing strategies for developing nations.

How will consumers in developing countries respond to marketing stimuli around consumption in the future? What products would they buy and how would the purchases be made? At what stage of life would specific consumption be adjudged as right and which outlets will be approached for these purchases? What role will religion play in these? These are some of the questions that relate to consumer behaviour. It is not outlandish to indicate that psychological factors would be relevant in these contexts. Essentially, psycho-logical factors underpinning consumption are perception, attitudes, motiva-tion, learning and memory, the self and personality, as detailed in Chapter 2. While religion in itself has a significant degree of interpersonal relationships, the way in which it drives consumption will be a function of the adherent's perception of the beliefs that underpin the religious ethos. Similarly, literature evidence holds that consumers' attitudes influence intentions, and ultimately their behaviour (Ajzen, 1985; Zhao et al., 2014; Joshi and Rahman, 2019) such as, in the context of this book, the choice of religious-oriented products. Similar influence of the psychological factors on the worldview of consumers could be deduced in relation to their personality that makes them uniquely different and their motives and drives for the purchase. Moreover, learning is fundamental to consumer behaviour as most behaviour exhibited in relation to the consumption of goods and services is learned. So, in a simple form, we conceptualise learning as changes that take place in the consumer as a result of experience (De Mooij, 2011). The internet and digital technologies are making learning in respect of consumption and market knowledge between developed and developing nations more prevalent and evident (Zhao et al., 2013; Gbadamosi, 2019). Hence, it is expected that such trends will continue for a long time to come including the issues and consumption activities linked to religious values.

Group and group formation have been at the centre of consumer behaviour for a very long time. As shown in Chapter 3, consumption activities continue to be patterned by people's need for affiliation. As a matter of fact, apart from the spirituality element of religion, the involvement of some people in religion is significantly underpinned by their need to love and be loved which propels their consumption activities as linked to religion. A meticulous look into the collectivist cultures will reveal a lot about what people cherish in 'togetherness' such that it defines numerous aspects of their lives. Evidently, phenomena such as culture, family settings and other social classifications will continue to drive consumption, arguably in relation to religion in the foreseeable future. The social stratifications in societies as often depicted in the form of social classes and how they influence consumption decisions of members are noteworthy. Such differences, showing that some societal members are at the top of the pyramid while there are some in the middle and others at the bottom, are well established. Using this to delineate relationships among people is what some religions such as Sikhism denounce. Nonetheless, the stratifications have interesting implications for consumption that cannot be ignored. For instance, it is noted that middle-class members are more in tune with the more modern religious affiliations when compared to their lower-class counterparts. At the macro level, it is noted that while developed nations tend to become less religious due to their individualistic cultural pattern (Malhotra et al.,1994; Stolarski et al., 2015), this is at variance from developing nations where cultural orientation is more towards collectivism (Barash, 1967; Addai et al., 2013). Given that consumer behaviour could be a defining factor towards differentiating between a successful marketing strategy and one that is not, the knowledge of how reference groups impact consumption in developing countries vis-à-vis the religious beliefs of the consumers will be crucial for firms of different categories interested in this context.

Over the years, a number of seminal papers have reported a pattern that describes the consumer decision-making process. Essentially, they argue that consumers pass through a number of stages before the eventual choice of specific products and services consumed (Engel et al., 1968, 1995; Howard and Sheth, 1969; Sheth et al., 1991). These stages are conventionally noted as need recognition, search for information, evaluation of alternatives, decision and post-purchase evaluation. Interestingly, there has been significant scholarship on this over the years that moderates this postulation in one form or another. For instance, there are contentions that these stages are not rigidly applicable to all market offerings and cases as depicted. As this conventional process depicts a rational model of decision making, there are other models such as emotional models that do not follow this convention. Specifically, it has been argued that stages may be skipped in some circumstances as in the case for low-involvement products and some of the extant literature also hinted that this could vary with the type of consumer involved (Gbadamosi, 2009). Another noteworthy point on this is the diverse range of needs that could be characterised in a number of ways. Some are categorised as basic needs while others are higher-order needs. One of the detailed explications of needs is that of Abraham Maslow whose work produces the hierarchy of needs of the five states of physiological needs, security needs, social needs, esteem needs, and self-actualisation. At each of these stages in this model, and in classifications proposed by other scholars, the issue of religion such as halal products often associated with Islamic religion and vegetarianism that constitutes one of the core values that underpins Hinduism are applicable. Similarly, apart from the need hierarchy, as indicated in Chapter 4, the overall stages of the decision-making process are indeed amenable to interpretations and explanations relating to religion and consumption. Meanwhile, increasing evidence shows that this pattern of consumption does not only exist in the contemporary developing nations but is also gaining momentum by the day.

Another phenomenon that connects different parts of the world together, especially in recent times, is the notion of brand. In a metaphorical perspective, brand speaks, differentiates and connects (Gbadamosi, 2015). It communicates the features of a market offering in terms of what it offers and how it offers it, and through this distinguishes the products and services from those offered by competitors. The dynamics of brands and branding activities have changed dramatically in the past few decades. The global marketing environment has been connected in various ways with activities of several players such as multinationals linking developed to developing nations. For instance, the iconic global brands manifest the culture of consumption which brings consumers at one end to those on the other through socialisation (see Chapter 5). Accordingly, globalisation and consumerism are fusing and closing gaps between nations. The global consumer culture (Arnould and Thompson, 2005; Cleveland et al., 2016; Taylor, 2018) typically illustrates this by stressing how brands and their paraphernalia travel across regions uniting consumers. It is therefore understandable that brands have been conceptualised to function culturally, politically and ideologically (Schroeder and Morling, 2006). The notion of branding is now being applied to cities, places and nations to communicate heritage as part of an additional message to the discourse of branding. Great examples, as noted for the United Arab Emirates, Saudi Arabia and Kenya to mention but a few, emphasise the value of place branding to the local and wider community. Meanwhile, the scope of branding narratives also extends to that of religion in various ways such as modesty in consumption and loyalty to specific brands acknowledged within specific religious circles.

In all of the themes covered in this book, ranging from various influences on consumer behaviour, digital marketing, to branding and brand culture, the notion of marketing ethics remains paramount (see below more discussion on the ethical dimension). In its fundamental sense, the issue of ethics revolves around what is right and wrong that is expected to guide the interaction of marketing and consumption activities (Gbadamosi, 2019). The core philosophical discourse of business ethics is conceptualised under the templates of teleological and deontological perspectives. In the teleological perspective, marketers are guided by the outcome of the actions taken in the decision scenarios whereas the deontological standpoints indicate that there are independent moral codes to which actors are expected to adhere (Hunt and Vitell, 1993). Considering it from the angle of the marketers, issues of marketing ethics could be traced to any of the key marketing mix elements. For example, offering defective products, unethical marketing communication messages, unethical pricing, marketing research, exploitation of disadvantaged consumers, high-pressure selling and greenwashing are some of the commonly discussed ethical issues that often direct criticism to marketers (Kotler and Armstrong, 2018; Gbadamosi, 2019). Meanwhile, consumers could also be unethical in various ways such as in the cases of shoplifting, overconsumption and poor attitude to recycling. On either side of the marketing divide (selling and consumption), participants are guided to follow some degree of ethical codes based on established codes stipulated by the relevant industry, government and regulatory agencies, and other factors such as religion and the parties' religiosity. As shown in Chapter 6, religions can be very prescriptive in several ways such as in cases of what to eat and what to abstain from, dress codes and the general lifestyle to follow. In several cases, these are linked to guidelines in the holy books associated with the religions such as the Bible, Torah and Quran. Consequently, one may ask, which of these moral codes will be applicable to businesses organisations or individual consumers? For business organisations, while there may be reasons behind adopting either teleological or deontological philosophical viewpoints, in reality, most organisations are guided by both approaches in their transactions (Hunt and Vasquez-Parraga, 1993; Akaah, 1997). Logically, to a great extent, similar contention could be made for consumers, in that religious beliefs and values could also pattern their ethical behaviour in addition to several other codes statutorily stipulated for such transactions or consumption behaviours. There are several examples supporting this in many developing countries such as China, India, Pakistan, and Mexico.

Meanwhile, a discussion of consumer behaviour would be incomplete without adequate reference to how technological advancement has changed the pattern of things over the past few years. Technology has been a dominant part of consumption especially when considered in relation to the process of the consumer decision-making process. The changes are palpable! Consumers' need for convenience, for example, is now being met in a number of ways through the use of digital technologies. The surge in internet transactions for goods and services is a typical example of how this has revolutionised consumption patterns. Another related development is the wide array of opportunities available to consumers to obtain information about the market offerings needed and the ease of making evaluations to know which options to choose based on the applicable criteria. This advancement in technology enhances the activities of all stakeholders in value-oriented marketing transactions including consumers, marketers, channel members, suppliers and others. Hence, the increased use of social media such as Facebook, Instagram, LinkedIn and Twitter facilitates conversations and transactions of brands. Interestingly, as highlighted in Chapter 7, consumers of various religious groups are also brought together through these digital means and adopt them in one form or another to facilitate their consumption. Segmentation, targeting and positioning becomes a very useful strategy for marketers to explore these digital means including social media tools for reaching consumers (Danaher et al., 2020; Sun et al., 2020). By and large, the use of digital marketing and religion for decisions around consumption activities is becoming increasingly acknowledged as part of the key drivers of consumer behaviour in various geographical contexts. The experience of the use of digital media during the Covid-19 pandemic period in various parts of the world is testament to the fact that technology will continue to play a significant role in consumption in the twenty-first-century developing nations.

REVIEW OF RELIGIOUS PERSPECTIVES TO BUSINESS AND COMMON DIMENSIONS DERIVED THROUGH MORAL VALUES

Before we start on this section, there have been arguments regarding the rationale about how influential or even logical it would be to refer to religious feelings to explain human decisions. Most historians argue that religions have been very important in influencing human decisions and developing civilisations. For example, it has been argued that Christianity has been a huge influence on Western civilisation (Johnson, 2000).This ranges from the North African St Augustine (one of the most influential early Christian fathers, who argued about the need to think in terms of the city of God that goes beyond materialistic imperatives) to the 65.4 per cent of winners of Nobel Prizes who identified their religious preference towards Christianity (Shalev, 2003). In a similar vein, during the Islamic civilisation most scientific achievements were by people who also classified themselves as Muslim. The same arguments may be extended to most civilisations (e.g. Fieser, 2017).

When we discuss the rationale for including religion in the business perspective, there are two levels of consideration. First is whether there is a philosophical rationale to decisions based on religion. Second is whether a marketer should accept the argument about the imperative of religion in consumer decisions. The later issue will be discussed in the next section. Regarding the first point, as argued by Kok-chor Tan (2017), what is at issue here is not what is rationally justifiable to a philosopher but whether it can be pursued and realised in compliance with the requirements of justice or 'background standards of justice'. For instance, although utilitarianism or liberal egalitarianism may be quoted as potential justifications for some religious arguments, this may not be considered necessary if people still accept the influence of religion on their lives. Hence the argument becomes socio-cultural rather than necessarily rational. Accordingly, and since marketing is about understanding the needs of

Table 8.1   *Bases for ethical arguments*

Ethical perspective	Type of argument	Purpose	Criticism
Secular philosophical bases	Utilitarianism	Maximising social good.	Who decides?
	Deontological	Heeding universal rights irrespective of consequences of actions (e.g. all humans are equal).	Are there exceptions (e.g. giving gifts is wrong)? What about clashes between two moral duties? Or historical acceptability?
	Social contract	Maintaining social harmony through equity, cooperation and mutual benefits. Rulers should be blind to position in society.	Risk that this rule disadvantages further the most disadvantaged?
	Virtue	Counter relativism in ethics. A virtual person or organisation has integrity, fairness, trust, respect, empathy and transparency.	Lack of agreement on what is virtuous and how it should be applied or operationalised?
Religious philosophical bases	A higher being understands better what is best for the salvation of creation.	Living according to the precepts of the sacred books.	Texts may not be debatable. Different interpretations.

Sources: Murphy et al. (2012); Fourali (2016).

consumers and serving them profitably, this rationale becomes justified. In the next section, the religious perspective to business is reviewed.

THE IMPERATIVE OF RELIGION AND ITS VARIOUS PERSPECTIVES IN CONSUMER DECISIONS

At its heart, religion is about justice and life's purpose. Consequently, it is about right and wrong. Overall, there are two categories of bases for making ethical decisions and choosing a behaviour including what to consume (Murphy et al., 2012). These are secular philosophical bases and religious bases. Table 8.1 briefly describes these two categories and the derived main arguments (e.g. Murphy et al., 2012; Fourali, 2016). The table lists four key sources of secular arguments (utilitarianism, deontological, social contract, virtue based). However, the religious category of arguments is broadly exposed. It needs further clarification, especially since it is the main focus of this chapter. Nevertheless, it is worth noting that the arguments are not anti-thetical to each other. Hence an argument may combine more than one view-point even including both secular and religious perspectives. The difference between the arguments may be just a matter of degree of focus. Additionally, such arguments may not disagree with the idea of being evidence based. It is possible to stress that all arguments, secular or otherwise, are life affirming. Hence one might have an ultimate basis for determining the adequacy of any argument. Accordingly, both religious and non-religious arguments can be combined and speak to the priorities of each listener/reader.

In this presentation in our gaze to the future, we review religious traditions with a view to determining their principles and how they help enlighten each tradition's business perspective. We will review the Jewish, Christian, Islamic, Confucian, Bhuddist and Hindu traditions. In this presentation we will first review the monotheistic religions (Jewish, Christian and Muslim traditions) and then proceed to cover the others. It is clear that religious orientations, like any ideology, have had their fair share of scandals, but these should not detract us from their ethical principles that usually portray the highest principles for human life.

Jewish Perspective on Business and Marketing

Jewish business ethics encourage fair trading. They are guided by the Hebrew Torah and can refer to a number of commercial situations (Murphy et al., 2012). Overall, the purpose of the law is to discourage deception in its various guises (Jewish Encyclopedia, 2011). Accordingly, business people should:

- Ensure accurate calculations and measurements.
- Avoid money deception (such as exploiting situations of scarcity to charge unreasonable prices).
- Avoid deceiving others and keep promises.
- Avoid misrepresenting products and services (e.g. quality).
- Avoid providing false or incomplete information.
- Avoid using persuasive techniques to sell commodities that a buyer does not need.
- Avoid usury. Although such law appears to have been breached when trading with non-Jews, this exception was only for situations where these gentiles were willing to charge usury. Hence it was seen as justifiable (Jewish Encyclopedia, 2011).

Christian Perspective on Business and Marketing

Given the multiplicity of Christian orientations, we will refer to the Catholic social tradition (e.g. Klein and Laczniak, 2009). This can be derived from the National Conference of Catholic Bishops' (1986) report called 'Economic Justice for All'. The conference put forward seven major principles that have a direct bearing on business/marketing transactions. These suggestions have been criticised (Reece, 1989) for being rhetorically unconvincing and over-looking the reality of the United States economy. Nevertheless, the principles are a useful reference point for understanding the Catholic perspective, and to some extent the Christian orientations.

Human dignity
According to the National Conference of Catholic Bishops (1997), this principle is reflected in the statement that the economy exists for the person (who has an inherent worth, irrespective of race, colour or creed), rather than the person existing for the economy. This means the aim of business is to distribute wealth equally as much as possible.

Common good
This principle highlights the need to focus on the needs of all stakeholders so that the basic necessities, including access to education and affordable health-care, are all met. Additionally, harmful products such as cigarettes should not be marketed.

Subsidiarity
Generally, this means that decisions should be devolved to the lowest prac-tical level. However, in Roman Catholic thinking, it means that whenever possible decisions should be devolved to the individual level. For example, customer-facing staff should be allowed to make decisions at their level as they are more aware of the situation on the ground. However, if there are persistent and unfair practices the government should weigh in to offset the unfairness.

Preference for the poor and vulnerable
This principle is reflected in 'Love thy neighbour' and the aim to remove disadvantage.

Worker rights
This highlights the right to productive work, decent working conditions and fair wages.

Solidarity
This principle highlights brotherhood. This means that marketers should develop affordable products.

Stewardship
This principle highlights the importance of businesses contributing to the care of the earth and aiming to remove all 'collateral' harmful outputs.

Islamic Perspective on Business and Marketing

As for Christianity, we will focus on the most widespread Islamic orientation: Sunni Islam.

Despite the media's general tendency to link Islam with an extremist destructive view, by definition Islam connotes two concepts: peace and total submission to the will of God. This is reflected in a Quranic verse (49:13) that states that 'The noblest of you in the sight of God is the best of you in conduct'. Consequently, anything that promotes human welfare is strongly encouraged. Among the most prominent Islamic principles are unity, equilibrium, free will, responsibility and benevolence (Saeed et al., 1997). There are strong overlaps with the above principles listed in the National Conference of Catholic Bishops (1986). Perhaps in the Muslim context the following dimensions need particular attention (Ali, 2011):

- Aim for a profit that benefits the company while avoiding harm to society and the environment.
- Avoid usury through imposing interest and consider valid alternatives.
- Avoid consumerism/profligacy. This means maintaining modesty in spending.
- Avoid bribes. This means being very cautious in our transactions to ensure there is a difference between bribes and gifts.
- Show generosity through providing optional products to cover various levels of affordability.
- Avoid deception and fraudulent activities as they lead to market turmoil.
- Ensure transparency and truthfulness that will enhance trust towards organisations.
- Competition should be fair and not destructive such as being involved in practices that can drive rivals out of business.
- Honour commitment and promotional promise.

Confucian Perspective on Business and Marketing

Confucian ethics is similar to virtue ethics discussed above. In particular, trust-worthiness is highly rated (Murphy et al., 2012). The aim of Confucian ethics are to walk on the path of Dao, or truth, which means to live according to the supreme metaphysical force that dominates everything in the universe including the universal moral order (Tsai, 2005). The way of the Dao is supported by three ethical principles. Internally, it is supported by 'jen' (humaneness) and 'yi' (righteousness). Externally it is supported by 'li' (following rules of propriety and right behaviour). Social harmony supported by altruistic attitude is also encouraged in Confucian ethics (Tsai, 2005). In terms of moral business transactions, these principles can be translated to mean that business action should be supported by humanism and social responsibility.

Bhuddist Perspective on Business and Marketing

Bhuddism puts forward five principles that should be heeded at all times:

- Do not harm.
- Do not cheat.
- Do not lie.
- Do not promote intoxication.
- Do not get involved in sexual exploitation.

Consequently, some activities are discouraged. These include: armaments, intoxicating drink, poisons, animal slaughter, gambling and slavery (Murphy et al, 2012). However, Bhuddism promotes respect for the preservation of the resources and beauty of nature; encouragement of private enterprise, self reliance and economic freedom; and the personal and social value of full employment with a living wage (Wee, 2001).

Hindu Perspective on Business and Marketing

Hinduism is hard to define but one definition that is put forward is that in Hinduism the fulfilment of life desires (including achieving wealth) is to be subsumed within spiritual (Moksha) and social responsibility (Dharma) concerns. Consequently, true business success is measured by how much such business contributes to both spiritual and social welfare. In the light of this prioritisation, service is more important than unscrupulous competition.

There are five restraints and five observances in Hinduism that inform the practice of business and marketing (Dunn and Jensen, 2019). The restraints are truthfulness, not stealing, non-violence, sexual moderation and non-possession.

The five observances are surrendering to god, satisfaction, purity, austerity and self-knowledge. Given current practice in sexualised products, it is good to see specific mention of sexual moderation. The dimensions of non-possession and austerity again seem to support an attitude of social help and spiritual fulfilment.

Common Threads among the Various Perspectives

The above review highlighted key ethical justifications currently referred to in business and marketing practice. It then proceeded to focus on the religious dimensions and identified underpinning ethical values associated with six religious traditions reflecting Jewish, Christian, Islamic, Confucian, Bhuddist and Hindu religions. A number of common threads can be glimpsed throughout the six traditions.

- They all seem to give priority to social concerns over individual concerns.
- They all seem to refer to a variety of stakeholders beyond the usual shareholders, organisation staff and clients to include all people that may be potentially affected by business practice.
- All four key ethical arguments (utilitarian, deontological, social contract and virtue) appear to be referred to.

Despite the above commonality of ethical arguments between religious and secular perspectives, there appear to be clear differences. Whilst in the secular dimension the force of logical arguments appears to be the primary determinant for deciding which path to take, in the religious arguments there is a dimension that overrides the logical argument. These are the spiritual and sacred elements. Indeed, the spiritual dimension seems to be very personal.

In a way this goes against the perception of ethics as just a formula to apply based on some religious or secular advice derived from selected 'experts'. Ethical views have been seen as primarily 'synthetic' thereby overlooking the 'heart dimension' of what constitutes being religious (Otto, 1969). Religion at its heart is a very deep relation to a universal being. As a result of such relation, there is an element of sacredness associated with how humans relate to others, especially human beings (Otto, 1969). Indeed, in religion it seems that any argument that is not underpinned by a higher purpose may fail. In Deuteronomy 6:5 there is a command: 'Thou shalt love the Lord thy God with all thy heart, with all thy soul, and with all thy might'. In Islam its equivalent 'Verily, my Salat (prayer), my sacrifice, my living, and my dying are for Allah, the Lord of the worlds' (Qur'an 6:162). If we consider that 'the Lord' or 'Allah' is the higher purpose that all religions have been referring to, then one might find some common ground between the various religions. Obviously, the reverse is also true: if the aim is a lower purpose (e.g. a quick profit) then that would reflect the 'chosen Lord'.

In the above section we reviewed the importance of religious principles in guiding people's behaviour. In the next section we will review the key factors that influence a consumer and try to locate the religious dimensions among these factors.

KEY FACTORS INFLUENCING CONSUMER BEHAVIOUR DERIVED FROM MODELS AND COMMON THREADS

Religion has been seen as a recurrent factor influencing behaviour throughout several studies on management and marketing (Johnson et al., 2017; Fourali, 2016). In management studies 'culture' has tended to be studied as part of a number of other dimensions, with religion as one of the cultural elements. For example, Johnson and colleagues (2017) produced a successful book on culture that sees religion as a subdimension of culture which in turn is a subdimension of the macro and micro analyses that need carrying out to understand a given organisation. In marketing, too, most frameworks about explaining consumer behaviour tend to refer to culture as one of several dimensions (Fourali, 2016; Schiffman et al., 2012; Brassington and Pettitt, 2006). Nevertheless, given the complexity of influences, the consumer behaviour frameworks can only refer to broad dimensions associated with factors influencing consumer behaviour. Typically, these factors tend to be organised in terms of external influences, their interaction with internal influences and the resulting consumer behaviour. In turn, these three dimensions tend to be reflected according to input, process of decision making and output (Fourali, 2016).

What perhaps appears to be lacking from the various studies is the rank ordering of the importance of each of the elements that make up the list of factors that influence behaviours. Again, this may be due to the fact that different populations may attract different rankings. Nevertheless, there appears to be a general view that core beliefs (variably referred to as 'taken for granted assumptions' or even 'paradigms') are key to understanding how a company functions (Johnson et al., 2017). In this respect, Johnson and colleagues (2017) highlighted the decisiveness of leadership and teams' individual beliefs in influencing how responsibly the company may operate. This is a particularly important point as whilst for some people their core beliefs may be secular values, for others such values are intermingled with their religious values. Indeed, there seems to be an ongoing iterative interaction between personal and religious values as suggested above. Such core beliefs in fact are widely accepted within current counselling and psychotherapy psychology (e.g. Ellis, 1994; Beck et al., 2015). Despite the difficulty involved in measuring the contribution of religious beliefs in accounting for consumer behaviour, this by no means suggests that such attempts should be overlooked. Hence the next section aims to suggest a way of undertaking such a task.

CAN RELIGION BE SYSTEMATICALLY REPRESENTED IN MARKETING PROJECTS?

Given the importance of religion in consumer behaviour it seems natural to seek ways of systematically ensuring that marketing philosophy takes into account this dimension. In a way this is already done by various global companies.

In order to do that it seems to make sense to adopt a marketing planning framework. This is because marketing plans tend to summarise the various elements that marketers tend to consider when designing the plan. According to marketing management literature (Wilson and Gilligan, 2013; Fourali, 2019), five types of questions can be asked to help guide the strategic plan. We will apply these questions to help enlighten the religious dimension as shown in Table 8.2.

Note that there is nothing new in terms of requesting organisations to adopt these principles. For instance, McDonald's provides halal burgers in Islamic countries and McAloo in countries with a predominantly vegetarian population. What is new is to ensure that the religious issue is systematically addressed, thereby preempting likely offences to certain religious groups.

The strategy for business success has to be cooperative and aim for a win-win approach as much as possible as such an approach is strongly advocated by most religions.

It is important that religious values are evaluated according to their preeminence in the value framework of each religion. For example, it is important to recognise that any follower of the monotheistic religions, by definition, places the highest value on ultimate surrender to one God. This dimension is particularly stressed in Jewish and Islamic beliefs where any suggestion of idol worship would lead to their alienation.

THEMES FOR THE FUTURE OF CONSUMER BEHAVIOURAL RESEARCH

It seems that we have moved from 'Can you market brotherhood as you market toothpaste?' as suggested by Wiebe (1952), to 'Can you market God as you would market any other product or service?'. The only problem with this approach is that marketing brotherhood tends to be less controversial than marketing a particular version of a 'god' or religion. For multinationals with increasing presence and operations in developing nations, ignoring the sensi-

*Table 8.2   Application of the marketing plan to religious marketing
planning*

Marketing plan stage	Clarification of stage	Application to religion
Stage 1: Where are we now?	Analysis of organisational strengths and weaknesses	Determine if religious-compatible principles have been applied
Stage 2: Where do we want to be?	Vision, mission and objectives, target groups and competition (or cooperative strategy)	Match vision, mission and objectives with religious objectives. Decide on which religious groups may have been overlooked and aim to serve them. Decide on strategies to adopting cosmopolitan cities (i.e. multiple religions)
Stage 3: How do we get there?	Determining operational criteria on various alternative offers	Determine priorities and how best to implement the strategy in the form of a larger marketing mix offer, as process and staff attitudes are as important as other dimensions
Stage 4: Which way is best?	Alternative offers are evaluated in terms of overriding values, practicalities and potential adverse effects on various subgroups	Testing the options with various groups with a view to deriving the optimal solution. It is advised that a fuzzy logic approach is adopted (Fourali, 2016) when evaluating the options
Stage 5: How do we ensure arrival?	Monitor the situation with a view to taking corrective actions	At this stage ensure that effects and responses from all affected groups are monitored. Corrective action needs to consider adverse effect on other groups

Sources: Wilson and Gilligan (2013); Fourali (2019).

tivity of that subject could yield adverse consequences and many ramifications. This is especially so as the argument in this book is that religion is a complex phenomenon but with great relevance to consumption in developing nations.

In this section we will review the various themes in this chapter and try to identify possible areas for future investigations about religion.

There was a time when just buying a fully vegan toothpaste or cheese was difficult, but these are now considered standard items in any supermarket. At the moment we can find kosher, halal and vegan items. Is this enough? There is a need for a transparent process for identifying and making available religiously sensitive alternatives. Given the possibility for misunderstanding or outright bias against certain religious traditions there remain challenges to companies that may miss out on opportunities given cultural misunderstanding. As an example, Nike did not join the bandwagon of developing sports

Table 8.3   Marketing mix from a religious perspective

Marketing mix	Example
Product/service	Does the product include only ingredients acceptable to the religious requirements? For example, is there a halal or kosher mortgage which does not involve any dimension of usury? Or does the food avoid all ingredients that breach religious requirements and is all the information transparent?
Price	Is the price ethical and are there options for people with different affordability levels?
Promotion	Does the promotion respect the religious ethics? For example, does the advertisement tacitly appear to promote an ideology that goes against the values of the religion of interest, promoting instead an individualist view of the world?
Place	Can the person access the product in a way that respects the values of the religion? For instance, is the location of production controversial in terms of religious discrimination?
People	Are the people delivering a religiously sensitive service? For example, is the outfit or attitude respectful to the values of the religion?
Process	Did the process of producing the product or service avoid all aspects that may contravene a particular religion? For instance, does the bank that wants to attract representatives of a certain religion invest in arm-producing projects?
Physical evidence	Does the environment respect people of a religion? For example, a holiday company may need to think twice if they offer a hedonistic environment for people who are promised spiritual upliftment.

Source: Fourali (2019).

articles of clothing that respected the wishes of Muslim women until relatively late. As a result, the company missed huge business opportunities and allowed other companies to beat them to that market.

Clearly, in order to apply values-sensitive initiatives of any sort, including religious initiatives, a revised extended marketing mix should apply. To give an example, the details given in Table 8.3 could apply.

Clearly, a simple adjustment of the standard marketing mix may not be enough, and a more radical approach may be adopted just as was done for other 'new marketing disciplines' such as social marketing, when newly designed alternatives to the standard commercial marketing mix were offered (Fourali, 2016).

However, it is important to ask, is a simple adaptation or even a radical reformulation of the marketing mix enough? Like any fully thought-through initiative, there has to be a comprehensive multipronged approach to minimise any alienation against a particular religious group. This is easier said than done especially if some expectancies appear to clash not only between but within different religious traditions. Despite the best of intentions, some organisations may not be ready to undertake the selected challenge. Obstacles can come in various guises including personal, cultural or even inadequate processes that may lead to what has become known as 'institutional discrimination' that leads to loss of opportunities. This may be seen as an extension to the concept of marketing myopia (Levitt, 1960) in that the bigger picture is overlooked. In some cases, such a situation simply reflects contradictions between the higher aims and the reality of the implementation of those aims in the form of operations, very much as argued in the gaps model of service quality (Wilson et al., 2016) when identifying the various gaps between what a company aims for and the various levels of obstacles that may prevent the realisation of the ultimate aim. This issue may also cover 'internal marketing', that is an organisation may make the double error of missing opportunities to understand and serve its customers as well as its staff.

To illustrate such short-sightedness that may particularly affect the service industry, let's consider a real-life example based on a recent development that hit our screens about Al Rayan bank (Greaves, 2018). Although there has been quite a lot of news about Sharia-compliant investment, these tended to apply primarily to the Muslim community. Just to clarify, Sharia-compliant investment refers to an Islamic approach to investment that bans riba (or usury) and only accepts investment returns in terms of profit (or expected profit rate) as opposed to the annual equivalent rate. The difference is that in Islamic law, a halal (just) return cannot be generated from interest (i.e. money making money). In other words: under Islamic law, money is banned from generating money (i.e. interest) and instead the expected profit rate is generated from profits made through investing in ethical companies. Additionally, Islamic banking bans investment in non-ethical/self-destructive products (e.g. tobacco, gambling, etc). It is clear that one does not have to be a Muslim to agree with the fairness of this approach (already present in the Old Testament) but also the dangers of unfettered schemes for creating interests that many claim were the cause of the recession of 2008. Al Rayan bank presents itself as not only a fully Sharia-compliant bank but also it has for many years produced returns that are on a par with if not better than what non-Sharia-compliant banks offer.

In the light of the fact there are about 1.9 billion Muslims (many of whom are located in Western countries) it does not make business sense for banks to ignore this Sharia-compliant investment alternative. Also, when the competition offers returns on investments (called profits) that are at least as good as those offered by supposedly unfettered investment banks then it becomes akin to irresponsible management to ignore the opportunities that Sharia-compliant banking could bring.

Despite such clear rational reasons for banks to consider this type of investment, there still seems to be a reluctance from several banks to get into Sharia-compliant offers. A committed marketer working for an investment institution should not disregard the opportunities of this alternative approach to investment but, rather, should undertake a sober analysis of the pros and cons of such an approach and if the evidence warrants great advantages then the advice is to make the case with management for adding such a product to its portfolio of products. The application of such an approach requires clear leadership and an unbiased analysis of the situation and the development of strategies and tactics that maximise the possibility of success. For example, ensuring that everybody who works in the Sharia-compliant section of a bank is deeply informed about the requirements and aware of their meanings for the target population.

Clearly the above is just an example that can be developed much further in the light of a proper marketing plan supported by a well thought-through offer in the form of an attractive marketing mix (Fourali, 2019).

The above example can be extended to many products and services that require genuine leadership right from the top, particularly in the light of strong cultural and personal biases that can interfere with the analysis and development and application of business opportunities.

A VIEW TO THE FUTURE?

There is an argument that technology not only supports various scientific achievements but also the development of more robust ethical, including religious, decisions. For instance, it is believed that an artificial intelligence (AI)-led decision-making process may be more objective and minimise injustice. However, it is clear that the famous adage 'garbage in, garbage out' may apply here, since AI is dependent on algorithms that in turn are dependent on humans. Hence the bias of the designers of the algorithm may be reflected in the decision-making process of AI machines. This is what led to the current trend to agree on ethical ways of developing AI. In this respect Microsoft and IBM agreed with the Vatican to safeguard the rights of all humankind in various devices including facial recognition devices (Espinoza, 2020). The issue was seen as particularly important as it was argued that designers have a duty to provide explanations that would clarify both how algorithms come to their decisions but also the purpose and objectives of the decisions.

However, is there a future for the debate about values? Given the so-called tendency of humans to think and act selfishly (Andreasen, 2006), there is clearly a strong argument for doing so. The argument for doing so can also suggest that relying on the good will of industries to adopt clear values may not lead anywhere. In this respect, Jenkins (2018) argued that ten years after the financial crisis that destroyed the lives of many people and is generally seen as the consequence of the irresponsible behaviour of financial institutions led by banks, the industry is yet to show adequate signs of assuming its responsibilities to prevent future financial disasters. Consequently, a new list of United Nations principles for responsible banking have been drawn up with a view to inviting banks to subscribe to them. These are broadly about working to achieve the United Nations 17 sustainability goals, social responsibility, transparency and establishing governance structures that ensure responsible targets are met. Clearly cynicism is rife and it will take a lot of evidence-based changes before people are convinced about the authenticity of the overt manifestations of the banking inclinations for change. Accordingly, there is a need for regulatory bodies to proceed from the perspective of 'if things can go wrong, they will go wrong' to minimise the exploitation of any loophole by unscrupulous business people who have always shown their ability to side-step the purpose of principles and even legal injunctions (see Gentilin, 2016).

On the other hand, there is another argument that states that humans have values wired into them that may have been prompted originally by the survival instinct that provided the opportunity to live within social groups (Sober and Wilson, 1998). Such values include wisdom, courage, humanity, justice, temperance and transcendence (Peterson and Seligman, 2004). From this perspective, it is not only that values are very compatible with religious values, but they should generally make it easy for initiatives to agree on key values to be successful.

Recent events associated with Covid-19 have shown lots of terrible things but also lots of opportunities for improving the human condition. For example, it demonstrated that all humans are interdependent, wherever they may be. It also showed that what used to be necessary religious measures (e.g. catechism) are no longer so in the light of deleterious consequences on fellow human beings. Religious liturgies have been dropped (e.g. Christian Sunday services or Islamic Friday prayers) as the dangers of such services have become clear in helping spread the dreadful virus. Whilst the arguments used to be about the necessities for such services, people quickly realised that it is all about 'horses for courses' and suddenly 'original principles' at the heart of every religion such as 'thou shall not kill' or 'love your neighbour as yourself' were very quickly recovered and raised to the top of the hierarchy of principles.

Harari (2020) argued that technology has been one of the key weapons in fighting off the threat of Covid-19. Telephones have been used to help locate likely infected people. He argued that it would be a small step to imagine a world where there will be so much information available about people (customers) that the organisations holding that information can determine the needs of a person before he/she knows them. He imagined that just as our smart phones are being used (misused?) for deriving important information about

Table 8.4   *Future directions enhanced by technological development*

		Surveillance (distrust)	Empowerment (trust)
Nationalist (us versus them)	Material welfare	surveillance-nationalist-material	empowerment-nationalist-material
	Spiritual welfare	surveillance-nationalist-spiritual	empowerment-nationalist-spiritual
Global solidarity (all in it together)	Material welfare	surveillance-global-material	empowerment-global-material
	Spiritual welfare	surveillance-global-spiritual	empowerment-global-spiritual

Source: Fourali (2019).

us, it is likely that these devices may develop to include information about our health or even our emotions that can be fed into algorithms to determine a reliable report on our needs. He predicted that such a situation would lead to two choices by states: a choice between totalitarian surveillance versus citizen empowerment, and a choice between nationalist isolation and global solidarity.

Such options can be contrasted into a two-by-two matrix ranging from high distrust/surveillance, high nationalism to high trust/empowerment, high solidarity. Clearly the first focuses all power within the state whilst the other allows a more trustworthy consultative approach that appears to be more inclusive. Perhaps a religious dimension may be introduced here: more specifically, a third choice to be made in the form of materialism versus spirituality (Fourali, 2019) as shown in Table 8.4. Although it is clear that spirituality is different from religion, it is hard to imagine any religion without a spiritual element (a sense of wonder, the sacred, purpose, the beyond and justice). Accordingly, a 'religious perspective' may review the elements of the matrix to include an extra, spiritual element.

In Table 8.4, the most benign option, aiming for human empowerment and inclusiveness, also allows a spiritually led perspective. A spiritually led perspective does not necessarily exclude the materialistic perspective but perhaps prevents practitioners from losing the primary purpose of values. Such dimensions may be either secular or religious in nature. In fact, at the core, if the intention is serving the 'spirit or spiritual dimension' of values, such as the sacredness of human beings, there is no difference between the two perspectives. It is hoped that a marketer would adopt a more responsible attitude that is compatible with the latter perspective.

CONCLUSION

Evidently, consumption is central to life. It connects all geographical contexts from developed nations to developing nations. Accordingly, a plethora of studies has been conducted to provide various sketches of its ramifications. Despite this, it also becomes increasingly compelling to explore precise aspects of this phenomenon as a way of making specific contributions to the extant literature. This brings in the relevance of the study of the influence of religion in the consumer behaviour of developing nations. Arguably, having a thorough understanding of the past is an important input into knowing the present, and even the future. This explains why people are considered 'backpackers' as they carry the remains of their experience and those they had in relation to others from one location to another over the years (Schmidt and Garcia, 2010). Accordingly, it is not outlandish to project the place of religion in the consumer behaviour of contemporary developing nations. For developing nations like Mexico, Ghana, China, and others, religion can no longer be treated as an afterthought.

So, adopting a systematic approach to providing a solution using a marketing mix in this context becomes essentially relevant and will continue to be germane in the foreseeable future. An example is the importance of communication and, particularly, companies' reputations in attracting certain religious groups. When considering this issue, at times, there may be the risk of focusing only on tangible products (e.g. food or clothes). Similarly, there is an argument that some industries appear to be ignoring salient issues in marketing when trying to serve various religious groups. Consider the movie industry: how many times did they stop to consider the religious sensitivities of certain groups when developing their movie scripts? Much has been said about the influence of Hollywood in diluting local cultural standards, yet how can a truly global industry overlook local differences? Are we getting to the stage when, just like products such as burgers or drinks are adjusted for local needs, in the same manner local sensitivities should apply to services such as the film industry? The answer seems to be in the affirmative. This may look like a far-fetched step but marketers have always advocated the need to 'think outside the box'. We may even get to the stage when religious 'products' may take the challenge to offer better quality than the more broadly available products. In this respect, one may list the bank Al Rayan which, after introducing its very competitive, Islamically sensitive banking service, discovered that it was attracting many clients who were either non-religious or even belonged to a different religious tradition altogether. The reason is simple: people know what is an ethically grounded product irrespective of its name or the company providing it.

In fact, it is hoped that marketers' religious activities will go beyond a 'horses for courses' approach and that their considerations will become pervasive to all marketing activities. This not only encourages avoiding unnecessary errors that can lose customers but also create serious reputational challenges that eventually will affect the bottom line.

Finally, the issue of religion is not going to be a silver bullet. As demonstrated above, it is an issue that should become part and parcel of marketers' considerations. At a time when research specialises and there is a tendency to oversimplify outcomes, it is important that marketers keep their head above water and continue to address the myriad of influences, including religion, so as to avoid missing the wood for the trees.

It is hoped that this book and more specifically this chapter can become a rallying call for marketers to meet the challenge of developing their discipline to make it more relevant and inclusive to all human needs and in this process address one of the remaining bastions of marketers' hesitations: providing ethically supported religious products in both developed and developing countries. This challenge can be tough and has to be met with in-depth understanding and wisdom but the rewards are worth it.

REFERENCES

Addai, I., Opoku-Agyeman, C. and Ghartey, H. T. (2013). An exploratory study of religion and trust in Ghana. *Social Indicators Research*, *110*(3), 993–1012.

Ajzen, I. (1985). *From Intentions to Actions: A Theory of Planned Behavior*. Berlin: Springer.

Akaah, I. P. (1997). Influence of deontological and teleological factors on research ethics evaluations. *Journal of Business Research*, *39*(2), 71–80.

Ali, A. (2011). Islamic ethics and marketing. In Ö. Sandıkcı and G. Rice (eds), *Handbook of Islamic Marketing*. Cheltenham, UK and Northampton, MA, USA: Edward Elgar Publishing.

Andreasen, A. (2006). *Social Marketing in the 21st Century*, Thousand Oaks, CA: Sage.

Arnould, E. J. and Thompson, C. J. (2005). Consumer culture theory (CCT): Twenty years of research. *Journal of Consumer Research*, *31*(1), 868–82.

Barash, M. (1967). The role of traditional religion in a developing nation. *Archives de sociologie des religions*, 37–40.

Baumgartner, H. (2010). Bibliometric reflections on the history of consumer research. *Journal of Consumer Psychology*, *20*(3), 233–8.

Beck, A. T., Freeman, A. and Davis, D. (2015). *Cognitive Therapy of Personality Disorders*, 3rd ed. New York: Guilford.

Brassington, F. and Pettitt, S. (2006). *Principles of Marketing*, 4th ed. Harlow: Prentice Hall.

Bullard, G. (2016). The world's newest major religion: No religion. As secularism grows, atheists and agnostics are trying to expand and diversify their ranks. *National Geographic*. https://api.nationalgeographic.com/distribution/public/amp/news/2016/04/160422-atheism-agnostic-secular-nones-rising-religion (accessed 25 June 2020).

Cleveland, M., Rojas-Méndez, J. I., Laroche, M. and Papadopoulos, N. (2016). Identity, culture, dispositions and behavior: A cross-national examination of globalization and culture change. *Journal of Business Research*, *69*(3), 1090–102.

Cusack, C. M (2010). *Invented Religions: Imagination, Fiction and Faith*. Farnham: Ashgate.

Danaher, P. J., Danaher, T. S., Smith, M. S. and Loaiza-Maya, R. (2020). Advertising effectiveness for multiple retailer-brands in a multimedia and multichannel environment. *Journal of Marketing Research*, *57*(3), 445–67.

De Mooij, M. (2011), *Consumer Behaviour and Culture: Consequences for Global Marketing and Advertising*, 2nd ed. London: Sage.

Dunn, S. L. and Jensen, J. D. (2019). Hinduism and Hindu business practices. *International Journal of Business Administration*, *10*(1), 33–48.

Ellis, A. (1994). *Reason and Emotion in Psychotherapy*, revised ed. New York: Birch Lane Press.

Engel, J. F., Kollat, D. T. and Blackwell, R. D. (1968). *Consumer Behaviour*. New York: Rinehart and Winston.

Engel, J. F., Blackwell, R. D. and Miniard, P. W. (1995). *Consumer Behaviour*, 8th ed. Fort Worth, TX: Dryden Press, Harcourt Brace College Publishers.

Espinoza, J. (2020). IBM and Microsoft sign Vatican pledge for ethical AI. *Financial Times*. www.ft.com/content/5dc6edcc-5981-11ea-a528-dd0f971febbc?…61-4fbb -9430-9208a9e233c8#myft:notification:daily-email:content (accessed 10 April 2020).

Fieser, J. (2017). *The History of Philosophy: A Short Survey*. New York: McGraw Hill.

Fourali, C. E. (2016). *The Promise of Social Marketing: A Powerful Tool for Changing the World for Good*. London: Routledge.

Fourali, C. E. (2018). Lecture on ethics in selling. London Metropolitan University.

Fourali, C. E. (2019). Lecture on serving customers in global markets. London Metropolitan University.

Gbadamosi, A. (2009). Cognitive dissonance: The implicit explication in low-income consumers' shopping behaviour for 'low-involvement' grocery products. *International Journal of Retail and Distribution Management*, *37*(12), 1077–95.

Gbadamosi, A. (2015). Brand personification and symbolic consumption among ethnic teenage consumers: An empirical study. *Journal of Brand Management*, *22*(9), 737–59.

Gbadamosi , A. (2016). Consumer behaviour in developing nations: A conceptual overview, in A. Gbadamosi (ed.), *Handbook of Research on Consumerism and Buying Behaviour in Developing Nations*, Hershey: IGI Global, pp. 1–29.

Gbadamosi, A. (2019). Ethics and sustainable marketing, in A. Gbadamosi (ed.), *Contemporary Issues in Marketing*, London: Sage, pp. 185–218.

Gentilin, D. (2016). *The Origins of Ethical Failures: Lessons for Leaders*. London: Routledge.

Greaves, E. (2018). Can Sharia savings accounts provide you an extra return on your cash? www.moneywise.co.uk/savings/savings-accounts/can-sharia-savings -accounts-provide-you-extra-return-your-cash (accessed 26 June 2020).

Harari, Y. N. (2020). The world after coronavirus. *Financial Times*, 20 March.

Howard, J. A. and Sheth, J. (1969). *The Theory of Buyer Behaviour*. New York: John Wiley.

Hunt, S. D. and Vasquez-Parraga, A. Z. (1993). Organizational consequences, marketing ethics, and salesforce supervision. *Journal of Marketing Research*, *30*(1), 78–90.

Hunt S. D. and Vitell, S. (1993). The general theory of marketing ethics: A retrospective and revision, in N. C. Smith and J. A. Quelch (eds), *Ethics in Marketing*. Chicago, IL: Irwin, pp. 775–84.

Jenkins, P. (2018). Can UN code help scandal-prone banks clean up their act? Ten years on from financial crisis, headlines hardly show a more ethical sector. *Opinion Inside*

Business. www.ft.com/content/a9fada36-ef43-11e8-8180-9cf212677a57 (accessed 11 April 2020).

Jewish Encyclopedia (2011). Usury. www.jewishencyclopedia.com/articles/14615 -usury (accessed 7 April 2020).

Johnson, G., Whittington, R., Scholes, K., Angwin, D. and Regner, P. (2017). *Exploring Strategy*. London: Pearson.

Johnson, P. (2000). *The Renaissance: A Short History*. New York: Modern Library.

Joshi, Y. and Rahman, Z. (2019). Consumers' sustainable purchase behaviour: Modelling the impact of psychological factors. *Ecological Economics, 159*, 235–43.

Klein, T. and Laczniak, G. (2009). Applying Catholic social teaching to ethical issues in marketing. *Journal of Macromarketing, 29*(3), 233–43.

Kotler, P. and Armstrong, G. (2018). *Principles of Marketing*, 17th ed. Harlow: Pearson.

Levitt, T. (1960). Marketing myopia. *Harvard Business Review, 38*, 45–56.

Malhotra, N. K., Ulgado, F. M., Agarwal, J. and Baalbaki, I. B. (1994). International services marketing: A comparative evaluation of the dimensions of service quality between developed and developing countries. *International Marketing Review, 11*(2), 5–15.

Murphy, P. E., Laczniak, G. R. and Prothero, A. (2012). *Ethics in Marketing: International Cases and Perspectives*. Abingdon: Routledge.

National Conference of Catholic Bishops (1986). Economic justice for all: Catholic social teaching and the US economy. *Origins, 16*(4).

National Conference of Catholic Bishops (1997). A Catholic framework for economic life. US Catholic Conference.

Oman, D. (2013). Defining religion and spirituality. In R. F. Paloutzian and C. L. Park (eds), *Handbook of the Psychology of Religion and Spirituality*, 2nd ed. New York: Guilford Press, pp. 23–47.

Otto, R. (1969). *The Idea of the Holy: An Inquiry into the Non-Rational Factor in the Idea of the Divine and Its Relation to the Rational (1923, 1928, etc.)*, translated by John W. Harvey. Oxford: Oxford University Press.

Paloutzian, R. F. (2017). *Invitation to the Psychology of Religion*, 3rd ed. New York: Guilford Press.

Peterson, C. and Seligman, M. E. P. (2004). *Character Strengths and Virtues: A Handbook and Classification*. Oxford: Oxford University Press.

Pew Research Centre (2012). The global religious landscape: Religion and public life. www.pewforum.org/2012/12/18/global-religious-landscape-exec/ (accessed 18 September 2020).

Reece, W. (1989). Why is the bishops' letter on the US economy so unconvincing? *Journal of Business Ethics, 8*(7), 553–60.

Saeed, M., Ahmed, Z. and Mukhtar, S.-M. (1997). International marketing ethics from an Islamic perspective: A value-maximization approach. *Journal of Business Ethics, 32*(2), 127–42.

Schiffman, L. G. and Wisenblit, J. (2019). *Consumer Behaviour*, 12th ed. Harlow: Pearson Education.

Schiffman, L. G., Kanuk, L. L. and Hansen, H. (2012). *Consumer Behaviour: A European Outlook*, 2nd ed. Harlow: Pearson Education.

Schmidt, M. A. and Braga Garcia, T. M. F. (2010). History from children's perspectives: Learning to read and write historical accounts using family sources. *Education, 38*(3), 289–99.

Schroeder, J. and Morling, M. S. (eds) (2006). *Brand Culture*. New York: Routledge.

Shalev, B. A. (2003). *Religion of Nobel Prize Winners: 100 Years of Nobel Prizes*. New Delhi: Atlantic Publishers.

Sheth, J. N. (1985). History of consumer behavior: A marketing perspective. *ACR Special Volumes*.

Sheth, J. N., Newman, B. I. and Gross, B. L. (1991). Why we buy what we buy: A theory of consumption values. *Journal of Business Research*, *22*(2), 159–70.

Sober, E. and Wilson, D. S. (1998). *Unto Others: The Evolution and Psychology of Unselfish Behavior*. Cambridge, MA: Harvard University Press.

Stigler, G. J. (1954). The early history of empirical studies of consumer behavior. *Journal of Political Economy*, *62*(2), 95–113.

Stolarski, M., Jasielska, D. and Zajenkowski, M. (2015). Are all smart nations happier? Country aggregate IQ predicts happiness, but the relationship is moderated by individualism–collectivism. *Intelligence*, *50*, 153–8.

Sun, B., Mao, H. and Yin, C. (2020). Male and female users' differences in online technology community based on text mining. *Frontiers in Psychology*, *11*.

Tan, K. C. (2017). *What Is This Thing Called Global Justice?* London: Routledge.

Taylor, C. R. (2018). Global consumer culture and advertising research. *International Journal of Advertising*, *37*(4), 505–7.

Tsai, D. F. (2005).The bioethical principles and Confucius' moral philosophy. *Journal of Medical Ethics*, *31*, 159–63.

Wee, V. (2001). Buddhist approach to economic development, in Buddhist Perspective in the Face of the Third Millennium, Proceedings of the Year 2000 Global Conference on Buddhism, Buddhist Fellowship.

Wiebe, G. D. (1952). Merchandising commodities and citizenship on television. *Public Opinion Quarterly*, *15*, 679–91.

Wilson, A., Zeithaml, V. A., Bitner, M. J. and Gremler, D. D. (2016). *Services Marketing*, 3rd ed. London: McGraw-Hill.

Wilson, R. M. S. and Gilligan, C. (2013). *Strategic Marketing Management*. London: Routledge.

Zhao, H. H., Gao, Q., Wu, Y. P., Wang, Y. and Zhu, X. D. (2014). What affects green consumer behavior in China? A case study from Qingdao. *Journal of Cleaner Production*, *63*, 143–51.

Zhao, Y., Yang, S., Narayan, V. and Zhao, Y. (2013). Modelling consumer learning from online product reviews. *Marketing Science*, *32*(1), 153–69.

Index

upper class 63
upper-middle class 64
upper-upper class 63
utilitarian motives 190
utilitarianism 207

value congruence 94
value-expressive influence 61
Valvi, A. C. 180
van Aardt, A. M. 88, 90
Van Cappellen, P., social affiliation 53
Van der Colff, N. 92
van der Geutgen, J. 156
Van Staden, J. 88, 90
Varieties of Religious Experience, The
    (James) 26
vegetarianism 87–8
Venkatesh, A. 128
Vesak Poya Day 98
virtual pragmatists 190
Vitell, S. 29–30

Wahyuni, S. 95
Wahyuni, T. 181
warranty 6
wealth acquisition 170
Weber, Max, *Protestant Ethic and the
    Spirit of Capitalism, The* 28

Welch, M. R. 53
Western brands 132, 141
Wetmore, D. 186
Wiebe, G. D. 215
Wikipedia 191
Wilkins, S. 85
WIMPY 165
Winter, B. 9
Wisenblit, J. 2, 202
Wolf, M. 130
working-class group 64
worldview 27–31, 36, 38

Xiao, B. 186

Yagboyaju, D. A. 11, 12
Yom Kippur 81
young consumers 189
Yousaf, S. 90
YouTube 187, 191

Zakat 31, 169
Zanna, R. 90
Zheng, C. 181
Zikmund, W. G. 80
Zoroastrianism 17, 188